CHALLENGE YOURSELF TO CHANGE

CHALLENGE YOURSELF TO CHANGE

365 DAILY INSPIRATIONAL MESSAGES TO BRING OUT THE BEST YOU

Joseph Saxon, Jr.

Midas Publishing Company
Columbia, South Carolina

CHALLENGE YOURSELF TO CHANGE
365 DAILY INSPIRATIONAL MESSAGES
TO BRING OUT THE BEST YOU

Published by
Midas Publishing Company
Columbia, South Carolina
saxonj51@gmail.com

Joseph Saxon, Publisher
Yvonne Rose/Quality Press.info, Book Packager

Paperback ISBN #: 979-8-9917362-0-6
Hardcover ISBN #: 979-8-9917362-1-3
Ebook ISBN #: 979-8-9917362-2-0
Library of Congress Control Number: 2024922519

Acknowledgements

I would like to personally thank and send my deepest gratitude out to all of those who have helped with the production of this book...

My good friend, Michele Rene Brown; my mentor, Andrew Moore; Ms. Yvonne Rose from Quality Press, who has helped immensely and guided me throughout this self-publishing process; and Stephanie Robinson, Brandon Craig, and countless others who have added to the content and creation.

Without these people constantly, and consistently pushing me, guiding me, and reminding me of my own goals, not only this book but many other things in my personal life would have never been accomplished. These are the people in my life who are springboards, that continually catapult me to the next level, and I will never forget to reach back and help pull them up. As they continue to push me into a greater me, I, in turn, will push and build them. We are locked into an invigorating cycle of opportunity, growth, and support. Thank you guys for being my rocks.

Introduction

Never in my wildest dreams did I think I would ever write a book. While in school, I never had the attention span to even read an entire book. As a matter of fact, I didn't read my first book from cover to cover until I was 35 years old... and although I have now become a more avid reader, it is still a struggle, and I must force myself to finish the books I start.

Challenge Yourself to Change: 365 Daily Inspirational Messages to Bring Out the Best You began as a simple conversation between my good friend, Michele Renee Brown, and myself. We would often talk about a myriad of subjects, ranging from babies to zombies, the Bible to our favorite childhood cartoons. At times, especially due to our work schedules, we couldn't finish entire conversations, and there were times when I had to look deeper into the subject. Many times, this "research" led to messages I would send back about what I'd found on our chosen subjects, and maybe even a few personal thoughts, just to give her time to thoroughly read, and understand my point. It got to a point where we were having more frequent conversations, and therefore.... more messages back and forth.

As I talked to other friends, about problems or life situations that they had experienced, everyone seemed to be talking about the same things, or having the same issues at the same time; so, I would send all of them the same messages. Eventually, I started adding people to my contact list, and one day while in the gym, three people mentioned how I should write a book… and thus, the book was born. I made it up in my mind that the book would be whatever the message was for that given day.

There is no rhyme or reason to the messages, and there are messages that are very similar to each other, but this is how they came to me, and that's how I wanted the book to be. Maybe someone will be dealing with something again later so a similar message may help.... all of us don't pass the test the first time around. I ask that you look past any unprofessional writer's mistakes and instead focus on the messages. I would like to personally thank you for your support and purchase of my first printed publication, and I hope my words can help to bring a bit of insight into your life.

DAY 1

There are people in your circle who can get u where you want to go and can get you the things you're looking for. And if they don't know it themselves, then SOMEONE you know can at the very least point you in the right direction. Begin to open up to some of your closest confidantes, let them in, share your dreams with them, and see if any guide you to someone or something that can help get you closer to your goals.

NOTES:

DAY 2

When babies are learning to walk, we encourage them, support them, and intently watch them, trying to get them to take more steps....bigger steps. I am sure that they are just simply trying to emulate everyone around them and do what everyone else is doing. Just like we encourage those babies, we should encourage those people around us who are trying to do better or different things. We wouldn't tell a baby, "Well, you've been trying this walking thing for a year, and haven't figured it out yet, so stop altogether" Not only should you NOT tell those around you these things, but you should also tell yourself these things. Never give up on your dreams, and never stifle yourself, and say you can't do it. Setbacks, stumbling, detours, and standstill traffic are all part of life's journey. Continue to push forward, and accomplish your dreams, no matter how many times you FEEL as though you're starting over. Every time you THINK you're starting over, you're actually starting from a better position, because you now have more experience and knowledge, and both of these will be able to help you in your future endeavors, and along your future journey. Just like those babies, find yourself someone to emulate. Find someone who is where you want to be and begin doing whatever it is they do. If at all possible, talk to them, and ask for their help and guidance.

NOTES:

DAY 3

Life is filled with ups, and downs, highs, and lows. Quite often we may ask ourselves, *why can't we just have it where we are even across the board, where everything just stays the same, if it's all going to balance out anyway??* Things that stay the same aren't changing, aren't moving, and definitely aren't growing. If you have no highs or lows on a heart monitor, that is called a flatline...DEATH. Build your knowledge base enough so that when you begin to implement what you're learning, you can build higher and higher, so that when you do hit your lows, even those are higher than your highs used to be.

There was a study done with lab rats, one group had everything they could need....the perfect temperature, more than enough food, the right ratio of male to female, comfortable living, and no predators. Those rats died off within 3 generations. The ones who had predators, and had to scrounge for food, where survival of the fittest won, lived many more generations. Don’t wish it was easier....wish u were stronger. **(COMPARE WITH DAY 70)**

NOTES:____

DAY 4

Whether you are a leader at home, at work, or even in your relationship, leadership is of the utmost importance, and should not be taken lightly. A herd of sheep being led by a wolf can do far more damage than a pack of wolves, being led by a sheep. As the captain of a ship, you direct where the ship is going. Not many on the ship can see with their eyes where you're leading them, so they must trust your word, your judgment, and your skill set, to get them to the final destination.

People are putting their trust, their hopes, and their dreams into your capable hands. Lead with care, determination, love, peace, and gratitude. Being in leadership doesn't mean that you know everything....so ask if you're unsure. Quite often, at least one of your subordinates knows the answer. Ensure to guide and teach with a bit of patience to the younger of the herd and be instrumental. If you're in the position of being led, sit back, and learn all you can. Be sure to ask as many questions as may pop into your head, because one day you will be at the helm, and you need all the experience possible to help guide you through to your final destination.

NOTES:____

DAY 5

You are a product of that which u consume. It is very difficult to have a bodybuilder's body if you eat pizza, burgers, ice cream, and cookies at every meal. Similarly, it's very difficult to have a positive outlook, or positive thoughts if all you feed your conscious, and subconscious is hate, death, negativity, and hopelessness. Feed your body a better diet, physically, mentally, and spiritually. Begin to read more books about subjects you are interested in or want to do. Stop telling yourself "It can't be done" or "I'm no good." If something comes up that you don't know how to do, ask yourself HOW can this be done, instead of automatically shooting it down. Watch far fewer death, gore, sex-filled movies (maybe more sex filled) and watch more knowledge-based movies, like documentaries. The better the things you put INTO your body, the better results you can get FROM your body. It doesn't have to be an overnight change; as a matter of fact, I can bet you that it absolutely, won't be an overnight change. One more piece of fruit today, watch 30 minutes less TV, and use that time to read instead; then stand up and do 10 squats. It doesn't take much to start the path to a better life, but it does take determination, and you starting. Make the choice and start today.

NOTES:____

DAY 6

Elephants are some of the largest, strongest land animals on the planet. It's hard to stop them when they are angry. But in the circus, they are controlled and held in place by a piece of rope, attached to a stake in the ground which your average 8-year-old could probably pull up. The way they control these massive creatures with such little effort, is they tie them to the stake when they are young, and weak. At this young and weakened age when they try to fight and pull away, they aren't strong enough. This thought sticks in their minds the rest of their lives, and when they are big and strong enough to finally pull the stake out, they don't even try because they are mentally defeated by an untrue limiting belief.

What untrue limiting beliefs are u holding onto, that are holding you back?? Who are you listening to, that told you, you couldn't do it, or you weren't good enough, or u were too ugly, or it's in your genes to be that way. You can do, you can be, you can have whatever it is you wish, as long as you KNOW u can do it, speak it into existence, and put the work in to get it. Stop letting that stake in the ground, or someone else's thoughts of THEIR limitations hold back your massive dreams.

NOTES:____

DAY 7

In different languages, certain phrases and words just simply don't translate, especially when it comes to more....offbeat words or slang. When we speak to people, everyone has their own interpretation in their head. What we say just may not be interpreted the way we thought we said it. Quite often things need to be broken down into smaller morsels and expounded on to get through to people. Take the time to not only break down what you're trying to say to someone, but to also listen, and ask more questions to get a better understanding of what someone else is trying to convey. True communication is far more than talking, it's about understanding and making sure all other parties involved understand what's being said.

NOTES:

DAY 8

In order to achieve and master anything, we must first master ourselves, with self-discipline. To reach our goals, we must learn to DELAY some gratifications. It is very difficult to lose weight, AND simultaneously eat what you want, until you change your mindset and decide to delay that food for a while to reach your goals. You must have the proper discipline to push back from the table when u want more, to save when you want to buy, to read when you want to watch TV, or to work out when you want to sleep; but rather decide which you want more… your dreams, goals, and opportunities.....or not getting them. Discipline is the bridge that will lead you to your dreams.

NOTES:

DAY 9

Make sure that you are prepared to pay the price for what you're asking for. It usually won't come in the way you think. I purchased an older suburban years ago, (it was always my dream car) and I always said that I wanted to restore it. I thought about it, wrote it down, and fantasized about what it would be like riding around in it. Over the years, it's taken me all across the country and back, to and from different jobs, it's broken down on me mid-trip, on the job, and sometimes I didn't even get out of the city without spending my entire check on repairs. At one point I had to overdraft my account to fix the truck to get me to a job. And during the entire time, all I could think about was going to get a new car, scrapping this one, and starting over. It was rough, gas was extreme, repairs were extreme, and even up to this day, I am still spending cash on repairs (12 years later). I recently had to get the drive shaft replaced (that's the thing that connects the steering wheel to the wheels*). I'VE NEVER EVEN HEARD OF THAT BEING DONE BEFORE!!!!!!!!!!* Then a thought popped into my head, and I remembered what I'd wanted so many years ago when I said I wanted to restore it.

All this time, I've simply been getting exactly what I asked for. It wasn't easy, it wasn't pretty and it damn sure wasn't how I thought it would come, but I've been getting what I asked for. Had I junked the car, or sold it, that would have ended my dream and my wishes for restoration. This is why you write down what you want to manifest, so u can continually look at it, and remind yourself of your goals, and for what you're fighting. Nothing you want to manifest is going to come easy, and probably not even in the manner you think it will get there, but it's coming. And don't give up on your dreams and goals. Just like all the repairs, and breakdowns, were actually restoring the car and making my dreams come true, so too are the hardships in your life making your dreams manifest. You just can't quit before they come to fruition.

NOTES:____

DAY 10

YOU have to learn to enforce the boundaries in your life. People will see your boundaries, hear you say what they are, and then test them repeatedly, just to see if they can blow past them.

Takers can see givers coming from a mile away. Takers will use your generosity, or lack of discipline to get as much from you as possible. If you don't stop them, or say anything about it early, when you finally do say something, they will tell you they thought you guys had been on the same page the whole time. Takers have no boundaries when it comes to taking, they will take from you until you have nothing left, then blame you for not having more, and move on to the next one.

I'm not strictly speaking about materialistic things. People will take your love, compassion, gratitude, peace, charity... it doesn't matter. People will take what they lack. So, it is up to YOU to protect yourself. Stop believing that someone close to you in your life would never treat you a certain way, because you would never do that to them. Set your boundaries and keep them firm. You can loosen them up later down the line as need be, but for now, hold firm. People in your life treat you the way you have taught them it's ok to. If someone is treating you foul, it's because you've allowed it, and taught them through your lack of boundaries that it's ok.

Stand up for yourself and begin to push back!

NOTES:____

DAY 11

Everything that you're going through, is building you, and preparing you for everything you've asked for.... stay the course.

NOTES:

DAY 12

Working on personal growth is paramount in your life's journey. Personal growth is the very foundation you are building the rest of your life on. No, it won't be easy, and no, it doesn't happen overnight, but a step a day puts you light years ahead of where you would be a year from now if you never take those steps. Do not listen to those who see you working and say you'll never reach your goals, all they want is more company in their miserable existence of a life, at the bottom of the ladder rungs. One choice to change will lead to more choices of change. We've all heard of "gateway drugs" where you start with this seemingly harmless drug like weed, that leads you down the rabbit hole to crack. Well, begin to make some "gateway choices" that will lead you to better decision-making, more money, more happiness, and more peace. You can make the choice today, to be either your greatest asset or your largest liability. Begin to pour into yourself FIRST, before pouring into others, feed yourself. Choose to be better, and be prepared to put the work in.

NOTES:

DAY 13

This picture resonates with me and speaks on so many levels. Organization and setting up a game plan in life are essential, and a necessity. That singular large fish can be ANYTHING....any problem, you have in your life. If it's your finances, and your bills are all scattered abroad, you don't know how much you owe, what the interest rates are on different debts, when due dates are, and it all feels so overwhelming. Then you must organize with a budget. All a budget does is tell you when you will be able to be free and do what you want. It lines up all the information about debts you owe and the fastest way to pay them off. It's not a scary thing to look at your situation and devise a plan to NOT be here anymore, that is part of growth, and maturity....to face your obstacles with a can-do attitude.

Organization works on the job, in your relationships, at the gym, and even in your health. First Find the major problem; second, think of a few different ways to handle that problem; third pick the best option that works for you, write it down and look at it; and do at least ONE thing towards that goal every day. Make 1 phone call, save 1 dollar, take an extra trip to the car, or do 1 sit-up. Just make sure you're making positive progress toward your goals, and organization every single day.

NOTES:____

DAY 14

Waiting to start something until the stars align will cause you to wait a long time. The time will never be right to start. The right time to start anything u want to do is TODAY. Every day you wait is another day closer to the grave you get, and another day less that you have to enjoy your dreams. The sooner you start, the sooner you reach your goals. Your life doesn't change overnight, or from 1 move, but starting leads to another move, and another move, until you get to the point where you're living your dream, and you don't even recognize it, because you've changed so much and its now simply everyday living to you. STOP WAITING and start your journey TODAY.

NOTES:

DAY 15

it is easy to spot a yellow car, when you're thinking of yellow cars, and it's easy to spot an opportunity when all you think about is opportunities it's easy to spot reasons to be mad if all you think about is being mad. You get and become what you constantly think about. So, be careful.

NOTES:

DAY 16

Life is a journey, of mostly smaller steps and non-noticeable moves that make larger moves. Be grateful, and thankful for where you are and what you have. Go over your lists and see that, although you may not have everything you want, you have more than what you NEED. If you aren't grateful for the things you have now, it will be hard to notice the smaller steps, and smaller accomplishments; so, when you finally make it, you still won't be happy and satisfied. Take the time to stop and smell the flowers today, look around, and be appreciative today. Enjoy it when you save that $2, or walk those extra 100 steps throughout the day, and when your larger goals are met it will be a day of pure joy.....but it starts with small praise.

NOTES:

DAY 17

Don't look at or focus your attention and energy on your present situation, except to make changes and adjustments, to make it to your final destination. You must look PAST your present situation and see what you CAN be. You are not the finished product you're supposed to be. Eggs flour, sugar, flavoring, butter, milk, and oil are nothing spectacular apart, but if you crack the egg, use portions of the milk, pour out sugar, and add everything into a bowl, you get a tasty mix. Put all of that into a pre-made dish and add a lot of heat for a long time until you get a cake. If your life were this cake, what stage of your life would you say you are in?

Are your ingredients being broken, opened, poured into the bowl, knocked around, and beaten up to get a good mix, or are you being turned upside down to go into a safe place, so that you can be thrown into the oven to make you??????? Life is always about the difficulties it takes to prepare you for the next level...the next stage of your evolution. Even after you've made it through your trials, you still need time to settle, relax, and cool. Just know that everything is preparing you for your next level, and your final destination.

NOTES:____

DAY 18

Throughout our entire lives, we've been taught to work hard, save money, and get out of debt. But that equation, IF it ever works, takes a lifetime to accomplish. The real equation is to find something to put your money in that makes money for you, with little to no work, and save THAT money until it's enough to repeat the process again and again. Buy a home you can afford but that is too big for you, and rent out rooms, instead of renting yourself. Start a small business for tax write-off purposes, Lyft, Uber. Buy and sell stuff on eBay or Amazon, sell plates, or snacks or just go ANYWHERE where a lot of people are, ask them what they need, and find a way to monetize that. No matter what you do, GET...MOVING. We must unlearn what they've taught us and learn the older hidden way of building.

NOTES:____

DAY 19

Education comes from more than "traditional schooling." Education is everything that you learn throughout your entire lifetime. Never stop learning, never stop growing, and never stop trying to be a better person than you were yesterday. Education can come from books, mentors, trial and error, or from just simply asking more and better questions. Increase your knowledge and education daily. Whatever you want to know more about or be better at, apply yourself.... on the job, finances, health, auto repairs, teaching, and side hustles. There are books, YouTube videos, and experts on just about any area you choose to study. It's simply up to you to apply yourself.

NOTES:

DAY 20

YOU are the sole architect of your future. Whatever YOU build, is what you will live on. The more you want, the stronger your foundation needs to be. You need to put more into YOU than you do other people's places and things. You cannot continue to build others if you are not sound yourself. Any business that is not stable and continues to build other businesses will fail. People are the same way. We feel as though we MUST be there for our friends, our families, our jobs, our coworkers, church, etc. while lacking ourselves, and we continuously dig ourselves deeper and deeper into debt. Learn to work on YOUR knowledge, YOUR finances, YOUR happiness, YOUR peace, and YOUR joy. You can't give what you don't possess, and you can't give abundantly, what you don't have abundantly. Take care of YOU first.

NOTES:

DAY 21

In the summer, when we were little, we would all go outside with a magnifying glass, and use that simple piece of glass to focus the sun's rays to burn ants, start small fires on paper, or burn grass or something else. We have the ability to do the same exact things with our own lives. Concentration and focus will spark things in you that you can't even presently imagine. Your mind is the sun, your heart is the concentration, and the words that u speak and write down are the focus. With variations of these different ways of thinking, speaking, believing, and doing, you can focus your wants and start massive fires of abundance, healing, health, wealth, solidarity....whatever it is that you choose to manifest in your life. Focus, manifestation, meditation, prayer.... whatever u want to call it, it is available to us ALL. Use it, believe it, and watch it work in Your life.

NOTES:

DAY 22

If u believe that u can do it, it can be done, if u don't believe....it won't. If u believe you're broke and can't do any better, the only thing your mind will see are the avenues to keep you broke, and not doing better. If all you think is that you have no time, your mind never sees any more time to do anything. When you begin to believe differently, your mind opens up other avenues. Your life is a direct reflection of your thinking and actions. Begin to surround yourself with positive people instead of the ones who always tell you, "It can't be done", or "That's too hard." Instead, find the people that will say "You can do it," "it's not as hard as you think," or "I'll work with you". These are the ones who will feed into you and push you to be and do better.

NOTES:

DAY 23

Everything that you have is precious.... your heart, your mind, your love, your peace, your kindness, and everything else that you find positive. It is all precious, and all worth protecting. SOMEONE finds what you have so valuable, and intimidating to them, that they are willing to destroy it in your life, just to shine a little bit brighter in their own lives. Not only should your materialistic things be locked away for safekeeping, but your spiritual, mental, and emotional things should be locked away as well. All things of value need protection, and only those to which you allow access should even be able to see those sides of u. Protect your inner-self at all costs.

NOTES:

DAY 24

Don't believe what you see.... see what you believe. Your entire world is shaped by YOUR thought processes and YOUR actions. Make them positive, affirming ones, and begin to conquer the day.

NOTES:

DAY 25

Structure and discipline are key in anything. If more money is what you want, then not only do you need structure and discipline to know how to get the money; but you also need structure and discipline in knowing how to keep it, as well as making it grow, and passing it on. Structure and discipline should become so ingrained in you, that it becomes no longer a chore or duty, but simply a part of your life.... like breathing. It should be automatic to save some of every bit of money coming in to put towards investments. It should be automatic, to wake up and be thankful for everything that you already have. It should be automatic to read and gain more knowledge daily....so much so, that if someone sees you not doing any of these things, they automatically question, "What's wrong with them today?" You should be living your goals in such a way, that when u live contrary to those goals, you are automatically corrected by those on the outside.

NOTES:

DAY 26

A well-balanced diet does wonders for the human body. It can keep you from getting sick, it will help you recover faster when you do get sick, it can help heal the body when accidents happen, and it can help you grow bigger, or even get smaller. The right diet under the right circumstances and the human body can achieve just about anything. The converse is also true. The wrong diet can and WILL bring sickness, poverty, unhealed wounds, and even unfulfillment. As u read these words, I'm sure you probably pictured what you ate this morning, or maybe last night, but there is more to your diet than simply food. Your diet consists of everything that you put into your body. The food you eat, the drinks you drink, the movies/shows you watch, the music you listen to, and the people you hang around and allow to influence you.

A proper mental, spiritual, and physical diet is of the utmost importance, and I would even argue far greater than a physical food diet. The better things you feed into your mind; the better things will come out. Cut back on the drama-filled shows, the music, and movies filled with hate, violence, anger, and malice. All that's doing is planting seeds of negativity, and the more you feed it, the deeper those roots will grow in you. Begin to fill yourself with positivity.... positive images, books, and music… and surround yourself with positive people; and slowly you will begin to heal internally, which will undoubtedly lead to an external transformation.

NOTES:____

DAY 27

In life, we all face issues, problems, division, and what seem to be insurmountable odds, but it is within each and every one of us to fight back, defeat, and conquer any obstacles that are put before us. We are where we are in life, based mainly on our own decisions, which means that....you are where you WANT to be, and if you don't like being there, YOU have to make some decisions on what it takes to get out of it, and on to a better life. For many of us, when we want to change ANYTHING, it takes time, it's a difficult process. We may start it, stop it, pick it back up for a while just to drop it, and repeat the process over and over until it finally catches. If we do this for our own wants and needs, for something that we know will better our life, and it's that difficult for us, how then can you expect that you can change anyone else into doing what you want?????

We can't work on or worry about other people; our best option is to simply work on OURSELVES. If you're getting punched in the face, you can ask the bully to stop, demand they stop, find a cop, and tell them, write letters to Congress, and wait for laws to be passed, or even pray that God will take this burden from you. But in the end, you're still getting punched in the face the whole time. The simplest thing to do is to change YOU and move out of the way; the next simplest thing is to fight back. So, move out of your own way, stop overspending, stop excessively eating, and stop filling your mind with foolishness and hanging around those same negative, draining, got-nothing-going-for-themselves people. And begin to fight back. Start working out, eating better, reading, listening to books on tape, staying off of social media, replacing TV time with book time, start saving an extra dollar a week. You can start ANYWHERE, just make sure you start with YOU.

YOU are the problem.

NOTES:____

DAY 28

YOU are a very special, and important being. There is a 1 in 400 quadrillion chance that YOU would be born. You've already hit the lottery, and now it's simply up to you to capitalize on it. Plenty of lottery winners are broke 5-10 years after winning. They have not changed their mindsets and have not adapted to the money. The time to prepare is BEFORE you get something. Don't wait until you have the blessing to try and figure it out.... you'll destroy it trying to figure out how to take care of it. Start learning about the things you want out of life TODAY so that when they do come, you will at least have some semblance of knowledge of what to do with them. And one of the first things you should begin to do is serve others. It is difficult to accept anything else if you are already full. The cup must be emptied before you can refill it, or otherwise, your water will be wasted. To make room for more, the water must be drunk or poured into others' cups. Pour into others' cups, so that you too can be refilled with the things you are looking for.

NOTES:

DAY 29

The barriers in your life, that you consider to be brick walls in your path to success, are simply illusions. These are things you have either been taught or taught yourself that are barriers to your success. Successful people know that there are no barriers. If you can come up with the idea, it can be done, it simply takes WORK, and a new train of thought.

Excuse: I just don't have time to work out.

A) Make time. People work out every day and have the same problems, issues, jobs, and all.

Excuse: I can't afford a down payment on a house.

A) Buy a multi-unit apartment. Your tenants can pay the bills and u will live for free. Rent out a room/space where you are now. Not only will people rent rooms, but people will also rent out your free space for storage. Sign up for ANY delivery app nowadays. Uber/Lyft, DoorDash, Walmart, and sooooo many others.

It may not be easy or convenient, but you can do anything you put your mind to. It doesn't take money to make money, it simply takes SOMEONE else's money. Put your mind to it and begin to brainstorm, write down every idea you can think of, for whatever challenge you may be facing; then think of 10 solutions to each one. You'll be amazed at what you can come up with.

NOTES:____

DAY 30

The higher you build a structure, the smaller it must become, because if you get high enough, and the building begins to sway, it can snap, and the immense weight of all the construction material, can cause havoc on your foundation. The higher u want to go in your personal life, the smaller YOU have to become. Everything, and everyone, can't go with you. Your destination is the new you, and a lot of the old you, old friends, and old places are simply too much weight to bear and will cause you to topple over, and/or crush your foundation.

You've got to learn to see who's helping, you, building you, and supporting you on your rise to higher levels. Those who aren't feeding into your success, are feeding into your failure, and downfall. Leave those not feeding the positive by the side of the road. You don't have to be mean about it, just a simple, "I can't go out with y'all, I'm busy" is all it takes. The more time you spend on your goals the less time you'll have for anything and anybody else, except those things that push you further.

NOTES:

DAY 31

A ship that sits in port is safe. It won't be knocked around too badly by the waves, it can't run aground, it can't run into other ships, it won't get lost, and it can't get swallowed up by sea monsters. But unless you start those engines and put them out there on the water, you will never even know what they are capable of. It'll never reach any ports/destinations, it can't help anyone in trouble, it doesn't bring much joy to anyone just sitting there, and unless it's being used as a museum or something it's probably wasting more money than it makes. Your life is that ship.

Do you want a safe life tied to the pier, or do you want to take the chance at a better life, hitting more destinations, more goals, more dreams? You....are....built ....for this. It's what you were made for. Don't spend your life wasting away stuck in unhappiness, and unfulfillment. Untie yourself from the people, places, and things that are keeping you stagnant. You will run into problems, but when you learn to look at problems simply as opportunities to advance, you'll see things in a different light. You ARE bigger, you ARE better, you ARE stronger. Pull out and go to your next destination.

NOTES:____

DAY 32

Being equally yoked is not just about having the same religion. Being equally yoked is in all things. You don't want to be in a relationship, whether sexual or business, with someone you're not on the same page with. If you study, save money, believe in building for the future, and want to travel. It would be very difficult to have a relationship or business with someone who doesn't study, spends every dime they get, plus some, and is living for today because they may not make it till tomorrow, and they never want to leave "their city".

Equally yoked is finding someone you can communicate with, see each other's viewpoints, build each other, be each other's peace, and work on disagreements positively. Equally yoked counts in friendships, sexual relationships, business partnerships, and any in other "ships." If you want to better yourself, continue to surround yourself with people who are bettering themselves. Take a deep look into yourself and find out who you really are, and when you meet new people see if they align with your criteria of your wanted yokes. If you are unequally yoked, either you're gonna bring them down or they are gonna bring u down, and neither of those situations is ideal.

NOTES:____

DAY 33

I saw a quote today, that said, "The person that knows HOW to do a thing, will always have a job, and the person that knows WHY you do a thing will always be his boss." The more you know, the more you have the possibility to grow. Simply having the knowledge and/or know-how of how to do something isn't going to get you far in life. It's knowledge PLUS application MULTIPLIED by determination, that will allow you to meet your goals. Amass as much knowledge as possible with reading, seminars, mentors, and classes. Then put that information to work. Do your due diligence, but don't wait forever to put things into action. That fear you feel that's keeping you from venturing out isn't nearly as bad as the real-life situation. Push forward and push through.

NOTES:

DAY 34

You have to learn as much as possible about as many subjects as possible, in as many fields as possible. Inspiration usually doesn't come from whatever area you're studying. Quite often, it's tied to an idea, or a thought of different fields, and then it's translated into the particular field you are studying. Somehow your brain ties 2 completely different fields together to help you see the light. The more good things you put into something or someone, the higher the possibility there is that you may get better things out.... sometimes even unknowingly. I never in a lifetime would have said I would be sending out daily inspirational texts (books as some say lol), but the more I read, the more things just began to overflow, and I had to let them out.

The more you study, the more you plant fertile ground, and seeds inside of you, and if you continue to nurture and cultivate that fertile ground and seeds, they will begin to sprout, and flourish. Simply begin with the subjects you find interesting, and they will lead to others over time, and you will begin to ask yourself " Self.... how have I not found this, this interesting before???" Continue to put in the work, and you'll look up one day, and see just how far you've come.

NOTES:____

DAY 35

Who u pick as a partner, whether business, marriage, dating, or hopscotch is of the utmost importance. Partners can build you, or they can destroy you; they can motivate you, or discourage you; they can lift your spirits, or drag those same spirits through the pits of hell. Partners know more about you than the average person; we tend to spend more time with them than most people; and they know how we operate, how we move, how we think, and what we may do in any given situation. If you are in league with the wrong person, they could use this information to stab you in the back.

Quite often people don't "change" or "switch up" on us, we just have never seen them in that situation. Many people act differently when they have money, and when they don't; when they are sick and when they are healthy; and even more so, when YOU have money, and when YOU don't. Look to find partners and people to surround yourself with, who help you with nothing to gain; and who, even when times between you are bad, are still protecting you from vipers trying to bring about your downfall.

NOTES:

DAY 36

On this day, we celebrate "love". Love of those special people in our lives, who are there, supported us, maybe helped build us, or whatever YOU consider this day to mean to you. But I suggest that we, first and foremost, stop and figure out what it means to love OURSELVES. Find out what your love languages are (and not simply from the love language website) but learn what really makes you tick. Many times, we are looking for the love that someone told us we should accept and want. Maybe flowers, or cards, and dinner don't work for you. Your idea of love may be to take me to a monster truck show or a trip to see the Aurora Borealis in Alaska. It could be a walk in the park or help with a project. Whatever it may be, learn to love yourself, so that you know how you want others to love you properly. Love is also more than a sexual relationship. Love those in your inner circles and build on those relationships. These will possibly be some of the greatest connections you will ever hold.

NOTES:____

DAY 37

Many times, in life we all fall. We stumble, we skin our knees, and hurt ourselves in all kinds of ways.... some worse than others. Oftentimes, there are people in our lives who we may ask, "Why weren't you there when I fell?" or "Why didn't you help me when I fell?" or "Why didn't you help me up?".

1) it is NOBODY's responsibility to do anything for you. If a person chooses to help you, then that's great, you may make it up a little faster and …

2) just because YOU don't see the help, doesn't mean that it didn't come. It may be possible, on their way to help you, they fell themselves; or, maybe even though you fell, they positioned themselves under you to soften your blow, and that blow hurt them far more than it hurt you, but the only thing that you can see is that you still fell. Be thankful for the helpers in your life and begin to be the change you want to see. Become a helper to others. It doesn't always require money.... maybe time, a listening ear, or a home-cooked meal. You never know, sometimes it could be as simple as a wave and hello. Just strive to be a better person than you were yesterday.

NOTES:____

____

____

____

____

____

____

____

____

____

____

____

DAY 38

I have been going to the gym consistently for about the last 9 months, I've been eating a little better, and just making better overall health-wise decisions. Usually, I would work out for 1-3 months, then stop; then go back and repeat the process over and over again. But this time, I decided I was going to be consistent. I wake up early and go before work and during this stint, I've heard people say things like, "Oh, u say you're working out, but I don't see a difference in you. If you really are going to the gym you're just wasting your time" or "what are you eating that health food for, we all gonna die anyway?".

Many negative things have been hurled my way, but I had already made up my mind that I wasn't stopping. Even when the scale started going BACK UP, I knew I had to keep going. Today I see a difference in myself, I'm seeing looser clothes, better appetite control, and healthier skin, and looking in the mirror I can really see a change. I just have to keep going to reach my ultimate goal. Don't live up to the expectations of others. Set your reasonable goals, write out the game plan to achieve those goals, and follow the plan. The plan can be adjusted at any given point in time but have a plan.

Outsiders will say and do anything to keep you from reaching your goals, but you are the one who must stay strong. Get accountability partners, friends, colleagues, or ANYBODY who can help motivate, push, and guide you to where you want to be. Every day won't be easy or the best, but every day done in the service of your goals will not only be worth it, but it is another brick added to your new home.

NOTES:____

DAY 39

I am tutoring a young man, and I've helped him start a small business. Every week, he goes out and asks the neighbors if he can take their trash to the curb and bring it back after it's been dumped. He's also started picking up the small debris from out of their yards as an added bonus. When he gets paid, I make him take 20% and give it to me. 10% goes towards an emergency fund, and 10% goes to his business account, in case he may need anything for the business or chooses to invest in something else. I save his money, and unbeknownst to him, I also match the money he puts in. When it is needed, more than he puts in will be there waiting for him. During this process, I'm also teaching him banking, sharpening his math skills, and organization, and getting him used to having business meetings.

Life, quite often, is the same as this situation. We have to get out and put in the work before things happen. He was given an idea and MADE to do it weekly. It wasn't willingly at first, but now that he's seeing his own money, he is beginning to be enthused by it and is putting in more willing work. Everything that you do will not bear instant fruit, but you are planting seeds, and those seeds, once matured, will bear far more fruit than you could imagine. 1 apple seed can produce a tree that gives you 500 apples every season, but first, it must be planted, protected, and cared for, for a while until it has matured. Much like the young mentee, he is planting seeds that he cannot even begin to see right now. The harder he works, the more seeds are planted, the less attitude he gives, the more those seeds are watered. In due time, he will see the fruits of his labor. Continue to plant seeds of faith, truth, love, happiness, joy, peace, and diligence, and you will receive the fruits 100-fold in due time.

NOTES:____

____

____

____

____

DAY 40

Begin to journal your life. Start anywhere.... with your workouts, your feelings, and your daily interactions. Journaling allows you to remember things that would have normally been forgotten. Throughout my day, I jot down notes when inspiration hits, which guides me back to my daily messages. Even when I know it's a great message, and I'll remember it, if I don't at least jot down a note, it gets lost in the hustle and bustle of the day. Journaling also helps you keep track of your progress or lack thereof in any given situation. You can look back and see how far you've come from your starting point, or where you need to make any adjustments.

Every once in a while, stop, and take a look back over your notes. Quite often, you will be inspired by your progress, and it will probably push you a little harder. If you're saving money, and you look in your account, and see that you've saved 1k, 5k, or 20k, it will excite you and make you want to go that much harder. You can use your journal the same way; but first, you must get started. Again, it doesn't matter where you start, as long as you start. Beginning ANY process will take you places you never thought possible.

NOTES:

DAY 41

Everyone has different definitions of everything, whether it be love, marriage, debt, saving, investing, or whatever. When speaking with someone about a given situation, make sure you are both coming from the same vantage point or frame of reference. You don't have to agree but try to understand where they are coming from. As an electrician, I have to make sure things are straight all the time, but if I'm measuring off of this wall that's 2 feet from me, and you're measuring off of a wall 10 feet away, our measurements will never line up, and we will never get things straight. Now if I know that your wall is 10 feet away, I can compensate for that, and we can make things work. Our measurements still won't be the same, but I now know where you're coming from and I can make the necessary adjustments, to reach both of our desired goals.

Telling a person that they don't love you because they aren't doing something the way YOU think it should go may have u by yourself for a while. Tell them how YOU view love, and what it looks like to you. Ask them what love looks like to them. Get a better understanding of someone else's reference points, and maybe things will work out a little better for you, or you can continue to fight against one another and get nowhere. A simple question can lead to huge gains...."What does happiness, peace, joy, love, fulfillment, respect, or ANYTHING look like to you", and watch where it takes you.

NOTES:____

DAY 42

I had a conversation this past weekend that led to the word "submission" and it reminded me of a sermon I'd heard many years ago that I agreed with. He said "If you submit to the things you agree to, then it's agreeable not submission; submission doesn't even begin, UNTIL you disagree. Can u truly be submissive if all you do is what you agree with???? The definition of submission is the action or fact of accepting or yielding to a superior force or the will or authority of another person. *Yielding to the superior force or will of another.* If you agree, you are not yielding to the will of someone else. At work you yield to the boss all day, every day; on a team, you yield to the coach; in business, you yield to lawyers and accountants.

If you're with someone with whom you feel you can't submit, whether male or female, then why are you with them?????? No type of relationship is a monarchy, but more often than not, a democracy. Submission is not a negative word, it's simply how you see it. I believe that we can do better and go further with more trust and a bit more submission. Try it on for size and see where it gets u. Look at where NOT submitting has gotten u.

NOTES:____

DAY 43

In life, many people strive for perfection when trying to do things; or they wait until the perfect time or opportunity comes along. There will be very few times, if any in your life, when all the stars align, and everything works out as you think it should for you to start. Focusing on PROGRESS is a much better goal than perfection. If you get 2% better a month at anything, that's 24% better a year. In less than 4 years you will have doubled your current position. You may say "That's a long way away", but what were you doing 4 years ago????? As you progress and do better and acquire more skills, you may be able to progress faster than 2% a month.

No matter how fast or slow you progress, you're still that much further than you would have been had you done nothing. Be in contention with yourself, and yourself only. Be a better person than you were yesterday. If you focus on progress, you can look back, and see how far you've come. If you focus on perfection all you will ever see is how far you still have to go, and how you still have yet to reach your goals. Progress is the key.

NOTES:

DAY 44

How do you eat an elephant....1 bite at a time? This saying tells us that any large insurmountable goals that you see in your life can all be handled if you break them down into smaller bite-sized goals. How do you purchase a $500,000 home???? You first have to find out what that note would be (let's say $2500). So, how can you come up with 2500 every month and sometimes you may have to do some things you've never thought about? Take the payments you're paying now for housing (1000), begin some sort of business that brings you extra cash, start a seminar, or a YouTube channel, begin to write books, do Lyft/uber or any other delivery app, buy/sell on eBay… just start getting your creative juices flowing.

Once a week advertise on Facebook something that you can do that you're good at, that you can market and charge people for. Maybe instead of buying a $500,000 home, you can start out buying a $100,000 home, stay in it, move in a year or two, and rent out the first home.... Then repeat the process until you reach your goal and move into the "big house." if you want to lose 50 extra pounds, don't look at it as 50 lbs. Say to yourself, *I will lose 1lb a week for 52 weeks* (smaller bite-sized goals). How do you lose 1 lb. a week???? Walk more, make better eating choices, maybe join a gym, get a partner to help push and motivate you, buy a bike, and take the stairs at work. You can break down any goal into smaller ones. If you can't figure out how ask someone else, but it can be done.

NOTES:____

DAY 45

Sometimes it is meant for us to fail. Failure teaches us more about ourselves, and our opponents than winning ever has/will. In failure, many learn humility, peace, calmness, patience, gratitude, humbleness, and much more. Failure is quite possibly the biggest part of winning. All it takes is time, and the right mindset to see WHY you failed. Failure takes your mindset down a different path; you begin to learn how to overcome adversity and struggle. Your mind creates new pathways of learning and problem-solving, you begin to build up a thicker skin to ridicule, and u begin to get used to having ingredients, and dealing with less, which makes you that much more deadly. Failure is a companion that can catapult you levels ahead or knock you to the basement if you allow it to. Push through and persevere through the temporary pain of failure to make it through to the other side and see all the rewards that failure has in store for you.

NOTES:

DAY 46

Learn to work on and build YOURSELF before trying to attain fame, riches, or anything else. Without any peace, tranquility, happiness, self-love, or health, all the money in the world won't mean much. Learn to love yourself, first and foremost. Work on becoming healthier, happier, and more in tune with those things around you. Look for the peace, and positivity in things, and your goals, and dreams will begin to manifest themselves.

NOTES:

DAY 47

Most people are living their lives with a mindset that they "don't lose." Try living your life with a mindset of "winning"... because always "playing it safe" is a scarcity mindset. The more you educate yourself, things will become far less risky. The more books you read, the more you get with those in the business of what you want to do, and the more you focus, the "luckier" you'll find yourself becoming. Take the time to put in the work, be consistent, and watch things begin to shift and move in your favor.

NOTES:

DAY 48

Life is full of change. Most things that don't change in some way are dead or dying. Don't be afraid to say you've changed. You're not the same today that you were at 12, 25, 30, etc., so you may not be the same person, or have the same thoughts you had even yesterday. You have more experience, and more knowledge, and you've been opened up to more ideas which may have changed your thought process. Growth and change can be very positive, and uplifting things. Sometimes change may require that you leave some things you've held close for a long time, but migrating over to the new thing can replace that. Don't think of it as leaving an old thing, but instead just spending more time, and energy with the new thing that's bringing you more peace, time, energy, and money.

NOTES:

DAY 49

There is no need to cut anyone out of your life, just simply find better people to deal with. You will naturally gravitate to those things and people that give you more strength, more energy, and more guidance. If you find better things in life, you will naturally want to be there more often, and those people and things that aren't as good for you will naturally be around less and less. Find better, do better, be better.

NOTES:

DAY 50

If all you've ever had is bologna, you don't know how to handle steak. You couldn't season it, cook it, store it, or even afford it. You may even think steak is worse because it's tougher. Those who have only ever had bologna may not know that bologna is processed meat and has a higher chance of causing cancer, is less nutritious, and is only good for a snack every now and then. Many people have only ever dealt with Bologna people in their lives, and when steak people come around, they are so used to the poor quality of the Bologna people they don't know how to handle the steak people. The Bologna people have never uplifted them, supported them, spoken into their lives, built them up, and have only loved them as long as they could get something out of them. So, when Steak comes around and genuinely wants to do these things, they don't even know how to accept their help or love; they get pushed away believing they are being scammers or have ulterior motives. Learn to distinguish bologna people in your life and find more steak people.

NOTES:____

DAY 51

Many people say that it takes money to make money, it doesn't take money to make money, it takes an idea to make money. You can quite often use what you have to make more money. You may remember the young man who I am mentoring, we started his trash business. He makes money every week, and it took no money to start at all, just time, work, dedication, and mentorship. Look around in your life and when you notice something or someone that is lacking somewhere, see if there is a way for you to rectify what's missing and make a few dollars in the process. Train your brain to think of ideas and remedies. Don't listen to everything you've heard your entire life as gospel, because most of it is put into your head to keep u ignorant, broke, and subservient to the system. Begin with 1 idea a week and expand on that.

NOTES:

DAY 52

When you have a laid-out plan for your life, and set up a budgeted system for it, meaning budget your time, your finances, your meals....it becomes habit, even routine. So much so, that you don't notice the progress you're making. Once the initial mindset of lack leaves, you get adjusted to the new lifestyle, and living this way just becomes a habit. If you have a goal and a purpose that you stay focused on, you begin to worry less about the "things you can't do" and more about how close you are to your end results. This takes a mental shift though, and you must be determined to reach your goals. Stay focused, and stay determined, and you'll look up one day and see that you've surpassed the goals you set, and you need to set new ones. Keep pushing, and believing, and stop thinking about what CAN'T be done, and believe that you CAN get whatever you imagine done.

NOTES:

DAY 53

In baseball, if you have a 300-batting average, you're a god, can go anywhere and do anything u want, and will have some of the largest contracts in the league. That's a 30% hit ratio, so you hit the ball 3 out of 10 times you were up to bat. In basketball, if you shoot 44% from the 3-point line, you're the best shooter in league history, that's making a basket just over 4 times out of every 10. But in actual life, we expect ourselves, and those around us to hit homeruns every single time they go to do something.

A lot of things won't go according to plan, but you have to adjust and refocus. You will have failures, you will have setbacks, but if you are intent and focused on making it, you will achieve your goals. Don't think that everything will be a home run, especially in the beginning stages, just simply try to connect the bat with the ball. Make small goals that lead to larger goals. Instead of reading 1 book, read 2 pages today, make 2 phone calls, talk to 1 person, or make 1 post, but START. I've heard people say, "You can't lose if you don't try," and while this may be true.... you can never win if you don't try either. Get in the game, take your shots, and learn how to be better.

NOTES:____

DAY 54

Be careful about what you wish for because you just might get it. Often in life, we ask for, pray for, and even beg for things that we feel we want or need. And more often than not, we are given those things, but not in the way we expect, so we disregard them. We ask that our bills be gone, so we are given jobs but fail to plan, save, budget, or gain more knowledge. Very rarely will you be given the gift you ask for; you will more than likely be given the TOOLS you need to fix the situation. Preparation is also needed when asking for things. It's quite possibly the highest thing needed, because without preparation, even if you get what you're asking for, you won't know how to handle it, and you'll lose it. How can you ask for a husband if you are hanging out with all your single friends? How can you ask for a million dollars, and can't even handle your paycheck, how can u ask for better health, but don't work out, eat better, or do any health-conscious things now? Your blessing, and the very thing you're asking for, is inside of the preparation that you are willing to apply to it.

The children of Israel asked to be free from slavery, so Moses showed up. But it wasn't easy, Moses took them through the plague, and after the plague, they suffered just as much as the Egyptians did. They were in the dark, they couldn't drink the bloody water, their crops were eaten too, and they all cried for Moses to leave. They were now fighting against the very thing they had been praying for because it didn't come easy. When they were finally let go, they walked to the Red Sea, and Pharaoh caught up with them. They started whining and crying again, then they crossed the Red Sea and hadn't heard from Moses, so they cried AGAIN. They cried so much and so often that God said he wasn't letting NONE OF THEM into the land he had for them. You're getting what you asked for, but you aren't willing to put in the work. It takes more to gain freedom than just walking out the door. You must prepare for your freedom.

NOTES:____

DAY 55

Make up your mind about what it is that you want. Be willing and ready to go through a transformative time in your life. You can't bring the same mindset you currently have into the new thing you're trying to attain. If you want to be a millionaire, you can't think like a worker. Millionaires have workers working FOR them, it's difficult to be both. It takes a shift to see new things, another shift to understand new things, and another shift to do new things. Begin to prepare your mind and strengthen your discipline for the life and goals you have set for yourself. If I want to become a bodybuilder, I have to begin to think like one. I must read more books and articles about bodybuilding, begin to eat like a bodybuilder, go to the gym and hang out with and talk to bodybuilders, and train like a bodybuilder.

The problem is you want a bodybuilder's body, with a McDonald's mindset, a Burger King drive, and a microwave attitude. You must become the thing you want, far before you get it. To be a millionaire, and KEEP it, you must learn about saving, investing, numbers, return on investments, cap rates, percentages, blah, blah, blah. Many will say that that's too much and takes too much time. Then u will stay where you are, and maybe be worse off for the rest of your life, and you will have built a heavy burden around your children's necks because you haven't taught them how to be any better than you.

NOTES:____

DAY 56

How do you get the best return on your investments?????? That's simple, begin to invest more time, more effort, more dedication, and watch your returns grow. Increase your knowledge base about your investments, read books, and take courses, and your investments will begin to grow. Show me where you spend your time and money, and I can show you where your value lies. If your time and money are spent on your investments, that's what you value; and given enough time, they will begin to take care of you, instead of you having to always take care of them. If all you can afford is one seed, get a book on gardening from the library, learn what that seed needs, the best time to plant that seed, and then take care of that seed as you've been instructed. That one seed will sprout, grow, and bring back multiples of what you've planted. Now do you eat all the new fruit or replant them all for an even bigger harvest? Many people will eat the very seeds they should be replanting and be back at trying to collect another seed to plant as before. Sacrifice a few harvests to replant your garden, so it will eventually produce more than you can eat, and pass on that knowledge.

When I speak of investments, I'm sure the first thing your mind thought of was finances, but that was actually the last thing on my mind. When I was speaking of investments I was speaking of love, peace, help, happiness, joy, gratitude, knowledge, acceptance, patience, and contentment. If you have these things and plant them in abundance, the money will be there.

NOTES:____

DAY 57

Set goals big enough so that they require you to change. Your goals may seem like a thing to attain, but it's about the journey, and not the destination. The journey you travel on the way to achieving your goals is what makes you, what forges you, and what solidifies your character, and discipline. On the way to your goals, you should not only pick up more discipline, and more structure, but you should also be making mistakes, gaining knowledge and wisdom, stumbling, and recovering so that you can guide others around these very same pitfalls. Growth does not happen overnight, it's usually a slow and gradual process that is rarely seen unless you get away from people for a while, and when you return, they can see a difference. As your children grow you can't see it, but you see the effects of it.

The tighter or too short clothes, the outgrown shoes, new hairs, puberty; all of a sudden, they're looking you in the eye, but it's difficult to see their actual growth. And it's not about the final destination of graduation that we should be focused on, it's what we are putting in them up until graduation (the process/journey) that's most important. What good is getting them out of the house, if we haven't built anything into them, and they can't function on their own? Similarly, the million-dollar goal is nice, but what good is it, if you don't know how to save, invest, help others, or make it grow....? Not much, if you'll be back at work in under 5 years. Appreciate the journey, the growth, and all the headaches that come along with it, because you're simply being built stronger for your blessings.

NOTES:____

DAY 58

Don't accept anything in the good times, that you wouldn't accept in bad times. If it is unacceptable when you're losing, it should also be unacceptable when you're winning. I knew a basketball coach who allowed the guys to do a lot more foolishness and antics when they were winning games.... celebrating, not working as hard in practice, being late, letting grades slip; but once they started losing, all of these things suddenly became unacceptable, and intolerable. The problem with this is, that you've already conditioned the guys one way, and now you have to spend 10 times the energy to break that way of thinking and get them back on the right track. And some never will get back on the right track.

Many thought that the coach "switched up" on them when in reality he was just a bit more lax. Some couldn't reign themselves back in and ended up off the team. Similarly, don't allow things in your life i.e. lies, disrespect, stealing, stress, ungratefulness, and lack of reciprocity when you are doing well, and everything is looking up; because when things turn down, as they always do, these things become amplified, and YOU seem like the bad guy when you decide that you can't physically, mentally, and/or financially afford it anymore. Begin to draw lines in the sand in your life, and don't allow others to ruin your peace.

NOTES:____

DAY 59

Life doesn't just "happen" to the rich and successful. They PLAN and are very strategic about their lives. They have lifetime plans, broken down into 10-year plans, broken down into 5-year, 2-year, 1-year, monthly, weekly, and daily plans. Life only "just happens" to unsuccessful people. Professional sports players didn't "just happen" to get there, there was a plan laid out, workout schemes followed, practices, games, diet regimens, tapes sent out relentlessly to teams, and coaches, and self-promotion going on. It wasn't an accident that they made it to their respective leagues. Even the biggest busts could still beat YOU because they had been training, and following the laid-out plan. Begin to focus on your future life and plan it out. Log out a plan that leads you to where you want to be.

Do what you know how to do. Even if you think you don't know anything about your goal, do as much as you can. You probably don't know anything about being a millionaire or don't know any millionaires to talk to.... but you know they've got money in the bank. So, start there, and begin to put amounts of money in the bank, then start educating yourself about millionaires. You will learn so much on your journey, that it will change you into a completely different person, and your goals and dreams may even change along the way. But if u want to be more successful, keep planning the work, and working the plan. If you get in your car and just drive aimlessly, with a goal to reach Chicago, you MAY get there, but if you haven't looked at the map before, or pulled up Google maps you'll probably never reach your destination. Or if you do happen to stumble upon it, it will take far longer than it could have, if you just took the few minutes necessary to look at a map and write down the directions. Everything you want to do, and everywhere u want to go has already been done, and there's a road map on how to get there. Find the roadmap (the books) read them, write down what YOU plan to do, and begin to follow it.

NOTES:____

DAY 60

Life is filled with highs and lows. Mentally, physically, spiritually, emotionally, and financially. It's our low points in life, our valleys that allow us to ultimately reach our highest points and peaks. The further u pull the slingshot back, the further the pebble can go. If you duck out, every time things begin to get harder, and more difficult, you're stopping that slingshot from being pulled further back, which is also stopping YOU from being thrust further in your life. Embrace the fears, the pain, and the struggle, and learn to harness them, and use them as stepping stones. Learn in your valley, to use it while trying to reach your peaks.

NOTES:

DAY 61

Having a good friend(s) in your corner is priceless. They can be the best confidante, they can keep your secrets, and help you out of a bind. They can help so that you don't even get in those binds, and a good friend can even be trusted with your most prized possessions, your spouse, and your children. The Bible says a friend will stick closer to you than a brother. Even the worst of brothers will fight for, and protect you at least once, but the best of them never leave your side, and will die for you. Imagine having someone in your corner who will do more for you than that.

Build and cultivate better relationships and begin to make long-lasting bonds with those who deem themselves worthy of your friendship. Just like everything else your friendship bonds will be tested, the true test is whether the relationship will make it through the test, OR if once broken whether it can be mended. There is nothing like KNOWING someone will be there for you when you fall, and you don't always have to mend your own wounds from every battle life throws at you.

NOTES:____

DAY 62

Are other people's lives better because you were in them??? One gauge that we can use to see how well our life's going, or the impact that we have while we are here, is the effect our living has had on others' lives. Helping, guiding, teaching, building, and feeding into others' lives helps build YOUR life. It helps to surround you with a community, and friendships; and it fosters around all of you a better energy of sharing, and abundance, and a growth mindset. Begin building others around you and watch how you begin to get built from others.

NOTES:

DAY 63

Find your passions in life. Many people don't know what their passion is because they've been told what to do and what to think their whole lives. Start with this thought... what keeps you up at night, what brings you a smile, or brings a tear to your eye? These can be a guide to what your passions can be. Look a bit deeper than the surface, if you're worried about your bills, and they are keeping you up, it may be the lack of money, it may be the lack of self-discipline, so you overspend, maybe it's the lack of planning or a budget that's causing the bill problem.

Whatever it may be, look deeper than the initial problem you THINK it may be. Your life will not get better by CHANCE, it will only get better if YOU change it. Put in the work and begin to change what you see as problems in your life. Push the limits on your life. Stop dying every day, by not living the life you want, not aiming for your goals, and not even trying to reach a higher level. Stop believing the cards you've chosen are the only ones in the deck. You can do anything and accomplish anything you decide you want. Set your mind and begin the process. YOU....CAN...DO IT

NOTES:

DAY 64

We often focus on the more superficial part of life. I talked to a friend trying to lose weight, and they said the scale had gone up 2 lbs. This is the superficial part of health we focus on, but I think we should focus on everything else. I stated how I've been working out consistently over 9 months, and I've only lost about 15 lbs. BUT, I have gained so much more than the lost 15 lbs. My clothes fit looser, some of my grey hairs have actually turned back black, I'm noticing my body begin to take on forms I've never seen, I sleep better, my cholesterol, blood pressure, and sugar levels are down, and my testosterone is wayyyyy up. I'm not as irritated, or irritable, I'm more at peace, and I just seem to smile more. To me, these should be more of the benchmarks for healthier living. If we just stick in our minds that we are going to do something, work at it every day, no matter how small.

In life, just like the gym we focus on the next party, the next outfit, the next significant other, the next car we want to buy, or whatever else fills our head. Focus more of your energy on the less superficial things, like peace, happiness, joy, contentment, health, gaining more assets, and teaching future generations. There are so many other things we can focus our energies on, that would lead us to the promised land a lot quicker. Give it a try and see what u come up with.

NOTES:____

DAY 65

Concentration and focus are VITAL when trying to navigate this thing we call life. Many will say that they don't know how to focus or concentrate, but we all do; it's simply WHAT we choose to concentrate and focus on. We are raised and taught how to focus and concentrate on all the negative things around us. Unfortunately, the news shows only negative images, the movies we watch show destruction and terror, and instill fear in you; and the music we listen to is filled with negative tones and imagery. So, all we know to focus on is the negative....how much we are in debt, the bills that are coming due or late, what happens IF my car breaks down, my check is going to be short because I had to go to the Doctor. But we must take all of that energy and begin to shift it towards something else.

Listen to more positive music, watch less TV, and movies altogether, and when you do, make sure it's positive. Focus on the bills that you CAN pay, and deal with the rest either when you get more money or devise a plan for a side hustle. You worrying about things doesn't make them better; coming up with solutions to fix them, so that you don't have to worry about them does. Our brains are a warehouse, and as long as you've been alive you've been filling it with negative, self-doubting, self-hating material, so much so, that now in every aisle you go down, every box on every shelf is filled with negativity. We need to start refilling our mental warehouse with positive imagery. I can, I will, I am, I can do it. Focus on the GOOD in your life and begin your journey there.

NOTES:____

DAY 66

When we cook food, we all use seasoning. We throw a meal together, cook it, eat it, and store any leftovers to eat maybe tomorrow for lunch. If we eat it for lunch, quite often the meal is better because it's had time to marinate overnight in the fridge, and that gives the seasoning extra time to do more work. Life can be a little better when you get marinated. Sometimes in life, we see we are doing a lot of the same things at the same time as others, but not reaping what they are reaping. A little extra time on the stove of life will cook a bit more seasoning into you. Now you feel as though you've been left out in the cold, and darkness, and nobody is there for you. You've just been put in the refrigerator of life, and you're picking up more seasoning until you come out, and you're now well-seasoned and can make better decisions for your future.

Ensure that during your time of seasoning, you're preparing yourself for your ultimate goals, and you'll be ready when it is time to step up to the plate. Everyone's timing and seasoning isn't the same. Just remember to stay the course and make small incremental steps towards your goals daily. Pennies make dollars, steps make miles, snowflakes turn into avalanches, and raindrops turn into waterfalls.

NOTES:____

DAY 67

I've had so many people today tell me about the "small accomplishments" they've made recently. NO accomplishment is "small." If you made a plan, put it into action, sacrificed something, and reached your goal, that....is....MONUMENTAL. One goal leads to the next, and that's momentum to the next. Every accomplishment is a stepping stone to bigger and greater accomplishments. Never look at your accomplishments as miniscule or not worthy. Your goals are what keep you motivated. Now go and celebrate your HUGE ACCOMPLISHMENTS, and yell from the mountain tops what you have done.

NOTES:

DAY 68

There are a number of ways to figure things out, and how to get things done the right way. One way is to just go do whatever it is. Without any prior knowledge of the subject, research, or mentors to guide you through it, you will more than likely screw it up; but that's ok, because 99% of the time, the things we try in life aren't so monumental that we can't afford mistakes. Once you mess up, you will have a little bit of knowledge about how NOT to do it (at least one way). Mistakes are ok and also acceptable, but what's not ok, is never trying to do anything, or waiting for the "perfect time." If you don't start, you never will. If you always look for excuses, you'll never learn and grow. Don't look for excuses not to do it....look for reasons TO do something. Get out there and stumble if you have to, even fall, but just make sure you get back up, and keep going.

NOTES:

DAY 69

Many times in life, we ask for things and expect to get them, as if from a genie, where they wiggle their noses, and POOF it's there. Seldom do we think about the price that must be paid for what we ask. Recently I'd been asking that I would be able to become debt-free (as many people do).I didn't hit the lottery, or have a rich uncle die and leave me an inheritance, so my freedom from indebtedness came from MORE work. My job picked up on overtime, and I grabbed every hour I could, putting all the extra money toward bills.

I got exactly what I asked for. I don't miss time or take days off because "I don't feel like it" or "I'm tired" because I feel as though that's a slap in the face. You can't ask for something, and then turn your nose up at it because it's not wrapped in a pretty bow. EVERYTHING you're asking for is on the other side of harder work, longer hours, and more reading material. Be ready to put in some sweat equity for the things you ask for, and don't look to take days off, because it only prolongs your agony that much longer.

NOTES:____

DAY 70 (SEE DAY 3)

I read about a study done on lab rats, some years back. They had 2 different groups. Group A was given everything they needed. They had water, and all the food they could eat, the temperature was perfect, and they had no predators. Group B was pretty much the exact opposite. They had to hunt and forage, they put predators in the simulation with them, and sometimes they would take away their food and water for periods of time. Group A eventually died out; after about 3 generations, they just stopped mating. Group B consistently thrived throughout all of the test groups they did. If you have a "perfect" life you're setting yourself and your bloodline up for certain self-extermination. Trials and tribulations are not only most certain to come, but they are here for our betterment, to help us, to build us, to strengthen us. Adversity is not an executioner, but a teacher. Look past the slight discomfort and look to what can be learned from the situation you're going through.

NOTES:

DAY 71

We look at goldfish as small, cute animals to give to children to keep as a first pet. They don't cause a mess, there is no noise, not much to clean up after, and they don't cost much. But goldfish are only small because of the environment you keep them in. Since you keep them in a small bowl, they never grow to be full-size. If you ever let one into the wild, goldfish can grow to be as much as 2 feet long and weigh up to 8 pounds.

Stop limiting your growth by keeping yourself in an environment that isn't conducive to your growth. You stay around the same people who have nothing going for themselves or aren't motivated to do any better. You have the same conversations, that have nothing to do with the future you want for yourself. You miss the same seminars that could set you on the right track, and you spend all your free time NOT educating yourself about any subject that can change your life. You're safe and secure in your tidy little bowl, but if the smallest thing goes wrong, you.... just like that fish… will be flushed down the toilet. Begin to venture out so that you can start to grow into your potential. Get out of your same old routine that keeps you trapped and bound. Chains used to have to be clasped to your neck, hands, and feet to keep you from running away to a better life. Now....chains are called TV, comfort, and 9 to 5.

NOTES:____

DAY 72

The sunrise is a beautiful thing. All the colors and the sounds of the world are beginning to come to life. As you rise, you know a new day is beginning. You can see many of the same people doing the same things, or if you do something different like go a new way, or leave at a different time, you will see new things. Whatever it is that you see, you'll be able to see it clearly, because the sun is shining, and you're alert. As the sun rises on the East Coast, it still has a few hours until the West Coast can see the same sun you see; and halfway around the world, the sun is setting or has already set, and people over there can't see quite as clearly.

Life is the same way. You can have the brightest idea in the world, but because you live on the East Coast, and they are on the West Coast, they can't quite see your idea yet....it's not their time. They may be in the dark for a while. Find those who are looking at the sun at the same time, speak to those who speak life into others, find growth in people, and work with them. When you have people on the same page, with the same goals, at the same time, it's like strapping a jet engine on your back, pushing you that much faster to your goals.

NOTES:____

DAY 73

Keep going, no matter what. If you stop, it takes exponentially more energy to reach your goal. I was on the elliptical machine today, and my goal is to get 150 steps per minute. I wasn't really feeling it today, so I was pretty much just going through the motions. I was doing about 130 steps per minute. After about 2 or 3 minutes I began picking it up, and about a minute later I was at, at least 150. I realized how far I was behind my goal, so I began to pick it up, I started kicking it up to about 165 strides a minute. I wasn't completely focused on the workout; so, I would look down periodically, and I was back down, so I'd pick it back up.

It took me the rest of the workout (30 minutes) and a mad dash at the last 2 minutes to reach my goal. When u slack off, it makes it that much more difficult to reach any goal you set. If you stay consistent with your work ethic, you will get there. Even if u do stop, get started back, and complete your goal. It may take longer, but you'll accomplish your goal. Don't stop, and stay on track, continue to check your progress, and adjust accordingly!

NOTES:

DAY 74

Many people go to see therapists to figure out, or to "fix" problems within themselves. Usually, the therapist asks a bunch of questions to get to the root of the problem, and every so often throws in some small anecdotes or thoughts about what's being said. Most of the time, the therapist isn't telling you what they think or believe, but they are usually opening your eyes to other avenues so that you can figure out your issues for yourself. Even when you go to therapists, they open you up and allow YOU to solve your own problems. The answers you seek are normally either already in you or close around you. The more you put in yourself, the more answers you will have readily available. Continue to build yourself, continue to build your internal library of answers. You are the source of the solutions you seek.

NOTES:

DAY 75

Every year, we go through 4 seasons, and every year there some are people who are unprepared for each season. Springtime is the new beginning… everything begins to bud and grow, animals come out of hibernation, pollen is everywhere, and temperatures are beginning to warm up. Summertime, the heat is at its peak, everything is growing rapidly, and things are working as intended. This is the world on full display… everything is so moving and alive. Then comes fall, where everything begins to slow down, things start dying off, and animals begin their winter preparations. Finally, you have winter, where there is nothing… for the most part, there is no life, just desolation… and you must survive on your wits and what you've built the rest of the year. This happens every year....and every year there are some people who are never prepared. Just like the earth has seasons, so does your life. Every day, every week, every year will not be Summertime, when it's time to reap the good things. There will be falls, and winters, where there is nothing out there for you, so you must rely on what you've built up, stored, and collected between spring and summer.

During the good times in your life, stash some money away, start a business, build strong friendships, and relationships, pay your bills up a few months in advance, and begin reading more books so that you know and understand what to do when things begin to go south. The only way you can take advantage of opportunities when they arise is if you, first and foremost, notice the opportunity, and secondly have prepared yourself for that opportunity. If a House becomes available for purchase at a deep discount, but you haven't prepared your credit, don't have the down payment, and haven't paid down most of your outstanding debts to lower your debt-to-income ratio, you probably won't get the loan. You didn't prepare in the spring and summer. Start preparing today, for the dreams you want, so when they do show up, it's a seamless transition.

NOTES:____

DAY 76

Hurt people, hurt people. When we've been hurt so bad, for so long, it reprograms us and that is where our mind begins to start from....the hurt place. We know what was done to us, and we know how it feels, but somehow, we either, Consciously, or subconsciously begin to do the thing we hated having done to us, to other people. It must be pointed out to us, and we must make an effort to irradicate these tendencies. Talk to those close to you, tell them what your issues may be and to point them out if you begin to act on them; and ask them to help you make a change for the better in your life. You are the only one who can stop your generational curses and replace them with generational blessings.

NOTES:

DAY 77

In order to be proven, u must be tested; in order to be tested, you must be trained. When things seem low, you're confused and hurt. You're simply going through one of your many training periods in life, and it's getting you ready for your test. The tests never stop coming nor get easier, YOU just get stronger, and gain more knowledge and understanding. Walking hasn't changed since you were a baby; but now, your muscles are more developed, and you have more insight about it. If you go to the gym, the weights don't get lighter; the more you lift them, YOU get stronger. Those 100 pounds today are the same 100 pounds 5 years from now, the only question is....will it be just as heavy next year, or will you train harder, to be able to handle that load? Accept today's life challenges and overcome them so when the same test comes next month, you will be that much further ahead, that much stronger, and that much more resilient.

NOTES:

DAY 78

Make the choice... today's pleasure, or tomorrow's promise. If you just live for the day, it is very difficult to reach tomorrow's promise. To lose weight, the simplest explanation is that you have to burn more calories than you consume. If you keep tomorrow's promise in mind, you'll be more mindful of the things you consume, and how much exercise you're getting; and as long as you're consistently burning more than your intake, tomorrow's promise will be realized. If you go for today's pleasure, that will inevitably slow tomorrow's promise....at best, and may even, derail it altogether. Whether it is weight loss, finances, love, or happiness....make the plan, and begin to travel the personal road to your promised land. Everyone has had instances where they look back and say, "If I hadn't stopped I'd be...." don't let that happen again. Even if it's only a baby step toward your promise, IT MAKES A DIFFERENCE.

NOTES:

DAY 79

Even if you act the same towards everyone, and treat everyone in the exact same manner, you are NOT the same TO everyone. Everyone sees and views you in a different light, which is largely based on their own individual journey. My sisters and I were raised in the same house, by the same parents, in the same neighborhood, but yet we've all turned out different (me, a bit more radically different). You can be a savior to some and a villain to others; you can be an uplifting hand or an unwavering, overpowering slap in the face....all from the same gesture. All you can do is continue to do and be the best that you can be, and let the chips fall where they may. Even Jesus had enemies, and people who hated him, for no other reason than because he helped; so, understand that you are no better. Live your life, be the best person you can be, and let those who want to walk away.....walk away.

NOTES:____

DAY 80

The best way to change any situation you don't like is to change yourself. Personal growth and maturity will solve many of the problems you encounter. Growth and maturity will tell u NOT to go places or be around people who can put you in negative situations. Growth and maturity also teach you better ways to handle situations once you're in them, learning to accept a loss, and just continuing in your life, is the ultimate growth and maturity in my book. Growth and maturity are two things that don't automatically come with age. as some may think. My mom used to always say, "Ain't no fool, like an old fool." Growth and maturity must be sought after, they must be studied, and they must be taught to others. Begin building your strong foundation and take the time to be the change you want to see. You are the maestro of your life, so make changes for the better

NOTES:____

DAY 81

When we ask for things, there are 4 major reasons that we would get them (in my estimation) 1) your wants; 2) your needs; 3) your capacity to hold the wants; 4) your ability to care for the wants. To get something, there must first be a desire for it. You have to want something.... that's pretty simple. Your capacity to hold onto something. How much of the want can you hold? Sometimes you may ask, why did they get more than me, it may be because they can hold more. Larger vases hold more water. You don't know what someone is doing to work on themselves and make their vases larger. If you want to hold more, enlarge your vase by working on yourself. Begin construction on yourself. Be a blessing to others, help people, and work on your flaws and faults. Sometimes we don't see our own flaws, so ask those closest to you what they see as your flaws. You may agree, or disagree, but at least you've started the process.

Frequently we aren't given bigger, and better because we don't care for the smaller things that we currently have. If you see that your children destroy every toy they have, would you buy them an expensive VR headset??? We must take care of the things we already have in our possession, if we want to acquire more, no matter how small we think they are. If you say this car is old, so I'm not gonna wash it, clean it out, or fix it when things break, then that is now your new mindset, and you begin to look at everything like that. Even if you get a new car, you will eventually treat it the same way. How you do one thing, is how you do everything.

NOTES:____

DAY 82

Don't let good opportunities pass you by without at least giving it a shot. There are many things in life that we ask for, whether it be money, love, happiness, or whatever. When we ask for these things, we see them dropping in our laps, and us living our lives to the fullest with them. We are given most of the things that we ask for, but because they don't come as we thought they would come, we don't recognize them, so, therefore, we don't pursue them. We ask for money, or to be debt-free, but we don't take advantage of the overtime at work, and if we do, then we spend more of the money on frivolous things instead of sending it all towards paying down some of the debts we have.

You want more business opportunities but turn down all the deals that come your way, because they are sub-par, and what you think is beneath you to deal with. You want a good spouse but refuse to listen to the ones in your life who are trying to help, guide, and build you. The opportunities we want, and desire are all around us every day, we just have to begin to switch our mindset over to see them. They aren't big loud horns; they are small whispers because we aren't tuned into their frequency. Once someone tells you how a radio works, you can pick up whatever station you want, as long as you're within range. Success and opportunities work the same way. Once you start seeing the opportunities, they will continue to astound you with how many there are, and how they've always been right in front of you the entire time.

NOTES:____

DAY 83

Everyone has disagreements with their significant other, this is normal. The older we get the less these things should turn into arguments, and the more there should be discussions. There should be growth over time where you just shouldn't be arguing at 40 and 50, like you did at 20 and 30. Sit down and have conversations, see where each other is coming from, and how their mind actually works. The more you truly understand about your partner, not just their knee-jerk reactions, the fewer disagreements you may have. If I know hitting you in the knee gets me kicked in the shin, I'll be less likely to hit you in the knees. But we also have to see that I wasn't kicked just to be kicked, it was a reaction to what happened.

If you're having new disagreements, to me this is good. New disagreements mean that there's growth, we've conquered the old things, and we are moving into new areas, new genres, and new fields, and we have to learn from each other in these new areas. Selling McDonald's in America is different than selling McDonald's in India. There are different laws, different traditions, and different people. So, every time you move into another area of life, there will be new laws of that land you must learn; so, there will be a time when you must fumble your way through. But if you keep having the same disagreements about the same things, year after year, you are stuck in a space of no growth, and as I've said before, things that don't grow in some way, are dead.

NOTES:____

DAY 84

Those who know what to do are good, those who know WHY you should do it are valuable.... but those who know what NOT to do are wise and an invaluable commodity to your organization. You can teach a monkey to do many things people do every day, and that monkey will bring slight value to you. As long as he doesn't have to do any other tasks, think about anything, or nothing goes wrong then he works. But when the slightest thing changes, he's now lost and useless. The man who can think and knows WHY we do things the way we do, is more adaptable to situations, and when things go wrong, he can make changes and continue with the work; but when u can figure out many of the consequences, and you know why something SHOULDNT be done, you are invaluable.

Many choices we make in life, on the job, and at home, have consequences far beyond today. When you can look ahead and see many of the possibilities and outcomes that can come 6 months or 2 years down the road, you are now wise and have eclipsed the knowledge of the average person. Everyone knows you should go to work, but the smart ones know you need to save money for rainy days because they will come. But the wise know to save money only so that you have enough for emergencies. Anything over that should be invested into something that's bringing you cash flow so that you can live forever... because savings will eventually run out. The wisdom is to also teach future generations behind you about saving and investing to make their life easier, earlier. Now you have become an invaluable teacher to future generations.

NOTES:____

DAY 85

I grew up in Chicago, and just like every other city, we had our own slang, terminology, and accents. Of course, being from there, what everyone else did, and how they sounded was strange, and THEY were the oddballs. When I grew up, I joined the military and moved away. I've spent the rest of my years living in different parts of the South. Now when I talk to my classmates or family, I am the oddball who sounds like he was raised in the South his entire life. To me, I still sound the same, until I hear myself recorded, and then I believe I sound like a country Bama (lol). Awesome!

To grow in life, we have to be careful of the situations, people, and places we put ourselves around. Just like my new accent, what you're around long enough will automatically rub off on you, and you won't even notice it unless you can take a step back and see what you're becoming. If you sit in dung long enough, after a while it stops smelling. Constantly monitor your surroundings and be diligent about changes in your life. The sharpest knife cutting through the softened butter will eventually become dull if not sharpened regularly.

NOTES:____

DAY 86

If u give a man on the brink of starving to death a large mansion, you haven't done much of anything for him. You can tell him all the secrets of the universe, and how to be rich, loved, and happy; but he won't hear ANYTHING u have to say, because his immediate needs aren't being met. Once his immediate needs are met, you can talk to him in a better space where he may be able to hear and absorb what you're saying. A lot of times in life we are giving to people and wondering why they are not receiving in the manner we THINK they should. It may be because you're giving a starving man a house. Are you giving what is needed or asked for, or are you giving what makes YOU happy, and what YOU simply want to give? Meet peoples' immediate needs so that they will have a better listening ear.

NOTES:

DAY 87

My mother grew up with a bunch of brothers, and one thing they would do is beat each other up in their sleep. I don't know exactly how long it went on, but she left the house at 18 and married my dad. This year my mom will be 70, so she's been away from her family 3 times as long as she was with them, but I would suggest that if my mom is sleeping, you don't go shake her and wake her up, because she still wakes up jumping and swinging, as though she has to protect herself from her brothers. If I want to wake her up, I just pick up a shoe and throw it at her (it's my small way of getting back at her from when I would act up, and she would pick up the first thing she could find, which was usually a shoe, and chuck it at my head… lol).

Most of her brothers have died off now, but the effect they still have on her is immeasurable. Many things have happened to us over our lifespan… mostly when we were growing up… that affect us to this day. Some things we are aware of and some things we may not be. But the only way they can truly affect you is if you let them. Most of the things that shaped us negatively are dead and figuratively. And even if they aren't.... we can kill them (figuratively speaking. DO NOT GO OUT AND KILL ANYONE THAT HAS HARMED YOU). Don't go around the rest of your life saying, "That's just the way I am" or "I've been this way my whole life." YOU can change your life, and YOU can grow. You are a caterpillar who can change into a beautiful butterfly whenever you choose, but the choice is up to you.

NOTES:____

DAY 88

Growing up, my dad was a heavy weekend drinker. He would go out, usually to his bowling leagues, and after bowling many of them would sit around the bar and drink until everyone slowly started heading home. Most of the time, my dad was one of the last to leave. When he got home, he would sleep in the tub. I always thought mom just wouldn't let him sleep in the bed if he had been drinking, but what it was, was that he had thrown up before (I don't know how many times), and whoever had to clean it up must have said, "We're not doing this again." So, when he had been drinking and came home, he would sleep in the shower. Then if he vomited he could just get up, and shower, and not much cleaning was involved. We have the opportunities in our lives to change our path at any point in time. To prevent cleaning vomit, my father could have stopped drinking altogether, he could have drunk far less, or he could have stopped drinking after a certain time. But instead of treating the sickness, he chose to treat the symptoms and the aftermath. He said I'll keep drinking but I'll just sleep in the shower.

Many of us choose to treat our symptoms in life instead of our sicknesses. You treat the symptoms of low money by working overtime when you could treat your sickness of overspending, or simply being over-leveraged. Take a look at your bills... maybe that house, or that car, or those memberships are far more than you need and can handle safely right now. Take an inventory of your life and your situations, to see where you may be "lacking" and trace the lack back to the source. It probably won't be easy to change, but small adjustments over time lead to massive life alterations. Choose to find, and cure your actual sickness, instead of just the symptoms, and watch things begin to change for the better

NOTES:____

DAY 89

Where you are in life right now, is exactly where you chose to be. Your life is a culmination of your decisions.... or lack thereof. The better more informed decisions you make, the better your chances your life will turn out the way you want it to. You are in debt because of the things you chose to buy 1-5 years ago, you stay in debt because you choose not to funnel all extra money towards those debts, and you are overweight because of the food choices you make, and the lack of exercise. You feel as though you're stuck in a rut because you keep making the same decisions over and over again. Your job isn't the problem, YOU picked it, and YOU choose to stay every single day. Work on a plan of action and make better, more informed decisions.

Find out where you really want to be, then find 10 people who are already there, and begin to pick their brains. Read more books on the things you want to do. Take some classes or go to some seminars. Your life will not change if YOU don't change it. You have the keys to your own freedom, pick them up and use them to set yourself free. The library is open every day of the week. Free books, free internet, free computers, and a minimum charge for printing and copying. Begin forming your own personal chrysalis.

NOTES:

DAY 90

Are you interested in your goals, or are you committed to your goals? If you're interested in something, you'll do it when it's convenient, when you have free time, or in your pastime. If you're committed, you're going to do it regardless of what's happening around you. Are you still gonna run when it's raining and cold or are you gonna wait until conditions are "better"? Are you gonna save that $1.37 left over at the end of the week or are you gonna wait until you have more money to put away? Are you gonna give up your lunch break to read that book, or are you gonna wait till the weekend when you have more time available? Be more committed to the things YOU say YOU want.

You get up every morning and go to work to fulfill someone else's dreams and visions. You're committed to someone else's dreams. U may miss a few days, but unless something major happens you're at work. If you can commit to someone else's dream 8 hours a day, 5 days a week, why can't you commit to your own dreams 1 hour a day? Commit to your goals, and your goals will commit to you.

NOTES:____

DAY 91

If you pay in cotton candy, expect to get clowns 🤡. When it comes to life, the better the grade of people, the more you are willing to pay. Payment isn't necessarily monetary. Payment is whatever 2 people agree on. Payment can be love, peace happiness, joy, laughter....it doesn't matter, but payment MUST be agreed on. If you want a 5-5-bedroom, 6-bathroom house in a nice community with great schools, but want to pay only $10,000 for the house, you may die waiting on that house because you don't want to pay the price. And even if you do get the house, at the price you want it would be so much work, that it may scare you off.

First, find out the price for what you want; then if you still want it, pay the price, and move on. If you want a discounted version it probably won't last as long or as I said earlier you'll have to put a ton of work into it, which would take all of your resources away from everything else you want. If you're ok with that, go for it. If not, re- reevaluate.

NOTES:

DAY 92

One of the best things that a person can do for themselves, is find their true identity, and their true purpose. Find out who you are at your core, what really gets you going, and what drives you. If you could take away all of your bills today, and you had an abundance of cash, what do you think you would do with your life, where would you be, where would you go, would you try to help others, would you travel more, or spend time with loved ones??? If money is no object what could you do? Imagine that, ponder on it, really go over it, and put some thought into it.

Take all the time you need. Once you figure that out, DO IT. You don't need a lot of money to do anything, you simply start where you are. If you want to travel more, start by just going to the next town over, if that's all you can afford. Begin training yourself to set goals, and seeing what it feels like to accomplish them. Do you want more time with loved ones out of town???? Start by calling and talking to them, video chatting, and writing old-fashioned handwritten letters. If you want to pay off a big debt, you have to take a small amount out of every check and slowly pay it down. Your dreams are the same way. Take a little bit of time out of your time paycheck each day and begin to pay for your goals and dreams. Eventually, you can become that person you saw yourself becoming, and the person you were meant to be, just like large debts take time to pay off, becoming your ideal self takes time, persistence, dedication, and commitment from you.

NOTES:____

DAY 93

You can beat anything in this world....you can beat hunger, and poverty, overcome your childhood, how you were raised, an abusive spouse, loss of a loved one....WHATEVER. But the one thing that is the most difficult to overcome, is a bad self-defeating mental state. Telling yourself that you are worthless, you can't get it done, or you'll never be any better causes you more damage than 10 abusive relationships. To change anything in your life, all you have to do is change your mindset. If you see it, you can have it. Repeat to yourself daily, "I can do it, I can have it, it will be mine." If you say it long enough, you will begin to believe it. If you put action behind it, it will happen 10 times faster. The opportunities you want are there for you every day; it takes a different mindset to not only see them but also to take advantage of them. If you don't like it, say to yourself you will change it in a positive way until you begin to believe in yourself enough to make a move.

NOTES:

DAY 94

It is perfectly ok to have standards. You can have standards with your spouse, your significant other, your friends, coworkers, or children. Standards are simply the rules for your life and telling people how you expect to be treated. If a smoker comes into your home, you may tell them that the standard or rule is that there is no smoking in your home, or that they must take their shoes off at the door. If people cannot accept your standards, then you should think twice about keeping them in your space. Your mental stability, your health, your finances, your actions, anxiety, and many other things are all tied to the standards and boundaries that you set, and how far you allow others to cross those lines.

If a smoker smokes in your home and wears their dirty shoes in, you now have to smell smoke for days, maybe causing you headaches (health), and you have to spend unexpected time sweeping, mopping, vacuuming, and maybe even shampooing carpet because they wore dirty shoes around your home. OR you can simply say "No....you're not welcome in my space." It saves so much time, effort, headaches, and energy. Set your standards for all aspects of your life and begin to enforce your boundaries. It may seem odd or weird at first, but after a while, you will begin to feel a greater inner peace.

NOTES:____

DAY 95

In today's society, people have so much stuff. There are so many things advertised, that we just HAVE to have, and of course, we can't let the Joneses outdo us, so we must get even more. It seems that we as a society have forgotten what SACRIFICE is. Not only do we have to have the new big thing, but we must have it TODAY. People hoard so many things, and then they scream and complain to anyone who will listen that they are broke and cannot afford their bills. They refuse to get another job; nothing is ever quite the right fit. Every option interferes with their "schedule," they can't bring themselves to sell anything, and they keep the high car note and the high house payment. They buy even more shoes and clothes to add to the list of the ones they already don't wear, but amazingly can't find a way to put $50 a week into the bank.

Don't get complacent with debt, and struggle. Don't sit in it so long or sit around those who wallow in debt and continuously struggle and think that it's ok and normal to do so. You were not put on this earth to amass debt and pay bills until you die. Sacrifice a little more. You don't need cable. Get rid of that expensive car note that's killing you. If you Trade it in, you may have enough to purchase something like a house you can rent out, and then THAT can pay for your car. It's not an overnight fix, but you can pull yourself up, dust yourself off, and begin a new chapter in your life.

NOTES:____

DAY 96

I saw a fb post about dating. It came from a guy, and he said that if you wanted to stand out and impress a woman, send her money to get a meal and her nails done before you even meet her for the first time. On the first date, take her to someplace different, like a helicopter ride, or a hiking trail, and he named a few other things. To me, these are leading many down the wrong path. The purpose of dating first, or any other, is to learn from each other. If you start out this way, this is what is expected from that point on. To me, these things must be earned so that they can be better appreciated. I'd like to know that you are here for ME and not necessarily the THINGS that I offer.

The best way to learn that is through basic dating.... coffee shops, activities, dinners, conversations, and some time spent together. I am also a huge believer in reciprocity. If I am spending and buying all of these things, am I receiving what I am asking for in return, or am I being equally compensated???? We get ourselves into trouble in life when we run headfirst without weighing the costs of things. The Bible says that if you want to build a house, first you must see how much that house is gonna cost you, so you know if you can afford it. Do the research on things you plan on doing or getting into, BEFORE just jumping into them, not just relationships, but businesses, homes, and vehicles. Talk to those who have what you are trying to attain and see what they say. If you value their opinions, do what they tell you to the best of your ability.

NOTES:____

DAY 97

How do you see, and deal with adversity and failure??? Many people see these things as negative. I see them as very positive. Because you have failed at a task, it does not make you a failure. You have simply learned 1, 20, 50, 100 ways to NOT do something. Every time you attempt and fail you should learn a little bit more each time, so although you may have not reached your ultimate goal, it's not a complete failure because you've LEARNED something. Adversity is simply something in your way that you have to figure out how to get around. Adversity is meant to be a steppingstone, or a passageway to the other side, don't stop in the middle of it, and allow the passageway to become a prison. When you overcome adversity, it builds you up and makes you stronger for the next adversity you will face.

Adversity in life will never stop, but the moment YOU stop fighting against it you become weaker. Adversity in life is like the gym, the weight stays the same, but you just get stronger, and better at lifting the weight. It will be uncomfortable at first, but the longer you lift the weights, the stronger your body becomes, and you can lift more weight until you reach your desired body goals. Adversity works the same way, keep fighting adversity off. At first, it will be uncomfortable, but the more you deal with it, the better you will become at dealing with it until you can handle bigger problems and come up with better solutions. Soon you'll be good enough so that you can help others through their problems. Don't run from adversities, face them head-on, and don't back down until you've beaten it. You're only a failure when you give up.

NOTES:______________________________

____

____

____

____

____

____

DAY 98

Quality vs quantity is an age-old argument. Everyone wants quality at a quantity price. But you get quality by living a purposeful quantity life. Practice doesn't make perfect if you're practicing the wrong thing.... again purposeful, knowledgeable practice makes perfect (better). To live a quality life, you must first find the thing that you want your life to model after, then do your research on what it takes to get there. Read books, attend seminars, use mentors and coaches from people who have verifiable proof, they've been where you want to be. Come up with a plan, then put that plan into action, simple… right???? You have all the framework for the quality of the life you'd like to live. Now it's time to begin the quantity lifestyle that will lead to quality. Repeatedly read books, the same one if you need to, until it sinks into what you should be doing.

You have to continuously put money away out of every check until it becomes a habit, if you are looking to sell a product, you have to knock on door, after door, after door, repeatedly being told no until you begin to make sales. After each day, go back and review what you think you did good, and what you did badly, and make adjustments. Then do the same thing tomorrow and the next day. You can't get the quality beach body you want until you've learned how to get the quantity days at the gym. Even steroid users, still have to hit the gym every day. Your life is no different and must be looked at the same way. You MUST get up every day, with a purpose and goal in mind, that you can accomplish, and that will get you closer to your ultimate goals. A journal has helped me tremendously. It's hard to forget the steps you need to take when they're written down in front of you. Begin today by putting in the quantity, so that in time you will start to see the quality.

NOTES:____

DAY 99

Life isn't about the destination, it's about the journey along the way to the destination. Dreams, goals, and destinations are wonderful things to have, they are a guiding beacon of where you want to head, but it's more about the things you encounter and overcome, the person you are becoming along the journey to your destinations, and the people you meet along the way. Enjoy every step along the way, or you won't enjoy the final step when it's all done. I get just as excited every week, as I see my debt balances fall, as I will when I send the last dollar to my debtors. I'm excited about where I will be able to put all of this money, and how I can pay MYSELF. It will take a while, but I can see the vision, and with every extra dollar, I'm that much closer to my goal. I enjoy reading books and amassing more knowledge about how to build, sustain, and pass on assets to many of the people that help me, and the ones I help along the way. It's an invaluable journey, and by the time I reach my goal, there will be another goal, and another fabulous journey to begin.

NOTES:

DAY 100

I remember, when I was growing up, oil was cheap. Gas was under $1, it was actually 89 cents a gallon. All the gas companies were fighting for your money and seeing who could get the lowest price… that was.... until they came up with a strange new plan. Someone came up with a brand-new unheard-of strategy. They decided to come together as a whole and stop fighting each other. They said, "If we come together as one, we don't have to fight, or do underhanded deeds, AND we can charge whatever it is we want to charge, and NOBODY will be able to do anything about it." From that point on, the oil companies have made money hand over fist, making record profits at an obscene rate.

Be like the oil companies in your own personal life. Learn to cultivate relationships and begin building with others so that you can get more done and accomplish bigger and better goals. Even if you're doing fine on your own, think about what working in concert can achieve. Find like-minded individuals to build with, to work with, and to accomplish with

NOTES:____

DAY 101

Be cautious of your surroundings. Hang around bad fruit, and you can spoil too. The "good fruit" was doing everything it was supposed to be doing. It was attached to the source, it was getting plenty of water, and it got the right amount of sunshine and nutrients; but the one thing it did, was share a bit of too much time with a bad fruit. You can be doing all the right things in life, but you can still be taken down because of who you associate yourself with. The wrong crowd can not only influence you into doing wrong, but they can do wrong; and just because you're with them, you can get sucked into their whirlwind of disaster as well. Be cautious of your surroundings, and stay vigilant, bad fruit is only a breeze away.

NOTES:

DAY 102

Your time is one of the most, if not the most valuable things on this planet. People will give their entire fortunes for more time. So do what you can do with the time that you have. You can't save any extra time for tomorrow, so do the best with what you can do today because no one knows what tomorrow may bring. If you can look back and say, "I wish I would have done more, or given more, or gave my all here," then take the time and do that TODAY.

We are creatures of habit, and if you weren't doing it then, there's a good chance that you're not doing it now; so, put more into your daily activities. Change your mindset and go to work to actually get something out of it. LEARN your co-workers, go to one of them, and ask them to show you a skill they are better at than you. TikTok, Facebook, and all the other social media sites are meant to be distractions. The more time you spend on them, the less time you are spending on yourself. Use that valuable scrolling time to put into yourself. 1 hour a day working on self, will build a person that is better than 50% of the population in 10 years. Be better than 50%.

NOTES:

DAY 103

They say that you should trust the process, and I agree, but you need to know what the process is to trust it. Trust comes from familiarity, it comes from being reassured in past experiences, it comes from consistency. So, in order to "trust the process" you must, first and foremost, know what process you are trusting. If I'm trying to become the best football player ever, I shouldn't be talking to baseball players and trainers. If you're looking to do better in business, talk to those in the specific business you are interested in. Relationship??? Talk to those who you feel have successful relationships and are living the values you'd like to have in your relationships. If you sit down, and come up with something you want, and nobody you know around you has it, it's definitely time to change your circles.

Once you've found out what process you want, you must know what the process is, I have to have some rudimentary knowledge of what it is I'm asking for. I must study, I must research to see what the process is and learn it, so that I have a better understanding. In my studies, I can see how the process has worked for others, and where it has failed some. Now I can begin to understand what the process is, what it isn't, and exactly what I should and shouldn't be doing. Now I can put more faith and trust in the process, to help me attain my goals. Trusting the process works best when the process can trust you to do your due diligence and put in the work.

NOTES:____

DAY 104

Death is a business just like any other. Many of us don't want to talk about it, and we would rather sweep it under the rug or kick the can down the road, and we continue to do this until it's too late. Planning for your, and/or others' deaths are very important aspects of life. We shouldn't leave our family and friends trying to figure out IF you had life insurance, and if so where's the policy, and what company you had it with. Why should we leave our families to deal with grief, AND the business of death all at the same time? Grieving, and trying to figure out how things are gonna get paid for, is a horrible burden to leave.

We shouldn't be having fish fries to bury our loved ones. Everyone should have a folder with all important documents, account numbers, insurance policy numbers, companies, etc. To lessen the blow to your loved ones, pay for your burial and services ahead of time... Have these discussions with those you love, if they don't want to talk about it, continue to push the issue. At the very least, everyone should have a will; it's even better if you have a will AND a trust working together. And if you don't have any, get as much life insurance on as many people as you can afford. This is the main way, wealth is transferred. If everyone you knew had million-dollar life insurance policies, how long would it take for these senseless cop killings to stop??? The insurance companies wouldn't keep paying out because of itchy fingers officers. THEY would implement immediate change. Be about ALL of your business, but especially the uncomfortable business.

NOTES:____

DAY 105

Stop waiting for what you want and go get it. It won't come to you, the timing won't ever be right, and the stars ain't aligning. If you want it to happen, you will have to MAKE it happen. Anything that falls in your lap will fall right back out of it. How many years have you been on this planet still waiting for your opportunity to come? If you play checkers and keep waiting for the right moves to come to you, you'll be defeated, because the other player is setting up his pieces and his kill shots to take you out. Businessmen have plans to take your money, governments have plans to take your money, religions have plans to take your money, and schools have plans to take your money... The only person who doesn't have a plan for your money....is you, and amazingly you're the only one without any of YOUR money. Plan, budget, pay down debt, save, invest. Repeat every paycheck. This simple plan will take care of 80% of your problems. It may take a while, but how long did it take for you to get where you are now???? Plan to execute, then execute the plan. Stop waiting for the right time and MAKE the time right.

NOTES:

DAY 106

From the time we are small, fears run through our lives. We are scared of monsters under the bed, the neighbor's dog, talking to the opposite sex, rejection, and even not having enough for retirement. Our fears back us into corners, and we allow them to scare us into making unwise decisions. Then we feel scared to talk to anyone about our fears because we've opened up before and been hurt by the very ones we've trusted. But the more you keep your fears, doubts, and anguish in, the more it's eating you alive. Everyone needs an outlet, a vent, someone to talk to about what's going on in their lives. All you can do is vet someone to the best of your ability and pray they do not betray your trust and confidence. Find people you can be open, honest, and vulnerable with, someone, who you can not only share your flaws with, but can point out your negative traits and flaws. A soul mate has nothing to do with sexual compatibility, but rather whose soul can be intertwined with your own. This could be a friend, family member, or even a coworker. You are NOT the only one going through your situation. Open up to others and get the help you're longing for.

NOTES:____

DAY 107

I consider all dealings with people to be relationships, not just sexual dealings. Family, friends, acquaintances, and even someone you may have passed on the street and said, "Hey, you dropped something". In all your relationships, try to be as equally yoked (as the Bible says) or as balanced as possible. Now it may not always work out this way but learn to be more conscious of the dynamics in your relationships. Equally yoked and balanced doesn't necessarily mean that you find someone who is on the same page and thinks and acts as you do. Balance means that you have someone who doesn't see the way you do, doesn't necessarily do the things you do, or like the things that you like… the yin to your yang, the counterweight that balances the scale.

If you're a big-picture person and can see the grand finale, you need someone who can see the small intricate pieces that put it together. If I can see a successful business and I can gather the funding to make it happen and get the building built, I need a person who can staff the building, get the spaces rented out, decorate, order the flowers, and run the day-to-day of the business. In your relationships, learn to communicate with each other. Communication isn't just telling someone something, it's about ensuring that the person understands the message the way you intended it to come across and understanding their points. If you have common goals and a low ego, you can make many things work. Begin to think What does the other person want? What do THEY need to make this work?" Then, see if things change for you.

NOTES:____

DAY 108

I recently did a 1-day fast, no food, only water, and I have decided to do a fast every Friday, for the foreseeable future. I told a couple of people, and some even said that they would try to join in. I made a call after work yesterday to a good friend and he asked if I was fat-loading. I said, "What?" He repeated, "Are you fat-loading for your fast tomorrow?" I had completely forgotten about it. So, I had to get my mind together for the fast and change the plans that I'd made. People will tell you that you shouldn't talk too much about your goals, dreams, and aspirations, because there are those out there who will hear them (the haters) and try to do anything they can to stop you. This may be true, BUT, if you never tell anyone, there also will be nobody to remind you when you've forgotten or to remind you when you're slipping or have lost your way.

There will be nobody there to help or push you along the journey when you're tired because they don't even know that you're on a journey. Tell those close to you, about your plans... there are far more upsides than downs to telling folks around you what you're trying to accomplish. A confidante is someone you hold in close regards, and that you trust with your eyes closed and back turned. Surround yourself with as many confidantes as possible. It's more trial and error, and easier said than done, but once you have a few good people you will be unstoppable.

NOTES:

DAY 109

https://www.facebook.com/reel/898118644940737?mibextid=9drbnH&s=yWDuG2&fs=e

This clip from T.D. Jakes is a classic example of not only about 1 small difference between men and women but also about knowing how to navigate relationships and know your partners. We often find ourselves frustrated with the people around us, and it's not their fault, but ours, that we are frustrated. We tend to stay around the same people and try to MAKE them do the things we want and be the people we want them to be, even when it goes against who they naturally are and their upbringing.

Our issues are trying to turn people into who they are not, to please ourselves, instead of surrounding ourselves with those who we want and need. You are the CEO (chief executive officer, a business term) of your life. In business, the CEO makes decisions on how the business is run and the direction it is going to go in. They are responsible for bringing in more money and setting up future goals and strategies. That's YOU in your life. As the CEO, why would you take someone who is in the mailroom and put them over the accounting department, and then get mad at them for destroying accounting? You elevated that person to a level they were not ready for, not qualified for, had zero experience in, knew absolutely nothing about, and had no interest in learning about the position. The only thing they knew about accounting was who to talk to when their check wasn't right. This is how we run our lives and wonder why we are in a constant state of anger, frustration, and disappointment. Do an inventory, and begin to promote, demote, and fire people from the positions they have in your life. Anything that is well run, must have a well-run system behind it, and your personal system can't run well with the wrong people in the wrong positions.

NOTES:____

DAY 110

This is not a statement that I agree with. If it is meant to be, you must work to make it happen. Lions aren't the kings of the jungle by happenstance. They must work together, stay in packs, devour other animals, and hunt their prey. No animal just comes and lies down and says eat me, oh great king of the jungle. Every day they must prove again, WHY they are king. Nothing, even life itself, will just come to you. If you treat your significant other passively and don't convince them you love them, or simply wait for them to come to you, you WILL lose them. Your dreams won't just come to you, you've got to imagine the dream, write the dream down, plan the dream, save for the dream, build the infrastructure for the dream, and then begin building the dream. Life is NOT a passive sport. If you continue to wait for what you want, life will pass you by. Go GET what you want, take action, and never give up.

NOTES:

DAY 111

An emergency is usually only an emergency because we have failed to plan for it. Otherwise, it's usually just a mild inconvenience. There are studies showing that 50% of Americans can't handle a $500 emergency. So, if you are one of those people, and a $500 emergency comes up, you are stressed, you are anxious, nervous, and worried about how you are going to handle things, and what you should be doing. You will probably be looking to run up your credit cards, get loans (putting you deeper into debt), or maybe do some unsavory things. But for every single person I know, being in this position is a CHOICE. It is a choice because you choose to spend money in places you KNOW you shouldn't be spending it, and that's money that could be saved. You stay shopping online for completely unnecessary things and making the excuse, I/my child reeeeally needed this extra outfit, KNOWING they have enough clothes, or whatever else it is you chose to buy.

Prioritize your savings and investments. When you prioritize your savings, you can then use that to invest. With enough investing, you will then be able to use the returns from your investments to pay for your emergencies, and everything else you want; but it first starts with prioritizing your savings and being able to handle smaller bills and emergencies. Sacrifice your short term wants for your long-term ones. Save and Build your accounts, so that one day your accounts will be able to save you and build for you.

NOTES:____

DAY 112

When you're dealing with people, on a business or personal level, there should be some back-and-forth banter. Whether you're in the boardroom or on a date, not only should a person be telling you about themselves, and what they have to offer, but they should show just as much interest in you by asking you as many in-depth questions about you as time permits the bits of information they are giving to you about them. It is a skill to know how, and what questions to ask someone in any given situation. Begin to learn more about your partners and learn to listen more than you speak.

NOTES:

DAY 113

What does it mean to you???? What some words mean to you, they do not mean to me. What one word means in English, is not what the same exact word means in Spanish. Everyone has their own "language" and although the words we speak are the same or very close, there are times when the same word, in the same language, means two different things to two different people. Learn to expound, get clarity, and explain how you see the words or situations. They may tell you "You know what, I've never seen it that way." People who have been married for many years are living together speaking different languages, frustrated and ready to divorce, simply because they aren't truly hearing each other. He says, "Why did u do it that way, you were supposed to go the other way." What she heard was, "I told you not to do that, that was stupid, you can't do nothing right." What she replied was, "I thought it would've gone better this way, you weren't there." What he heard was "I'm grown, you ain't my daddy, I can do what I want, I work every day just like you do." What he thought he was saying was, "Hey, why did u do that, I thought we talked about this, and we agreed, that we were going to do it this way. This is going to cost us more time and money now and push the rest of our plans back." What she thought she said was, "Look, I know it's not what we agreed on, but you weren't there, I got a little scared, and confused. I didn't want to call and upset you because we already talked about it, so I made the best decision at the time. When they said ABC, I thought we were getting a better deal."

We must LEARN each other, and each other's verbal, physical, and mental languages. So many of our problems are simply misunderstandings. Next time you speak with someone, ask no less than 5 questions. What does that look like to you? How does that sound to you? How should I have said that to make you understand it better? What words work best for you? How would you have said/done that? … Or any other questions.

NOTES:____

DAY 114

We face obstacles every day, some large and some small, and some we may think are even insurmountable. But no problem, no obstacle, can stop you. How YOU see the problem is the only thing stopping you. There are people around the world in your exact same position, and they have found a way to overcome the exact same odds and problems. Whether you think you can, or you think you can't.... YOU'RE RIGHT. When an obstacle or a problem arises, don't fall back into fear, and self-doubt. Gather yourself and begin to think of how to overcome the issues. Talk to others who you think may be able to help or have been in similar circumstances. There is NO PROBLEM, that can't be beaten, with some thought, a positive mindset, teamwork, hard work, and persistence. Do not panic when problems arise, learn to be cool, and calm under pressure. Learn to Become adaptable to ever-changing situations. Keep levelheaded people around you to help you stay grounded when all around you is upside down. The obstacles you face are only as bad as you believe them to be.

NOTES:

DAY 115

Jokingly, I asked a good friend of mine for some money. She's usually pretty busy during the day, so she gets back to me when she can. Surprisingly 20 minutes later, I got a message from CashApp that said you have money. No questions asked, no excuses, not even a message asking *where do you want it?* It wasn't much, but it was exactly what I asked for, and it meant far more for her to give it than for me to have it. It is VITAL that you KNOW about those around you, those you hold closest to you. We cause a lot of our own frustration when we elevate people higher than where they should actually be. We often THINK that people are ride or die, and when times get tough, we find out they are hide and fly. I knew I could go to my friend for $40-50 and get it. I may be able to push $100, and that would probably come with a few questions, and a "Hey I need this back by such n such." I know I couldn't go to her for say.... $500, that's just out of her league. But I know this and wouldn't be hurt if I asked, and she couldn't do it.

I've got a pretty good idea of what the people around me can, and cannot do, and what they will, and will not do. Usually not because I THINK this will happen, but because I've been in different situations, and seen who's stood tall. If you've turned me down for $20, why would I expect you to hand over $100??? If you couldn't find the time to visit me when I was well, why would I ask you to come if I was sick??? If I gave you the information to fix your credit, and you didn't, why then would I ask you to go into business with me? Understand that things are connected, and you don't have to see the entire devil to know it's a devil.... quite often all you need to see is his tail. If I show you any piece of a rat individually, you'll probably be able to figure out that it's a rat, you don't need to see the whole rat. Use that same instinct when it comes to people. If you see glimpses of snakes, understand who they are. Stop setting yourself up for failure.

NOTES:____

____

____

DAY 116

One of the top things u must try your best to avoid when things go wrong...is panic. Panic is an emotion that only makes situations worse. Panic causes people to do crazy, irrational, and foolish things. Things that even go against their own safety. Just as we must train our physical bodies, for better health, we must also train our brains, for mental health. This helps us to keep all of our emotions in check, it helps us to prevent acting in a way contrary to what needs to be done, especially in a time of crisis. If you plan and train properly, many things that cause you to panic can be avoided, because you have properly trained yourself to see and handle adverse situations. As I've spoken about earlier, if you plan, and train yourself for financial emergencies, when they arise, they are not emergencies, they are merely inconveniences.

You have seen this situation in your mind, you've accounted for it, you've thought it out, you've saved for it, and the time is here, so you know what you need to do. This is no different from any other situation. When I was in the military, I worked in the engine room of an aircraft carrier. We ran simulation after simulation, after simulation, so much so, that it was just part of our daily routine, and when the emergency came up, everyone already knew what to do, because we had already trained ourselves. Ask yourself, *if your fears were to happen, what SHOULD u do?* The answers you come up with, are the things you should begin working on, to help prevent panic when the time comes. The better the preparation, the easier the battle. Begin to build a better you by working in your weakest areas. Emergency preparedness to prevent panic should be at the top of your list.

NOTES:____

DAY 117

I recently heard a guy complaining about someone ELSE'S relationship. He was at a restaurant and said how he heard another gentleman tell the woman he was with, "No, you can't get that because you can't afford it." For some reason, this really seemed to grind the man's gears. He then stated, "Ain't no way imma come to Chili's, and can't get whatever I want!" First of all, I don't understand why you're mad about someone else's relationship, it befuddles my mind. What works for them, works for them. He's not causing her any pain, hurt, or discomfort. Secondly, from what he says, he's giving her all that he has. Maybe it was a special occasion, maybe it was Wednesday, but he's giving everything he has at the moment, and to down a man for that is simply deplorable. Never beat a man when he is down, especially when he's legitimately trying to make moves.

NOTES:

DAY 118

When talking to, or dealing with Certain people, especially those closest to us, I don't believe that we should hold anything back, about who we are, what we want, or what we've been through. We shouldn't worry whether people will judge us or not. If those people judge you, you have just found out that they probably aren't worth being in your life at this point in time. If you feel that you can't accept the things in my past, OR you turn your nose up at the things I've done, the places I've been, or the people I've interacted with, then you can't accept me now, because those people, places, and things, are the very things that have shaped me into the person that you see before you. The prodigal son had to wallow in filth and swine to see the light. Jesus had to bear so much sin that God turned from him, but once they were clean, they went back home. We all have a past, and nobody is perfect;, if you love polished products, love the process and everything else that goes with it.

NOTES:____

DAY 119

A pet peeve of mine has always been people asking me questions about what I think they should do in a given situation, and then them doing the exact opposite. Then what makes it worse is when they don't follow what was said, do it their own way, mess it up, and then come back and ask how to fix what they messed up. Usually by this point, I'll either say, don't know, you should have listened the first time, or I know how to KEEP you out of trouble, I don't know how to GET you out of it.

I, like everyone else, am still a work in progress. I'm learning that it's not my job to get people to do things a certain way, it's their life, and they can live it as they please. It's my job to give out the information. Much like building a house, the information I give is a brick, it may be the first brick of a wall, or the last brick to finish the house, but it's only one brick of many. People are gathering bricks of information from everyone they come across, and I probably will never see the final completed project. It's just something I have to work on and come to terms with. All I can do is my part of the construction and pass it on to the next man to do his part. Recognizing a flaw in oneself and making a conscious effort to change is a goal I believe we should all focus on and strive to master.

NOTES:____

DAY 120

There is a lesson in EVERYTHING, the only question is can you see it? The more I focus on bettering myself, and becoming a better man, the more I see lessons in everyday things, things that you wouldn't think twice about. A stop sign.... stop what you're doing, think about the consequences, survey your area to make sure it's safe to continue to go, or it may not be your time right now, wait a while until things die down. A bottle of syrup, like buying myself nice things, something sweet, a treat to myself, but I know I can't indulge in it, or it will cause far more problems than I can handle. I can handle it more if I do the things necessary to keep it in my life. I want more syrup, so work more, take more steps, buy more things, and find ways to bring in more money. Everything is relatable, and everything can help, lead, and guide you. Even things that don't seem to be of any knowledge, or help today, may be tomorrow's message. Begin to look for YOUR message in the simplest things that you do every day.

NOTES:

DAY 121

Stay away from the naysayers. Everything you've ever seen and everything you've ever known was said to be impossible by someone. Cars, trucks, televisions, cell phones, satellites, guns, Bluetooth, etc. But SOMEBODY had that dog in them, that said, "I can do it" and they surrounded themselves with other dogs that said, "We can do it", and they pushed each other, day and night, until their goals were finished. Believe you can do it and keep those around you who believe you can do it. Get rid of anybody who says you can't. There is exponentially more power when dealing with more people on the same page, with the same desires.

People can only see as far as their fears will let them, so when you strive to do better, and you speak of being better, and going further, all they see is fear, because you've passed their limits of knowledge, and you're now operating in THEIR fear zone. They want to bring you back into THEIR comfort zone. Burst through their stratosphere and show them a new way, and if they don't want to follow, leave em behind. Those who push you, those who follow you, and those who encourage you, are those to keep on the team. They are your new fuel for the upcoming journey ahead. Stay strong and don't give up, keep moving forward.

NOTES:

DAY 122

Action is easy, positive action ain't. You can get up, and do anything, and make any kind of movement, but there is a difference between movement, and forward progress. Sit down, talk to your inner circle, and come up with an action plan. What do you want to accomplish in 5 years, 3 years, 1 year? In 5 years, I want to be retired (what does that look like) well I'll be living in a $500,000 home that's paid off, driving a $60,000 car bringing in X amount per month through an outside source (business/investments). Now break that down into smaller goals. 500k in 5 years is 100k a year for 5 years, $60k is 12k a year, which equals $8,334 a month, and 1k a month which breaks down even further to $2,084 a week, and $250 a week or a total of $2343/week. This is how much you need to save or bring in from somewhere every week if you want to live in a $500,000 house and drive a $60,000 car that is paid for in 5 years.

Now that you have your road map, begin to take action toward making these things happen. You can actually see your benchmarks. These are positive steps forward. Now money not spent towards these goals may just be spent in vain, and you may be running in place. If you purchase a new car through a bank loan, you're taking that much money away from your goals, and now you're back peddling. Keep your goals in view, and continuously work towards them, DAILY. Read books, attend seminars, pay for classes, and get organized. You are bigger, stronger, and badder than you can possibly imagine. All you have to do is believe in yourself and begin to walk in it. Change for the better is NEVER easy, but it's worth it. Start your change today.

NOTES:____

DAY 123

No Matter what, the storm will overtake you, the only question is.... will you run through it, will you sit and wait, or will you try to run from it??? The storms in your life are inevitable, learn to face them head-on. If you run from your storms, your back is towards the problem, and you can't see what's coming next. The longer you run away, the longer you will stay in the storm, and the more the storm will drench you. When you run from your problems, you don't learn much at all, except how to run from a problem, and all that does, is usually make problems worse.

If u stand fast, continue moving forward, and fight your way through your storms, you will find that you gain strength, you amass more knowledge of how to do things, and with this newly gained strength, and knowledge, you can help pull others out of their storms. You will forge new relationships, and with everything you have gained, it will make the next storm, that much easier to go through. Your strength can only be built through your drive, your self-determination, and your persistence. Take a step towards your storm and begin to deal with your problems today. The more you run, from them, the harder they will be to fight when they overcome you, because your problems are gaining strength, and you are losing strength.

NOTES:____

DAY 124

K-12, and higher education all come at a price. With k-12, it's paid through mostly property taxes of the surrounding areas. If you want better schools, you usually have to pay more in taxes. With these higher taxes, you generally get better facilities, equipment, and teachers. As you move on to college, you now have to pay directly out of pocket. You're still paying the same property taxes at your home, but now you have to pay higher education fees on top of that, plus finding a way to get to the school, and back again, food, and entertainment. Everything costs, and the more you want, generally the more it's gonna cost you.

One of the best educations you can receive is through life itself. Every single day, without fail, it's giving us lessons, tests, and quizzes to pass, and It's up to you when you pass the tests, but just like your other educations, it costs, and the longer you choose to not pass the tests, the more it costs you. It may cost money, it may cost pain, it may cost heartache, and it may cost shame, but know this....it will cost, and at times more than you ever even thought possible. Break your cycles, and learn your lessons quickly, so that you can keep your life's payments at a minimum.

NOTES:

DAY 125

Charles Schwaab said, "You don't get what you deserve/want, you get what you negotiate/fight for." It doesn't matter what you deserve, or how much you THINK you're worth if you continually put yourself on the clearance shelf and let any and every one take advantage of you. Many music artists, young and old, today, are now fighting for the rights to their music and catalogues, trying to get them back from the music companies, because at the time, they didn't know their worth, or just wanted to make a deal and be famous and on TV. The music companies knew their worth, and exploited them for as much as they could, as long as they could. The artists still have no rights to their music because they signed them away, but they can let others know about making bad deals and knowing their worth.

Don't get stuck in bad situations, fight and negotiate your way out. Tell your boss WHY u deserve a raise, point out all the work that you do, the stuff nobody else knows how to do, go on job interviews, get offer letters, and who knows you may find something better. But your boss isn't gonna walk up and say, "Take more of this money to do the same job". You have to push the issue. Speak up for yourself, and what you believe you deserve. It may actually turn out that you've overplayed your hand, and aren't quite where you THOUGHT you should be, that's ok too, because now you know where you sit, and you can adjust your plan to get a little further. Make the effort, it's well worth it.

NOTES:____

DAY 126

There are many strong people, bodybuilders, athletes, and military people who can do 1000 more push-ups than you, they can outrun you, and lift 10 times the weight you can, but with all of this in mind, you are still stronger. The strongest muscle in the human body is the one least worked or exercised by most. It's the brain. The brain is far stronger than any muscle you have, and it barely gets a workout. Where would your body be if your mind got the workout that your body did? Your courage, discipline, morals, higher thinking, skills, and abilities all come from your mind. The stronger you build your mind, the stronger you can build your life. Reading, challenges, puzzles, and solving difficult situations at work, and at home.

When it seems as though things aren't right, and falling apart, this is the perfect opportunity to build your master muscle. Contemplate the different scenarios that could come about… how can u do this, or that, what will happen if I do? Soon you'll be figuring out others' problems, without even thinking about it. Your mind can do things that you can't even conceive.... but you must exercise it daily. I was never a writer and not a good one now, but the more messages I write a day, the more information comes to me. For those who know me, writing daily inspirational messages would be the last thing they would think of when thinking of me; but I began working on me and building myself. You never know what you'll turn into when you work your master muscle.

NOTES:____

DAY 127

We are operating from a space of survival and desperation. Most of us don't know what it is to live from a freedom standpoint, a point where you don't have to worry about how much something costs, or when a bill is due. Our entire lives have been built on survival. That's how we were raised, and that's all that's shown to us. We MUST break that cycle of work, pay bills, make others rich, and die. Come up with 10 different ways to pay a bill off, then pick the 2 easiest ways and begin to pay that bill off with those 2 choices. Work like this until you are out of debt. If you feel you can do more than the 2 choices you picked, do more, there is no limit to your greatness. Once you taste a small bit of freedom, it becomes harder to go back into bondage. The more bills you free up the easier it becomes, then you will be able to invest in something that makes you money every month.

Once you have something that can pay all of your bills you experience true freedom. You'll be in a place where you don't HAVE to go to work to pay bills, and you can begin to enjoy life more and live from a love, and abundance standpoint. The fastest way to help someone else is to help YOURSELF first. Build your base and live from abundance so that you can pull someone else up and show them better. Crabs in a barrel keep pulling each other down, if they all stand on top of each other, someone will eventually make it out, but at the cost of others, because the weight of everyone was too much for those on the bottom. Find your way out first and throw a rope back to help others climb out, but you can't throw a rope until you make it out, or otherwise, you're just adding more weight to those building u up.

NOTES:____

DAY 128

Much like a boxer, we are in the ring of life, but many of us never had very good people in our corners, like trainers, motivators, and cut men (people who tend to your wounds when you get hit). So, we've been out boxing with no help, getting beat up. Many are discouraged and feel defeated because they've taken a few bumps and bruises, but every fighter gets hit, it's how you know you're still in the game. Every boxer goes through sparring sessions. These are people close to their opponents' abilities, so they can get a sense of their speed, strength, stamina, and defenses. This is usually several different people over a period of time. When they enter the ring, they go about 85% at each other, and they are wearing protective gear, but blows are still traded, there is still sweat, there are still bruises, and recovery time is still needed.

We go through our own personal battles every day refusing to have people in our corners that can help us. There are people who can see different things than us because we are too close to the problem. There are those who can help us recover from what we've just gone through, and there are those who can help prepare us for what's coming next. Don't refuse help from others, and believe that you are a loner, or that this journey is meant to be done alone because it's NOT. We all need a support system in our corners for when the bruising from battle comes, or we need to rest from the previous battle. It's difficult to make it to the next level if you've never had anyone show you what it is, or the easiest way to get there. Surround yourself with not only those willing to pour into you but those that you can pour into as well.

NOTES:____

____

____

____

____

____

____

DAY 129

The town I grew up in is a suburb of Chicago. It's never been cheap to live there, and since I've graduated, it just gets more expensive every year. The city is constantly building, and adding onto the schools there, so taxes continue to climb. I was speaking to a friend, and she said, "You'll have to have a 6-figure salary just to live here soon." I told her that's what they want. It's always been a nice place to stay, with manicured yards, no street parking, and no trash around. And in order to keep that up, the city must not only pay well, but it must also bring in above-average people to live there. This type of living isn't meant for everyone; everyone can't come, and everyone is not allowed. The more they add, the greater the value the city has, and the more they can charge. The higher the tax, the higher the percentage of people who like to keep their property values up, and with higher taxes, usually come better facilities, municipalities, schools, and libraries....more often than not, an overall better experience.

We should understand that this is EXACTLY how we should treat our personal lives. You aren't meant for everybody. They say to know your worth then add tax, that's what you should be doing. If you have too many undesirables in your life, begin adding tax. Ask them to do something for you, tell them you need help. See how many offer assistance, loan you what you need, or just give it up without a fight or questions. These are the high-value people that you want to keep around. If they never have anything.... drop em if they can never seem to help you.... drop em if they have an excuse for everything under the sun.... drop em... "Oh you're so strong I didn't think you needed help.".... drop em. Adding tax slowly weeds out those who can't afford to be around and leaves you with valuable PRODUCTIVE members in your small society. Expensive cars are all out of the reach of the average person and still have yet to go out of business. So, raise the cost of getting to you, then add tax.

NOTES:____

____

____

DAY 130

Life is a marathon, and not against others as to judge yourself by, but one where you are racing against yourself, and you can use others as guideposts or motivation. Too often we look at others as competition. We kick, scratch, bite, and claw at the very people we are to be helping, and uplifting. We should be focusing more of our energies on helping and supporting one another. We should be focusing on achieving our goals and you shouldn't have to tear down someone else's dreams to build yours. If you can look around today and see you're in pretty much the same place you were last year, you may be stagnant, not growing, complacent.

You should be progressing in the plans you've laid out, which means... you have to have some sort of plan laid out for your life. Debts are being paid off, money is being saved, classes are being attended, businesses are being started and books are being finished. There should be some sort of progress chart or checkpoints to your life's marathon. Your winning the race has nothing to do with other people, it's about accomplishing the goals you've set for yourself in a timely fashion.

NOTES:

DAY 131

Willpower breaks down more men than just about anything else on the planet. If you have that dog in you, that will NEVER quit; there is a very high percentage that you will get what you're looking for. If you have no willpower at all, you'll probably end up not liking your life very much and being someone else's lackey. There's a Denzel Washington movie called "THE HURRICANE" about a professional boxer who was wrongly jailed. The willpower this man had would make Ghandhi proud. He never stopped fighting, he never quit, he denied himself the smallest things so that the prison system could barely punish him, because they would have nothing to take away. You have to have the willpower to say no to things, not only externally, but most importantly internally. If you can deny yourself personal short-term gratification, for your long-term goals, you'll be able to accomplish 1000 times more than if you gave into every little whim.

Train yourself to go without something for a certain period of time. It can be food, TV, alcohol, spending.... whatever you think would be a struggle for you. If you're just starting out, do half a day, and work up from there. Every time you meet your goal, give yourself a small treat and move your time up an hour. Learn to go without, and nobody will ever be able to take anything from you, because you already know how to live without it. What are you willing to say no to today, so that you can be closer to your dreams tomorrow? Weekly, I fast on Fridays, and it's been ok. I can't look at the hunger I feel, I have to look at the health benefits of fasting, the way I'm strengthening my resolve, and all the other positive things that I gain from it. If all I choose to look at is the hunger and food I'm NOT getting, I will fail every time. But the food I don't eat today will undoubtedly be there tomorrow. The inner strength that I gain won't be though. If you have the strength to tell yourself no, you will be able to tell anyone no.

NOTES:____

DAY 132

I was at work today, and we are working pretty shorthanded. My supervisor decided that he was going to do the actual work, another man was going to be his backup, and I was going to be the "supervisor" for the day (basically stand around and yell at him for stuff he always yells at me about - lol) our supervisor tells everyone in the crew how to do, what to do, and when to do it, he is a little on the rough side, but he just takes some getting used to. Every mistake we make, he jumps on us and makes us do it the right way, no matter how minuscule, so that we know how to do it the right way. As we got into the work, he made a small mistake, and I corrected him; he made another, and I corrected that; then he made another, and another, and another, and....well, u get the point. I made sure I stayed on his head for every little thing, there were some sizable ones too. I corrected him in fun, and he knew I wasn't doing it maliciously. I know that everyone makes mistakes, and we've been laughing all day.

A saying I've heard when I was younger that's always stuck with me was "Show me a man who doesn't make a mistake, and I'll show you a man who's not working." The only people who don't make mistakes in life are the people who aren't doing anything and aren't trying. When we make moves and decisions in life, some will work out, and some won't. None of us have a crystal ball, and all we can do is put some thought into a decision, maybe ask a few people, and then pull the trigger. Hopefully, we've made the best decision possible for our future. If not.... hopefully, it's a decision that we can learn and recover from. Don't beat yourself up for making bad decisions, it simply means you're in the game. Just don't compound it by not accepting advice and making more bad decisions.

NOTES:____

DAY 133

There is a Black celebration of family, heritage, and community called Kwanzaa. It takes place between Christmas and New Year, almost like Hanukkah, I'd imagine. Every day, you celebrate a different principle, and one of those principles is called Umoja. Umoja means to strive for and maintain peace, and unity in the family, community, race, and nation. It's easy to maintain these things when the sun is shining and everything is going right in your life; but when the chips are down, your bills aren't paid, and you're in pain, can you still believe in unity and peace?? In times of adversity, can you think about how even though things aren't working for you, you may be able to make this situation better for someone else? You found a way to bless me with this situation that gave you pain, and you put a smile on my face.

Look to bless others not only on the good days but equally on the bad days, as well. This is how Community, relationships, strong bonds, and goodwill are built. When you bless others even through your own pain, every community you are a part of is strengthened 10-fold.

NOTES:____

DAY 134

I have several relationships that I hold very dear to my heart, and for these people, I'd do just about anything, if they asked. If they need me, I'm there. But I feel as though I can call on them when I'm in need as well. It's not just about when we are together having a good time, but in the bad times as well, when I've gotten laid-off and couldn't afford a meal, or when I was doing bad and couldn't pay a bill.

Relationships in life are very important. Relationships open up doors, that money, power, and prestige can't. People will take less, and sometimes even lose money, because of the relationships they value more than money. A good well-placed word will bring more peace to a person and their situation than any amount of money can. Cultivate more positive relationships in your life. Ones that can be around for the long haul, ones that can bring peace, happiness, joy, knowledge, and serenity.

NOTES:

DAY 135

I, like everyone else, have my debts, and they are of course.... bigger than I want them to be. I thought about different ways to get out of debt, starting businesses, getting side hustles, and second jobs, and I even prayed about it. And God answered my prayers. He dropped big bags of money out of an armored car, and I was set. Of course, that's not what happened. What he did do was give me opportunities to make more money. I began with ride-sharing and deliveries in my spare time and off-days, and since it was extra, all I kept was what it took to keep my car going, like gas, and any repairs that may have been needed. I began reading more business books, which helped with my taxes and allowed me to save even more money in taxes.

All the extra money went straight to the bills I owed. I did that for a few years, and over time whenever something extra came up at work, I did the same thing with that money. I purchased a house during COVID because prices were rock bottom, and it was $900 a month cheaper to buy than for me to keep renting. Then, I took that money and put it towards the bills. I had a house that was too big for me since I really only stayed in 2 rooms, so I began to rent out rooms in my house. Now THAT money was going towards bills, and now at work we are working overtime like crazy, and you know where that money is going.

God is always opening new doors, it's just up to you to notice and take advantage of them. Also, understand that every door is NOT a door of prosperity. Sometimes when that door opens up like Moses, it's a door opening up to the wilderness, and obscurity, but that wilderness is what's needed for you to grow and find yourself. I have such a drive to not be broken, because I've been broken, and REFUSE to go back. You have to travel the wilderness of life to amass more knowledge and strength. The door that was opened for Job led to death, destruction, and sickness, but he had to walk through the door that was opened. Every year winter rolls around, have you prepared??

Understand that this process not only took a shift in my thought process, but it has taken years, and I am still not finished. I've had setbacks, layoffs, firings, sicknesses, life drama, and everything else that could stop me. But those closest to me know, my mind is set on paying these things off, and that's my discussion, so much so, that they all tell me I need to have fun. But in my mind, fun is what got me here, so I will work it off, and then have "fun" in a more sensible way than before. The process has taken years, and I'm still at it, but I can now begin to see the finish line. In the early beginnings, you won't see much difference, you'll even tell yourself "Why am I putting this $2 towards this $50,000 bill? It's pointless" but it's conditioning your mind. Every time you put that $2 toward that debt, you're strengthening your mind telling it that you can do it, and when bigger sums of money come, you'll put bigger amounts into it. If you don't put that $2 on the debt because it's only $2, you're still strengthening your mind, but in the negative, you're training yourself that you'll never have enough to get started, and it will be harder for you to see opportunities, because even those won't be good enough.

The Bible says to be good over little, and I'll give you a lot, but we know we're bad with little and want even more to screw up. The baby steps can work if u allow them, it just takes time. It may not seem like you're moving forward, but you are. I'm only running now because I first learned how to crawl towards my goals. Don't let the small amounts trick you into believing you aren't accomplishing anything. The journey of 1000 miles begins with one step. Get 1 step closer today until you can take 2 steps.

NOTES:____

DAY 136

Life is a chemistry experiment, we have to learn what works for us, what meshes, and what doesn't. What works with these people, doesn't work well with this other group of people. When you do find out what works for you, it's hard to keep, because there's a shelf life. We and our environments are forever changing. This is why WE must be forever changing, forever growing, forever educating ourselves about our history, things we can be doing, and looking forward to, and even our health and fitness. Pick your mentors' brains, not for ideas that work (which is a good thing, don't get me wrong) but for the bad choices they made, the pitfalls they fell into, and the troubles they've seen so that you can avoid them.

Avoiding pitfalls and listening to those who've come before you about how to prosper, can put you light years ahead of where you could be. Remember, the good times have a shelf life, but so do the bad times; but it's all up to you, so work so hard that today's good times become tomorrow's bad times. Crush the game and pass on the knowledge you've learned to lighten someone's walk in life. Be the change you want to see.

NOTES:____

DAY 137

In order to get from our office, where we have our morning safety meetings, to our work area, we have to travel across a small bridge that goes through an area where geese have pretty much taken over. They see us, we see them, and everybody keeps it moving.... normally. The other day, I walked past as normal, and this goose hissed at me. I'd never heard that before, so I assumed it was trying to assert dominance or something, so I hissed back and flared my arms. Then it started flapping its wings and honking and I saw other goosesses (I know it's geese) flapping. It was at this point that I knew I had to get up outta there. As I hurriedly left, I saw some baby chicks waffling by, then I knew why I was getting this treatment. She was simply protecting her babies at all costs, and had I continued, I'm sure I would have surely gotten Molly whopped by a flock of goosesses. *LOL*

Learn from that mother goose and the flock around her. Protect what you've birthed into this world at all costs. This isn't just for women and children, but the businesses you've birthed, the home you've birthed, the peace, love, tranquility, happiness....anything you've built needs to be protected, and make sure you surround yourself with people who will protect what you've birthed, almost like it was their own. This is also a two-edged sword; you must also protect what they have birthed and be there for them. This is how we build an impenetrable fortress, where the only thing that can bring us down is us.

NOTES:____

DAY 138

Are you GOING through your problems and adversity, or are you GROWING through them??? You will go through trials and tribulations in life until you die, the question is.... will you go through the same situations again, and again? If all you can ever see is the pain and anguish you go through you are GOING through your situation and are doomed to repeat it until you figure it out. If all you can do is see the light bill is past due and you're sitting in the dark, even when the bill gets paid, you'll be living by candlelight again.

If you GROW through your situation, you're learning from it, you're picking up clues on WHY this happened, how can you avoid it from happening again, or at least mitigating the situation. Lights out???? How can you hustle up more money? Can you start a business, will people in your neighborhood pay you to help them clean their houses or garages, cut their grass, and cook their meals? Someone in near proximity to you will pay you to do something. This is GROWING through your situation. Learning, configuring, adjusting, adapting. Don't simply sit back with a wo is me mentality, fight with every ounce of strength you can muster. And lose the mentality "I don't want to do that." What you "don't want to do" will only be for a short time. I guess you'd rather stay in the situation you're in forever.

NOTES:____

DAY 139

When I graduated high school, I went straight into the military. A week after graduation I was in boot camp. running, jumping, getting yelled at for the simplest things, having to do push-ups and sit-ups because someone else screwed up. Dealing with Chicago heat while marching, and on runs. One thing I found out they would do is find someone they knew was not gonna make it out of bootcamp for whatever reason.... maybe he had a medical issue, maybe he had warrants they found.... whatever, and they would find the smallest thing he was doing wrong. Maybe not marching in step, or he was standing in a way they didn't like, and they would jump down his neck, tell him to grab his stuff, and get out of the barracks, they were sending him home. It was a mental thing, that scared a lot of people straight. It made them march that much better, or try that much harder, because they were scared of being sent home too.

Bootcamp was just a means to mess with your mind and break you down in whatever way possible, so that the military could build you back up in their image, according to their rules and their regulations. But they must get rid of a lot of YOUR ways and habits first. They must empty you first before they can fill you. Life beats on you, trying to empty you, trying to get rid of those things that have been put into you from birth, that shouldn't be there. It's trying to fill you with what you need for your journey, but you're resisting, so life's gonna keep beating. The life lessons are building and strengthening you for every single thing you've asked for. Learn from the lessons. Just because you've done it your whole life doesn't mean that it's what you need on your journey. Let life take that baggage from you and upgrade you. All you have to do is let it go, and accept what life wants to teach you.

NOTES:____

DAY 140

As you begin to work on yourself, you'll find that more, and more doors will begin to open up to you, people you may have wanted to date or go into business with, now begin to see you as a viable option. Your growth, your mindset, and your success expand your gravitational field and will bring more people.... some for the good, and some for the bad. It's a very rough thing to decipher, but you must learn to weed out who's there for YOU, and who's there for your growth and success. Those who are there for your growth and success, will most likely not be around when failure strikes (and it will, it always does). The hard part is deciding WHY they are here. There are those who knew you before, and weren't interested because you had no drive, no passion, no desire to do anything; and now, they see these things in you, which can draw them in.

I am around people all day who say what they want, and what they're gonna do, but never make any moves, haven't read the first book, won't even do a few Google searches. So why would I waste my time explaining anything to them, when I know they will probably discard the information? Because I know everyone grasps things in their own time, I may just be a seed planter, so I give a generic bare minimum answer and see where you will take that. The more you do, the more you can get. Some in your atmosphere now, are just waiting for you to do more, so they can give you more. One sign is those you know that you look up to, that you see as successful in whatever area. Those are the ones waiting for you to move. Life is a chess game, and I can't make a move or take a turn until you do. Learn that all doors that open aren't necessarily meant for you to walk through. Just because you're invited, doesn't mean you have to go. As you grow, see who's feeding into you. Are they the sun, the soil, the gardener, or are they coming by just to eat off of the harvest like birds, bugs, and locusts?

NOTES:____

DAY 141

If you are looking to make more money just to make more money, you will probably be pretty unfulfilled. Money never stops, it just keeps going on and on, "more money" isn't a very good goal. If you want "more money" you should tie it to a goal. I need more money to "allow more vacations, and time spent with family" or "freedom to travel the world on my own time." Specific goals can lead to a dollar amount needed. Once our goals are completed it tends to bring forth a better realization of accomplishments and fulfillment. For the average person, more money is simply more money that they will spend, or another bill they will make, which puts them in the cycle of working more to pay the bill; to make more money… and more money STILL hasn't solved their problems.

If you set a goal, it's easier to not get distracted, and focus your energies on the goal. If I know I need $5000 by the end of the year, to take a trip around the world, then I know I need to save almost $600 a month, which means $150 a week. If I know my goal, I can work my way backward to today, and work out EXACTLY what I need to accomplish it. Now that I can see what I need, I can take the necessary steps to complete my weekly goals. I know what needs to be done, now that's all that's left to do is pull the trigger, and put $150 a week away, and I'll have my $5000. My goal wasn't "more money" it was a specific amount that it took to take this trip. Think about WHY you desire "more money", what do you want to accomplish? Break down what it is you actually want and reverse engineer your dollar amount from there. Money is about the freedom to do what it is you want to do in life....taking trips at will, helping others, building future generations, building your community, etc. See how much your dreams will cost you and begin working on THAT amount. Start where you are and build off of that. Don't be afraid, just start. Everything you need will be added to you during the journey.

NOTES:____

____

____

DAY 142

I am reading a book today called The Real Estate Rookie, and there is a part in one of the chapters that speaks on how to find a suitable partner if you want to get into real estate. Not only how to find one, but things to look for, things to avoid, things that should be talked about, and how to have a proper exit strategy if one of the partners doesn't want to continue or does something unsavory. Reading over this chapter, turned on a bold thought in my mind, and let me see that she was not only explaining a business partner, but everything in her lists could be used for a relationship partner as well. It allowed me to see, that a majority of people have never been actually taught how to date, how to look for a partner, how to communicate, or handle rejection. One thing she says is, "Look for someone who compliments you."

Now we all think that means someone who does what we do, likes what we like, and so on. This may be true to a point, but to compliment you, is to balance you, and to do that they have to be heavy where you are light, they must be strong where you are weak, they have to be the yin to your yang. Many of the qualities and attributes of your best partners will be opposite of yours. Have you studied the person you want as your partner or are you going off of external factors? Don't simply look to see what this person "brings to the table." What do YOU have to offer, and is that something that person either wants or needs?? Learn to look for what you aren't. The Hulk NEEDS a calming soul, the lover NEEDS a fighter, and the protagonist NEEDS, an antagonist. Find your needs.

NOTES:____

____

____

____

____

____

____

____

DAY 143

Do you believe that you're worth it? Do you believe that you are worth the extra effort that someone should put in for your love, and attention? Are you worth the sacrifice someone would have to give for your admiration????? Most people would answer yes, and there are some who would answer no. If you feel that you're not worth it, then begin to work on yourself, and become the person you think is worthy of all the admiration. And for those who believe that they are worth every single thing someone has....then begin to sacrifice for YOURSELF, begin to love YOURSELF, begin to give yourself extra attention. Sacrifice your lounge time to work on your goals. Give yourself that love that you seek. Many times, we're looking for love, and we don't even know what it's supposed to look like, or even feel like because we are going off of someone else's interpretation of what it "should be."

Admire yourself. We want others to give us external love, and praise; then when we get behind closed doors we buckle, fold, and begin to beat on ourselves, because the personal love and admiration aren't there. If we learn to love ourselves, care for ourselves, and believe in ourselves not only will the things coming externally be simply an added bonus, but then we will know and understand how WE are to be loved and cared for more intimately because we've dated ourselves and found out what works for us. Believe in you, build you, work on you, and outside forces will begin to fall in line.

NOTES:____

DAY 144

When we are born, we grow physically from the time we come out of the womb until whenever our body tells us it's time to stop. It's natural, and we don't have to do much to encourage that process, except eat. People grow, trees grow, and animals grow, but internal growth is not so automatic. Internal growth just like physical growth grows up until a certain age, and then it too stops. Continual Internal growth must be forced, and pushed, and it must be intentional. Internal growth is spiritual, mental, and psychological, growth and maturity of your feelings, and learning to control your emotions. To become a "better you" all of these skillsets must be worked on, strengthened, and forged in fire. You must focus on internal growth and fight what your surroundings, your family, and your religion have forced into you. Internal growth happens when you see something inside of you, and you say "No more" I will not be what I have been, I will strive to be better.

Working on yourself is like driving on a long, dark, winding road. You can't see the entire trip; all you can see is as far as your light will shine. But the more you continue the journey the more you'll be able to see, and the closer you are to your destination. There will be curves, straights, and some places where you'll be at a standstill, but keep plugging and doing what you know to do. The road won't always be dark, the sun will rise, and you won't even need your own light, because there will come a time when you've put in the work, and you've surrounded yourself by so many of the right people, everyone's light is feeding everyone else. But you must continue to put the work in. Work on anything that you see as a deficiency and watch how things begin to change.

NOTES:____

DAY 145

You feel a weight on your back… it seems so heavy, and cumbersome. It feels as though it's gonna crush you and overtake you. You feel like you're being thrown around like a rag doll, all over the place, and constantly dropping stuff, losing things.... it's ok, it's all part of the process. You're complaining about the very blessing that's working in your life. In the Bible, when Moses took the children if Israel out of Egypt, they didn't just pick up their stuff and walk out, they left with a lot of the Egyptians' gold and wealth, as well. They had so much that every person, including women and children, had to carry what they could. They got to the point where they started complaining about carrying their wealth. The very thing that was given to them for their years of service was now seen as a burden to them, it was too much of a weight to carry around.

That very thing that was "holding them down and weighing on them" is what they could use as trade anywhere they came across, but they didn't want to endure the process of carrying it. The Bible also says that your blessing will be given to you pressed down, shaken together, and running over. You're simply being pressed down, shaken together, and running over. The more you press down a piece of bread, the more it will fit in your hand. It's ok, just keep doing what you know to be is right and taking steps to better yourself. Your blessings are working their way to you now, they are just going through the maturation phase right now, so they are ripe and ready when they get to you.

NOTES:____

DAY 146

Be very careful with whom you choose to build. There is a stark difference between "Those raised on survival," or those who had to "get out of the mud" vs "those raised on love." Survival is based on a fearful mindset, a mindset of lack, never knowing where your next meal is coming from. This trains the mind to not only hold onto things but to be more aggressive in gaining things, possibly even taking yours.

Think about it, if it's wintertime, and the only food there is, comes from 1 tree, there will be wars over this tree. This is how those who were raised on survival see life. It's ingrained in their psyche that there isn't enough to go around; so, many continue to fight and scratch, even when they've attained what they were looking for, sharing only to further their own agendas. Those raised around love, are usually more giving because their mindset is usually one that comes from abundance, a mindset that says there IS enough to go around for everyone. The love mindset is like living in a vast garden with plenty growing, and enough to share. Often these people give more than they receive, or sometimes even more than they have. As in any other part of life, balance is best; but understand with whom you're dealing and be aware of their background.

NOTES:____

DAY 147

We tell ourselves the craziest things, and we keep OURSELVES in bondage. Doing Lyft and Uber you come across a wide variety of people. There were two people that really stuck with me. One was a woman I came across, who said that she never learned to drive. I asked more questions, and she said she was too scared to drive. She'd get nervous every time she got behind the wheel, all she could think about was getting into a bad accident; but somehow when she rode with a complete stranger, and the thought never crossed her mind. The second was a man who chose not to drive because of the things that COULD go wrong. What if my car doesn't start, what if I have a flat, what if I can't pay the note.... what if, what if, what if. I told the man, "You're gonna have flats, and dead batteries, you may even get in an accident, but these are miniscule in the grand picture of things. You're letting a mouse stop an elephant."

The fear of the little outweighs the joys of the goal. As silly as these two scenarios sound, what are you letting stop you? Are you letting your paycheck stop you from being a millionaire??? You can't chase your dreams because you've got to pay these bills. I can assure you that you can take baby steps toward your goals while still paying bills. Don't let 50k and fear of the unknown keep you from becoming a millionaire, or whatever else it is you choose to attain. Don't be one of those crazy stories in someone's car, go for whatever it is you desire. Every move you make is an axe swing at a redwood. If you take one swing a day, I promise you that trees will fall, it'll just take some time. Keep swinging.

NOTES:____

DAY 148

Most of the world today doesn't know who THEY are. They have lived, loved, and spent 30, 40, or even 70 years on this planet, and STILL don't know who they are. Many have done nothing other than stay within the guidelines they were given....work, pay bills, make more bills, and die. You are special, you are an omnipotent being, and you are meant to do wonderful things in this world. So why are you worried about these people who don't even know who they are? Surely no one who doesn't know who they are can tell you who YOU are. Discard their words like an old rag and believe in yourself. Open yourself up to all that you can be. When you find your purpose, they will say that they knew all along what you would be. Their perception of you will change when you change the perception of you.

NOTES:

DAY 149

When I was in the military, I was stationed aboard an aircraft carrier, one of the largest military boats in the water. One day a storm was coming, and we had to get the ship running and pull it out to sea so that the rough waters wouldn't beat the ship against the pier, and cause damage to the ship or the pier. While we were out at sea, the water was really rough. Normally, I never felt the ship move, but this storm had us rocking and rolling. So much so, that there were shoe prints halfway up the walls, I couldn't hold anything down for a day and a half. After the storm, we pulled back in, and everything was right in the world.

As old as that carrier was, no water got inside of it, and it rocked and rolled, was getting tossed and spun around, but everything worked out just fine. YOU are that ship, the negativity, the problems, the irritations, and all of your issues are on the outside. They will knock you around, turn you upside down, spin you in circles, and do anything else possible. But as long as you don't let any water (problems) in your ship, you will be ok. You just have to wait out the storm. The end is coming. You had to be pulled away from where you were, otherwise, when these storms came, you'd get torn up by the thing you THOUGHT you were safe with. Learn to fortify yourself to keep all the negativity out. Read positive, listen to positive, watch positive, and begin to BE positive.

NOTES:____

DAY 150

To become better at basketball, you should practice and study basketball. To be better at baseball, you should practice and study baseball. You should practice and study those things in life that you want to become better at... So, if you want to be better at finances, you must practice, read, and study about finances. If you want a better relationship, work on the relationships you already have in your life. Giving you more money or another partner, won't help the problem if you don't know what to do with them. That's like giving a newborn, solid food.... you'll cause far more problems than you solve. If there is someone who exemplifies what you desire, ask them how they do what they do, sit back, and watch them every chance you can. See what they do, and especially what they DON'T do. YouTube a video on it, just ask more and better questions. The path to a better you is one step away. One step at a time, one day at a time.

NOTES:

DAY 151

Understand what you are asking for, and at what level you're asking when you're asking for something. Many people want to get married and pray for a spouse, and that's all they pray for. They never ask for someone who is compatible in any way possible. When asking for anything, go as in-depth and be as detailed as possible. If you search your past and recall the things you've asked for over the years, I'd be willing to wager that you've gotten most of it. It just wasn't how you expected it. All you asked for was a spouse, you got a spouse. You didn't ask that they were financially responsible, family-oriented, drug-free, not abusive.... you get the point. And what's the point in asking for what you want, if you're not good enough to handle it? Why would a financially intelligent person want someone who doesn't have 2 nickels to rub together?? If you ask for a bigger house, make sure you ask that all of the appliances will be working or taken care of (a home warranty can cover that), the foundation is good, it's pest and germ-free, you can EASILY AFFORD IT, and make sure that the house you currently have is at least clean and safe.

There are so many things that go along with what you want, but all we know is to ask for 1 thing that entails 50 other things. In all thy getting, get an understanding. Work on becoming a better you, and you'll begin to know what to ask for, and what to weed out. You may even find out that what you want today isn't quite what you'll need tomorrow.

NOTES:______________________________

DAY 152

Things left to themselves, only tend to get worse. A car left alone rusts away, a house left to itself will eventually fall down, and a bridge untended to will crumble into the water. A mind is no different. The areas that you don't use and are left to themselves will wither away into uselessness. If you don't challenge yourself, push yourself, and force yourself to grow, you will slowly but surely lose all of your potential. Not only will you lose your potential, but you will also limit the next generation and put a ceiling on their mindset. You can be better, but it takes hard work and persistence. Don't let yourself take steps backward, force yourself forward, force yourself into greatness… you can do it.

NOTES:

DAY 153

When I was younger I was the worst of my siblings, I got whoopins nonstop. I was always getting into something I had no business being into. I'm sure my parents thought the worst of me at the time. It got to a point where I'd ask myself, "Self....is this thing you know is wrong worth the punishment you'll get if you get caught?", and self would reply "It sure is, go for it!" My terrible 2's lasted till I was about 16. It's not that the whoopins didn't hurt, to me it was worth what I felt I wanted at the time. Pain in our lives is an absolute necessity. Pain lets the body know that there's something wrong and that there's a problem. It doesn't matter whether the pain is physical, mental, or emotional, you're being told that something isn't right. Pain in life is letting you know that there's an area that needs some attention… the more pain, the more immediate attention is needed. This is not to say that pain is a bad thing. Most people will say it is, but I believe pain is a good thing because it's pointing out the problem, and you usually get time to fix the issues that are present, or worse issues that can pop up later.

The pain in my youth beatings took some time to work, but they helped straighten out the problems of my youth so that they didn't build and compound over the years and make things far worse. I also went thru the pain of being so broke that I had to skip meals so that my children could eat when they would come on weekends. But that pain taught me valuable lessons, and I made sure to NEVER feel that pain again. We never know what the future may hold, but if you take the pain you feel today, and use it as fuel to build the future you really want, that pain can be the springboard to everything you've ever wanted. Or you can take the pain as pain and allow it to pull you into an abyss. Pain is natural, normal, and a very useful tool… use it to the best of your ability. When used properly you can make sure that you never feel that pain again.

NOTES:____

____

____

DAY 154

When you go to the gym, and you lift weights, you put the amount of weight that you think you can handle on the bar/machine and that's what you work out with until you feel better, think you've gotten stronger, and can do more. At no point in time, would you look at someone doing twice as much weight as you, and be upset that they can do it, and you can't. You know it would take time to get there, and if you want it, you'll work at it. But in life, we look at others' blessings and demand that we get what they get. Just like in the gym, Your blessings aren't based on what you want, they are based on what you can handle. You may not be quite ready for what you're asking for and lusting after. You must be built up before you can handle some things, or the same thing will happen in life as it does in the gym....you can be crushed under the weight.

Build yourself up, prepare yourself, and learn to work on being a better stronger you, not amassing more blessings. The better you are, the stronger you are, the more the blessings will come.

NOTES:____

DAY 155

Most people we come across are a complete mess. You, me, us, them....all of us. Some are either better at hiding it or have opened up and gotten some help. In a world built around social media, everyone seems to think that everyone else has it made and is living a grand life. There are so many frowns behind the smiles, and nobody is dealing with their inner issues. Open up to someone, and I'd bet they're going through or have gone through a very similar thing in their lives.

We are all works in progress, struggling to make it through this existence. Don't hide your pain and struggles, put them out there. If you go to the gym, most people will spot you, even ones who have no clue what they're doing. They will try to help in any way they can, and they will even tell you that they have no idea what they're doing, so what do you need them to do? Most people have no problem trying to help you, especially those who've been through what you're going through (and that's a good percentage of people) stop hiding, stop running, and begin to fight your fears. The saying "it takes a village" isn't just for children. It takes a village just to survive. Use your village, and if you feel you're in an unsafe or unhealthy village, begin working on building a better one.

NOTES:

DAY 156

There are people who want to "never want for anything" and they believe that that means they have money, abundance, and blessings overflowing. Although this is a possibility, it usually means that you've built yourself up, where you are knowledgeable enough to venture down a few avenues and get what you need, and wise enough to be content with what you already have. You don't need $1000 for groceries if you've gained the knowledge of how to grow most of them in your yard. You don't need $800 to repair your car if you've taught yourself how to repair your car.

You must be a good manager of what you already have, otherwise even when you get more you'll blow it. You can get money, cars, houses, relationships, jobs, or whatever, and if you can't properly manage them, you will lose it all. God will hold back your blessings until you can become a competent manager over the things he's already put you in charge of. This is not to say that you shouldn't strive, or work for more because you should, but if you aren't content with what you have, more won't make it any better. Learn to be at peace within yourself, then you'll have far more than you could ever dream.

NOTES:____

DAY 157

I travel a lot for work, and I remember my first long travel job. At the time I hadn't worked for a while, funds were beyond depleted, bills were stacking up, and I got a call from someplace I'd sent a resume to… I'd sent so many I couldn't remember. It was making good money and lasted for a while, but there was a problem...I was in Alabama, and the job was near Dallas, TX. I immediately accepted the job and told them I could be there in 2 weeks. I had to figure out how to get to Texas and live until my first check with absolutely no money. I'd asked folks for loans, and only 1 person gave me any money, she said it wasn't even a loan, I could have it. It was $300, which was enough to get me there, then I figured I could overdraft my account and pay for the room, and I would use the leftover cash to eat for the week, that's what ended up happening. I had to overdraft until my second check, but things eventually started balancing out (and yes she got her money back with interest).

Some see the glass as half empty, and some see the glass as half full. Either way, it is what it is, and you're not wrong, it's just how you see life. I tend to see the glass as 100% full and overflowing. Half water, half air. You need air more than you need water to survive, so why wouldn't you count it as adding to your cup; air is accounted for in anything else except our minds. For that job, I could have said I had no money, and nobody would give me enough, but the opportunity was there, I just had to reach a little deeper for it. What you're looking for is within your grasp; it just will take more work than what you're used to. Your glass is full of opportunities, but you probably are just looking at them as air and empty space. It's ok, we all have, but now it's time to start changing your mindset and seeing what's really available to you.

NOTES:____

DAY 158

Les Brown is a motivational speaker. He and his twin brother were given up for adoption when they were born. A woman adopted him, and according to his words his adopted mother was a wonderful woman, a great mom, and he couldn't have lucked up any better. But his entire life he was angry at two nameless, faceless people, who gave him up. He was well into adulthood before he learned he had to get rid of that anger because it was only destroying him. As good as his mother was to him, he couldn't get over his pain. She would have never been good enough if he didn't fix himself. Some people, some situations, some places, some things, will never fit right because there's something wrong elsewhere.... in another person, at another job, in someone else's house.

This is not meant to be taken as a statement of admonition, and to say that no fault lies within us, because it does, we all need to look inward first. I'm sure Les' mother screwed stuff up and was selfish or mean or whatever at times, but she kept pushing forward, trying to better herself and the situation; and it was Les who had to come to terms with his issues in order to move further ahead in life. Once he fixed his issues, his relationship with his mother became better. No matter what, it's always us, we need to always, and forever believe in and work on ourselves; but also understand that everything can't be controlled by us, and we must know that there are things and people that we simply have no control over.

NOTES:____

DAY 159

When we take on new endeavors in life, we often think that we have to have all of our ducks in a row first, or we think everything has to be a certain way in order for us to jump in. We are looking for the perfect situation, the perfect time, the perfect skillset, etc. If that's what you're waiting on you'll wait the rest of your life. The weeds won't part like the Red Sea and show you the right path; if anything, they will grow faster, and put more in your way, covering the path even more. The only way to clear the path is to begin to do it yourself. Put in the work, then take the steps. You'll never reach perfection, even the elite people in your chosen fields still make mistakes, they still make bad choices, and they still come across things that they have not seen.

It's ok to fumble your way through things until you get them right. You've fumbled through your entire life, so now fumble through a little more toward something you actually want. Perfection isn't needed, what's needed is progress, persistence, tenacity, and desire. This is a marathon and not a sprint. When you're at the starting line, you can only see all of the people and problems in front of you. Once the race starts, everyone spreads out, and you have more room. You can never see the end until you're there, all you ever see is the next few minutes of steps ahead of you. You keep running and you'll make it, but you have to get started, and not quit.

NOTES:

DAY 160

For everything you want, you need, you desire, you care for....there is a price to be paid. It may cost a little, and it may cost a lot, but it will cost. Sometimes we are so used to things, and things come so naturally that we forget a price is attached to them. Children, and many adults even, don't understand this because the price that it costs them is paid by someone else. The price I'm talking about isn't necessarily monetary. Often it can be a kind word, an act, a deed....it's whatever the supplier demands the price to be. The Bible says to know the price of a house before you start to build it; otherwise, you'll get to building it, find it's too expensive, and quit. You'll end up with an empty pocket, frustrations, and a half-built house.

Have you counted up the costs of the things you're asking for??? Have you prepared yourself for the unseen costs that may be associated? One unforeseen cost of houses is taxes, and many people who've never owned a house don't understand that your mortgage can change every year if the taxes continue to go up every year. Every year for the last 3 years my mortgage has risen by $100 a year. Are you ready to pay the price of that house you've been asking for??? The nagging, the questioning, the demanding, the over-spending, or not saving enough. Are you ready to do what an obnoxious arrogant boss says, who knows less than you at the new high-paying job you asked for? There IS a price for what you've asked for, and it must be paid if you intend to keep it. Are u ready to break out the checkbook?

NOTES:

DAY 161

At work, we have different small crews that all work on different projects. I was on one crew, and another crew was short, so I got sent to this other short crew. I was upset because not only was I going to a crew with a supervisor who was a jackass of immense proportions, but I didn't even get traded, I just got sent. Like, can you at least get a Coke and a smile for me or something??? Am I Kunta, and too much trouble?? During my first 10 minutes in the crew, we butted heads. So much so, that he called his boss on me. Nothing much happened because neither of us was wrong in our position, things could have gone either way. We went on like this for about a week or two, two rams head-butting each other; and then, we began to learn each other. I'd sit him down and have some conversations, swapping viewpoints, and although we still don't agree on a lot of things, it's about how we handle the situation. I get what I want and so does he. We've learned to accept each other for the jackasses we are and work around that. We are both workers and want to see the job accomplished, so we have a common goal and good work ethic. Everything else can be worked out.

Just like in business, most of these people don't like each other, but they have common goals in mind and good work ethics, so everything else falls in line. Get your business in order. You're going to have to deal with people you don't want to and listen to people you'd rather not, but make sure you're dealing with people who have the same goals in sight that you do, and who aren't afraid to put the work in to make things happen. Have side discussions and begin to learn others' reasons and intentions behind their actions. You may be surprised to find out WHY some people are the way they are. Fight with those who are willing to fight with you.

NOTES:____

DAY 162

Many people in this world aren't where they want to be.... mentally, physically, spiritually, or financially. That's ok, that's what drives us all....to be better than where we are and better than who we are. That is the motivation. Once you've set a goal and accomplished it, there will be far more to accomplish after it. If you want to lose 20 lbs., and lose it, then u may want to lose 20 more; or you'll want to tone up or have better stamina. Trust me, the lists don't stop, but you just have to reach that goal first. I had a financial goal that I wanted to reach. I thought that when I hit it, I'd be ok, and I could sit back and be on Easy Street… you know.... relax for a while. When I finally hit that goal and looked at it I knew that there was absolutely nothing I could do with that chump change, so I've got to keep going.

Once you've put in the work and have begun to study and focus; once you actually reach your goals, and attained what you've desired for so long, you'll find out just how little you knew in the beginning. You've expanded your mind and thought processes, and you've opened a new world of possibilities. You're a new person, and you begin to think as a new person, and every day you are breaking your personal best. Set your goals and smash them, be the best that you can be.

NOTES:____

DAY 163

I don't think we truly realize how cheaply we value ourselves. Think how much you would have if you had your dream job. How much would you make an hour? I had a coworker just get a job offer doing almost the exact same thing, and he was offered $80/hr. That's almost 3 times what he makes now. And I started thinking what I could do with that, and $100/hr. would be even better. Then I thought...*why so low?* How much did u think your perfect job paid? Why not $1000/hr., why not have businesses that poured out more money than you could count, where u never had to work at all again?

That's how little we value ourselves because we've never been taught how to REALLY dream. I want to be somewhere collecting checks on a sunny 63-degree day with a slight breeze, and a smile on my face, and not have a care In the world; with perfect health, a fit body, a good mind, and surrounded by laughter. That's my perfect job. Now think again, what's your perfect job? What would you be doing if everything you wanted to do was paid for? You would never have another bill. Shoot for the moon. As you probably just saw... you can't even begin to think high enough, you're worth so much more than you can even imagine. Open your mind to the possibilities.

NOTES:

DAY 164

Don't believe your own mind when it comes to the great things you want. Your mind will tell you it's an impossible task, that it can't be done, and that you're crazy for even thinking about it. Sometimes all it really takes is an "I can do it attitude" on my job, my supervisor's supervisor (also known as general foreman) left the job suddenly. The position was open, so I decided to tell HIS boss, that I was interested in putting my name into contention. He questioned me and asked if I really wanted to and told me that this was serious (I can be quite a goofball most days). I told him yes, and that I wouldn't have him looking like a fool (he used to be our general foreman until he was promoted a couple of years ago). He set up the interview for me, along with a few other coworkers. These weren't announced interviews, it was by invitation only; so, had I not asked, I would have only heard about them through the grapevine AFTER the fact.

I was the last to go, and I blew them out of the water with my professionalism, my answers, my intellect, and the questions that I'd had for them as well. With every answer, my former boss looked at me as if to say, "Who is this guy, and where has he been hiding?" We hadn't been notified either way of things, but I was told that everyone was very impressed with the way I handled myself, and even if they don't choose me, there are things coming down the pipeline that will surely have my name on them.

All of this to say...I'm not qualified for this job, there are other candidates with more time and experience, and who are better liked, but I opened my mouth and spoke it into existence. Even if I don't get the job I'll still get something that's better than what I currently have. If you don't ask, the answer will always be no. The worst that's gonna happen is someone tells you no, and you're right where you already were; but if you ask, the possibilities are endless. Apply for the jobs you're not qualified for and ask the girl out of your league on a date. Don't fear rejection, fear Being in the same spot this time next year, because you refuse to move.

NOTES:____

____

DAY 165

Do not be unequally yoked, stay to your own kind, or stick with your people all mean the same thing. Hang around like individuals.... unless you're trying to change. This isn't a racial, or religious statement, they are simply facts. I once tried dating a woman in her early 20s, I was in my early to mid-30s at the time, and we weren't compatible at all. In no way were we equally yoked. We didn't have the same types of conversations, listen to the same music, watch the same shows, or even like the same food. Needless to say, that didn't last too long. "You're kind" isn't necessarily a race or religion, it's who's on the same mental wavelength; those with the same hopes, dreams, and goals; and those that you can find common ground with.

We make life exponentially harder for ourselves when we try to hold onto those people in our lives, who we are not compatible with. A Christian and a Muslim can cohabitate if they can agree on a few basic things, it's not about the title. We are taught to seek out differences in life, instead of searching for similarities. If you constantly search for those who have many of the same future plans and ideas, you have a better chance of having stronger more meaningful relationships. If you don't have future plans, well... you are probably the one that's gonna get left behind.

NOTES:____

DAY 166

When speaking to people, whether it is in passing, in a long thoughtful conversation, or even for a job interview.... listen intently, and offer THEM something, even if you want something from them. *How can I be of service to you?* Things tend to go over much smoother that way. I had a gentleman at work, asking me for a haircut. The problem with this was, that we worked opposite shifts. He said, "Well, it's my b'day, so let me get a free cut; and I know we work different shifts, so you can just stay over until you finish my cut?" The problem here is that he offered nothing and was only in the market to receive. I cut his hair, for free, AND I had to stay past my shift, just to help him out but he didn't even want to come in early. Everything he mentioned was to help him.

If you go to people and only tell them about your problems, you're less likely to get things. If you show them how you can both benefit from what you're looking for, you have a far better chance of succeeding. If I want to borrow money, to put you at ease, I can allow you to hold something of equal value, plus make weekly payments WITH INTEREST until it's paid back. Now we both benefit from what I need. Even in a general conversation, just listen, sometimes that's all a person needs. Even if it's not something that you're particularly interested in....just listen, you never know what you may learn. Be more of a giver than a receiver, and you'll become more of a receiver than a giver. Don't be taken advantage of but give to what you feel is worthy of your time and energy.

NOTES:____

DAY 167

Is a leader, a leader if nobody will follow them??? I say with a loud and resounding voice... YES. There are many factors that can hinder someone from being followed, but that doesn't negate the fact that what they are offering is valid, and just because someone is following a person, doesn't make them a leader either. They could be following that person out of fear, ignorance, blind loyalty, or sheer stupidity. I was once asked if I believe we are led by the Holy Spirit. My answer was yes and no. The Spirit tells us what to do, and shows us the way that we should go, enlightens us, and strengthens us, which is what a good guide or leader should and would do, so in that aspect, yes...

But, in order to be led, we must CHOOSE to follow. You can lead your children, and even if they choose not to follow, that doesn't necessarily diminish you as a parent or leader. Some will say, "Well a good leader will find a way to break through," and I say, "Maybe." That person or group of people may be beyond my scope of knowledge to reach. Are you choosing to be led, and by who???? It's hard for a boy to be a man if he's never seen one, and it's hard for a leader to lead if he's never followed anyone.

NOTES:

DAY 168

Keep yourself in a position where you can take advantage of future endeavors. More often than not, we see what we want today, and don't give thought to tomorrow. We see the big house, the nice car, all the glitz and glamor, and we go get it and max out our paycheck to our heart's content. We live on the financial edge, assuming we will always have this money, and never run into any problems. The first problem is.... this is life, and eventually you will hit a wall; and secondly, we have no spare money in case a great deal comes our way that we can capitalize on. We stick ourselves in the rat race and then blame others. If you keep your bills low, you will have extra funds to invest, and over time those investments can begin to take care of you.

Today's choices don't only impact tomorrow's choices, often they completely derail them. Don't allow today's choices to put you in tomorrow's financial purgatory, where all you're doing is working to pay bills, making someone else rich, and waiting to die. Take a little less today, send that dream car back, get a cash car for now, sell the house that's keeping you broke, and move into an apartment. You're setting yourself up for future greatness. You can live great today, and be broke tomorrow, or live broke today, and be great tomorrow.... the choice is yours.

NOTES:____

DAY 169

Learn to break down your work into manageable pieces. There is a study showing that instead of giving children with ADHD more time to do things, like an extra hour added to a test, give them small breaks.... 5 minutes here, to walk around; 10 minutes there, to stretch; then come back and do a little more. The results show this way of giving extra time helps significantly more than just adding extra time to the end of the test and making them sit there longer. There was another study done on the average adult, and the ones who worked for an hour and took 5–10-minute breaks, were far more productive than the ones who worked straight through. The breaks refresh you, relax your mind, and prepare you for more to come, almost like taking a nap.

Break down your workday/ workouts/schedule into smaller time blocks, with more breaks, and see if you're more productive. You can break down anything.... after 40 minutes with your children, disappear to the "bathroom" for 5-10 minutes, and when you come back, see if you can handle the little hellions better. If GOD took a break 1 out of every 7 days, I know I need a break at least 1 out of every 4 or 5. If you divide 1 hour into 7 equal parts (like days in a week) it comes out to 8.5 minutes, so every hour you should be taking 8 and a half minutes to yourself. You get a break, your boss gets more productivity, and you take far longer to burn out....it's a win-win situation for everyone involved. It's the least you can do.

NOTES:____

DAY 170

You are special, you are magnificent, you are an individual; you were born to be different and stand out, so stop trying to be like everyone else. You won the lotto just being born. You beat the odds. There are hundreds of millions of sperm every single time a man releases, and YOUR sperm is the one that made it. You were stronger, faster, and better than hundreds of millions of other candidates. Don't stop believing in yourself now. You're a winner. All it takes is belief in yourself. Surround yourself with those who believe in you, and will push you, and build you.... those who want to see you grow and mature.

Think about this.... mankind is so special, that angels left heaven to marry us. Can you even fathom that? All we are trying to do is make it to heaven, and all the angels want to do is come down here to be with us. This is how valuable you are. It doesn't matter what you've been through, where you've been, or what you've done. All that is a little dirt on your past. If I take a gold bar and beat it, kick it, throw it in the waste treatment plant, chop it up into pieces, throw it in the oven, melt it, and sprinkle dirt in it while it's cooling....there isn't a person on earth who still wouldn't want that bar of gold. YOU are worth so much more than that bar of metal, and I wish that you would open your eyes and see that. You've been looking for a sign, and here it is. YOU....ARE.... IMPORTANT. YOU....ARE.... VALUABLE. YOU....ARE.... WORTH.... IT.....ALL.

NOTES:____

DAY 171

The man who asks a question is a Fool for a minute, the one who doesn't ask is a fool for life. There will be plenty that you don't know or understand in life; and in this era, we've been taught that that isn't ok. You've got to know everything, ignorance is a weakness, and faking it till you make it is what everyone does. Nobody asks questions anymore, and it's a cardinal sin to say "I....don't....know." But the exact opposite is true; if you don't know (which most people don't) simply state that, and I'd bet money that there is someone in the vicinity who will help you with your questions and lack of knowledge. You'll find that they may not even know what you're asking, and they may be willing to figure it out together.

That is what scientists and engineers get paid for....to figure out the unknown… and they get paid handsomely. Your payment, your rewards, and your peace are just part of your own ignorance. Once you begin to learn how the things that plague your life work, you can begin to change your future. It is ok to BE ignorant of something, but it's never ok to STAY ignorant about anything. Information on just about any subject is literally at your fingertips. Begin to inform yourself and block out self-doubt.

NOTES:____

DAY 172

When I was in high school I was on the football team. My senior year the coach put me on the offensive line, and I HATED it with a passion. Every day we did our drills, and calisthenics, and ran through plays, timing, and such. Every minute was like nails on a chalkboard for me. My lack of enthusiasm showed up on the field so much so, that I eventually got my spot taken. One day in practice the defensive coach told the head coach that he didn't want this big senior just standing there sucking up space, and he asked if he could use me for drills in practice. The head coach agreed and told me to go. This is what I always wanted... to be on defense, and when I got out there I was flying all around the field, making plays. I did better than just about anybody because by having been on the offensive side of the ball, I knew the formations, the tendencies of the players, and what things looked like. They kept me in that position the rest of the week, and that weekend I started in the game.

About 2 weeks later the offensive lineman who took my spot couldn't keep his grades up, and they put me back on offense. This time I didn't mind being on offense because I still got to start on defense, and I did a great job both ways. I started both ways for the rest of the season. Nothing changed considerably, not my ability, my talent level, my speed, or my strength; it was simply my peace, my happiness, my willingness to say I'll do it. It was my choice to be happy with what was there and make something of it.

This also showed me that the things you go through in life may not be for your present time. I learned the offensive line, and when I left, I didn't think I was going back; but because of the mistakes of others, I ended right back where I started. But this time I was different; I was looking through a different lens. Same person, same speed, same strength, but a different perspective. Your best life is a perspective change away. Choose to see things in a different light and walk taller.

NOTES:____

____

____

DAY 173

A lot of actors get so deep into character, that when the project is over, they need time to decompress. To get back to themselves, they are so deep into that character that they've read them, studied them, and portrayed them daily for months, and that character is beginning to stick in their consciousness. They've looked at and done the things this character has done for months, and it begins to actually change them. They are being self-programmed. How are you programming yourself????? What are you doing over and over that's causing things to stick in you? Are you repeatedly reinforcing positive, or negative behaviors and attributes??? Every day you turn on that TV instead of working on your goals, and dreams first.... you're reinforcing negative sedentary behavior.

Begin learning to watch what you say and do, and ask yourself, *how is this getting me closer to my goals?* If you can see it getting you closer....do more of it, that's a positive step. If it's not getting you any closer, stop doing so much of it… those are more negative steps. And it doesn't matter whether it's a positive or negative movement, but know this....every time you make a choice, it gets easier, and easier to make that choice next time. This is what makes our habits, and why we have such problems breaking them, because we've forced them upon ourselves and we've done them so many times, that it's pressed together and compacted inside of us so deeply that we may need years to unpack everything. Add 1 positive repetition to your daily moves today, write it down, and do it again tomorrow. While in the process, take away 1 negative action, write it down, and repeat NOT doing it tomorrow.

NOTES:

DAY 174

Do you know what to ask for, do you know what you really want??? I have been trying to be a better man, a better father, just an all-around better me. I was told that it was noticed and that the work is paying off. It was stated that I carry a heavy burden, and what could be done that day, that could help ease my load. I didn't know, I couldn't answer that. We will get so used to telling people that we don't want/need anything when they ask us questions of this nature. I usually say it...but I also get upset when people don't give me anything or do anything for me. I came to this realization about a year or so ago, and I made it a point to say everything I wanted when I was asked these things. I don't care how outlandish it is, I'm gonna tell ya. If you ask me what I want, I want an income-producing, cash-flowing property; I want to be retired; I want to travel at will; I want to laugh and be happy, and be surrounded by people who love me for me; I want unending massages.....and the lists don't stop.

I no longer am curtailing my responses to the people who ask, I am allowing the floodgates to open, because you never know what someone is capable of, but....you also have not, because you ask not. I'm asking for the moon, baby, and if you can only get me a paper airplane, I'll take it. But I am no longer going to not have what I want simply because I didn't ask for it. What do you want, what would your replies be if you were asked? Would you dictate your answers to the level of the one asking, or would you open the floodgates? Tell them what you want, look in the mirror and tell yourself what you want, talk to yourself about what you want on the way to and from work, point it out, circle it, highlight it, and put neon lights around it. Make it so visible that nobody will ever be able to say, "I never knew that's what they wanted."

NOTES:____

DAY 175

While growing up, many of us used to watch Bob Barker on The Price is Right. There was a game on there called Plinko (I believe that was the name), and with this game, you would stand on top of a platform and drop a round disc down a board with a bunch of pegs on it. The point was to try to get the disc into one of the money slots at the bottom, but every time your disc hit one of the pegs, it would go in a different direction. When it got to the bottom who knows where it would finally land, maybe on a money slot, maybe on a bankrupt slot. We often treat our lives like a game of Plinko, just being bounced around by the pegs of life landing wherever the pegs take us. You must be intentional about the life you want to live; you have to learn to carve out the niche in the life u desire.

Wealthy, and influential people don't just happen to get where they are off of happenstance, they plan their lives, and they work the plans. They have a roadmap on how to live their lives and the obstacles they must overcome to do it. They also put in the work. You can have the best plan in the world for weight loss, but if you don't put it into action, and eat less/workout more, you won't succeed. If you get your paycheck, just spend it frivolously, and say you'll pay the bills whenever they come up, you're setting yourself up for failure. But if you plan, make a budget, and pay bills FIRST, you'll have an exponentially better chance at reaching your financial goals. Don't play Plinko with your life, set a course and follow it. Be intentional about your life and don't end up in an unsavory position.

NOTES:____

DAY 176

A debate is basically a thoroughly rehearsed argument. You are given a subject, and you must study all sides of the subject, because you will show up at the debate, and you won't know until the debate begins if you are to argue for the subject or against the subject. So not only do you need to study all of the pros, but all of the cons as well, and as many loopholes on both sides so that you can argue and defend from all sides. When we have disagreements with people, all we do is argue. We normally not only don't know the other side of the argument, but refuse to learn, or even listen to it.

Begin to learn to debate, instead of arguing. See things from more than just YOUR point of view. The more information you can take in, the better perspective you will have, and you will find that it's probably not worth arguing about anyway. Once you begin to take a look at another perspective, you may realize that your actions, no matter how noble, have affected someone else in a negative way. A debate is simply an intelligent, rational, informed conversation; you can make it much further in life with intelligent conversation, than arguing, fussing, and fighting.

NOTES:____

DAY 177

When a woman gives birth, she is literally giving of herself to make this child. This is why proper nutrition is so important. Whatever the mother doesn't supply the baby in food, the baby will take from the mother's body. This is why there is a higher case of osteoporosis in women as they age because babies have literally sucked their bones dry. Life is much like this. When you are starting a business, in a relationship, or even raising a family....we give of ourselves. We take small bits of ourselves and give them away, bits at a time.

We can't see it, but the energy we give away is slowly sapping our energies from later ventures. Learn to be cautious of the energy you're giving away. Make sure energy is reciprocated. Just like a mother, if that energy isn't supplied from somewhere, you will slowly be depleted, and may not know until it's too late. Life is transactional, and if you don't believe so, I'd bet you're being taken advantage of. Ensure you're getting the nutrition needed to sustain your life energy.

NOTES:

DAY 178

Just about every building on this planet was built using some sort of blueprint. A blueprint is something that is drawn or written down, and it lets me tell you exactly what I want, how I want it, and where to put it. Every pipe, every switch, every tile, and every picture. In hotels and larger buildings, they even know what art is going to be on the wall, or on each podium, nothing is left to chance. So, whoever comes to work on this building, or system can pick up from anywhere and move without much interaction from the owners, investors, or management. No oversight is needed or anyone bird-dogging to see if it's the way the customer wants it. Once I've completed my tasks, or even during the task, someone can check up on me and make sure everything's running smoothly and being put in properly.

Where is the blueprint for your life? Where are the written down things that you can show to anyone who wants to come into your life and begin to help you build the building of YOU? Can you give someone the instructions you've written down and walk away, or will you have to tell them repeatedly what you want, and how to get it done, because they forgot what you said, or there was a mix-up, about what I THOUGHT u said or meant? The blueprint to your life should have goals, dreams, desires, written plans on how you intend to reach these things, and a timeline. Just like prints to a building, all of these things can be adjusted and shifted at any given time. If things aren't working correctly, or not fitting how you thought they should, send the prints back for an adjustment, but don't go rogue and try to build yourself without a plan/print; there's no telling what that will turn out to look like. Work on your blueprints of self and begin to follow the road map to your greatest desires.

NOTES:____

____

____

____

DAY 179

Whenever there's a cookout, there's usually enough food to go around. The hosts know who they've invited, and make sure that they are prepared for who's coming, and if it doesn't look like enough when people get there the good host may even go back to the store and get more of what's needed. Good guests will bring a dish or something of value to the gathering, to show appreciation, and also to take a small bit of stress off of the hosts....one less thing that they have to worry about. A great guest will even help clean up during, and/or afterward. The worst guests, show up with nothing (some may not have even been invited), eat and drink their fill, then try to take multiple plates home for others, and don't help clean anything.

Stop allowing people into your personal space, and into your life who are only coming to take to-go plates and sustenance out of your life; and when things get tough for you, they can never seem to add anything of value. They disappear like a fart in the wind. Stay away from those that are always around when it's time to eat, but never seem to have any time or money when it's time to do the grocery shopping. The "Oh, I ain't got it this time, I got you next time" people. Keep the good company in your life that shows up early to help you set up, who help build u up, and help prepare, those who come bringing things that will help you, and help take some bit of a load off of your back. Keep those people around who help you clean up the messes in your life, especially the ones who are there when everything and everyone else has already gone, and the party's over. Who are the people making withdrawals in your life that aren't making deposits? Who are the ones showing up with nothing, trying to take extra with them when they leave? If you aren't here to build and add value, you must go.

NOTES:____

____

____

____

DAY 180

I was reading a book recently, and it quoted a scripture from the Bible, Matthew 7:15-20. It basically says, Beware of false prophets, and you'll know the real and fake ones by the fruit they produce, or what they actually do, or what comes from what they actually do.... the outcomes. Some will say, well I'm not evil because I don't do anything bad; but it hit me....it says it can be determined who you are, by what you produce. Are you even producing anything to get judged by?

A good worker produces good work, a bad worker produces bad work, but a horrible worker doesn't produce ANY work. At least the one giving me a bad product is giving me a product, I can work with that. Even if you mess up, and produce bad work, get up, get in the game, and do SOMETHING; we can fix mistakes and losses, but you can't fix what you never had in the first place. Start producing some sort of fruit in your life, then you can worry about making it good.

NOTES:

DAY 181

When eagles make a nest, they put thorns at the bottom of the nest, cover it with branches and softer leaves, and then lay their eggs. When the baby eagles hatch, the mother nurses them until she believes it's time for them to leave the nest, once it's time to go, the mother bird pushes the babies out of the nest (many bird species do this) and watches them fall. Eagles usually build their nests very high up, and as she watches to see if they will take flight or not, she's timing it in her head. If she doesn't think they'll make it, she dives down, catches them, and brings them back into the nest; then repeats the process again, and again, and again. If the baby bird doesn't get it, momma pulls away all the leaves and branches and exposes all the thorns. The discomfort of the piercing thorns let's baby know they better do something really quick. Plus, if other eggs were laid, they have the pressure of their successful siblings, and they learn to fly very quickly once those thorns start poking.

Maybe you're in an uncomfortable situation because it's time for you to move, maybe you've been spoon-fed enough, and you're being told it's time to fly. You see everyone around you starting to take off, wondering when it'll be your turn....your turn is now, take off, and leave the safety of the nest. It won't be easy, but it'll be worth it. Take flight into the atmosphere and see how much better the world is than the nest. We were made to be eagles, and we choose to peck with the chickens. Eagles are known to fly up to 11,000 ft, that's over 2 miles in the air. Pain isn't always a bad thing, pain gets you moving, it pushes you, it lets you know that something isn't right. Use that energy to change your situations and build the life you're desiring.

NOTES:____

DAY 182

The flower loves to see the sunshine, for when the sun shines, it illuminates the flower's world, feeds the flower, and allows the flower to get pollinated. The sun loves to see the flower bloom, it knows it's taking what the sun is offering, and using it, putting it to good use, feeding bees, and giving off its beauty.

Whether you are the sun in someone's life or the flower, use what you have to make your surroundings a better place. Everyone can feed someone. Feed others like the sun feeds the flower, the flower feeds the bee, and the bee feeds the bear, and all mankind consumes its honey. Just because you can't give what was given to you, doesn't mean you aren't able to give. Do your best, so that you can be your best.

NOTES:

DAY 183

Everyone has a goal in life, some are large, and some are small, some can be done in a passing thought, and others will take years of hard work, determination, sacrifice, and dedication. No matter what your goals are, or how long it takes to finish them, focus and dedication are key. Distractions must be kept to a minimum. If you can't stay focused on your goals, and not be pulled aside by every shiny thing, it takes so much longer to accomplish your goals....IF you ever do. We must have on blinders like a horse so that we aren't distracted by the things that have nothing to do with our goals. Set your goals and then ask yourself, *does what I'm about to do, get me closer to any goal I am trying to achieve?* If the answer is no, you probably shouldn't be doing it.

The more time, attention, and energy you put into things outside of your goals, the less time you're putting into your ultimate happiness, and the more you're feeding the flames of your own failures. Imagine going on a trip and stopping at every other exit to see what's going on there, or stopping at every place where a billboard says there's an attraction. You'd never make it to your destination. When I'm on the road traveling, I only stop for gas, and you'd better eat, and piss there, because we ain't stopping again until that tank's getting dry again. Start with smaller goals to get yourself warmed up to the bigger goals. Don't turn your 6-month journey into a lifetime one. Stay diligent and focused.

NOTES:____

____

____

____

____

____

____

____

____

DAY 184

The grass (on the other side of the fence) is only greener because you aren't taking care of and watering yours.

NOTES:

DAY 185

When you're on a construction site, there will be a lot of noise, confusion, and mayhem. Everything is being built, shored, and supported, and there are 1000 projects going on at once. If you're not involved on that specific project, you're probably going to be lost if you walk up and just look to see what's going on. YOU are that project, and your mind, your body, and your life are that construction site.

Many people will walk up to you and tell you how you should be building yourself according to THEIR blueprints. But they may not understand the final goal or product that you yourself are trying to attain. Be cautious of other "builders" on your site who are just walking up, taking a glance, and trying to put their 2 cents in. Come up with a plan and work YOUR plan. Don't forget that plans can be adjusted, but the goal shouldn't be.

NOTES:

DAY 186

How do you make the people in your life feel? Have you talked to them, had conversations with them??? Do they feel safe, secure, heard, valued, validated????? Now, I understand that people cannot ALWAYS feel this way, in all situations, but the special ones in your life should feel these things more times than they don't. People leave relationships, jobs, friendships.... simply because they don't feel valued, heard, or appreciated. Find out what it will take to make those in your life feel more valued, and appreciated, it could be the simplest thing in the world that may cost you nothing. Don't forget that you too need to feel validated, important, and special, so you can't spend all of your energies pleasing others.... reciprocity is a MUST.

You cannot continue to give without taking at some point in time. Validate and value others while at the same time, teaching others how to value, and validate you. Plenty of people take less money on jobs, for more opportunities to be heard, or to have a better working environment, or simply because, they laugh more at the lower-paying job. Find out what really makes people tick and find out what really makes you tick. Put those things into action and watch how your surroundings begin to shift.

NOTES:____

DAY 187

Are u married to your goals and dreams, or are u in a marriage with them? Being married, and in a marriage, are 2 totally different things. Many people nowadays want to get married for the "title" of husband, or the "title" of wife, thinking that this life will work itself out. Then when things begin to get rough, they quickly look to blame someone else or take the first exit that they can find. When you're actually in a marriage, you are committed to the end, you're passionate about where you're going, and you're dedicated to staying and working through things. You're there to ride through the good, the bad, AND the ugly.

When you set goals, you have to see them through, because once you quit, no matter how difficult it was, the next time it's going to be a little easier, and the next time is a little easier, until quitting becomes second nature. Sit down and come up with a well-thought-out plan of action, then put it into play. If all you have is a half-thought-out hair-brained scheme it makes it 100 times easier to quit; but if you have a plan, and smaller plans in place to cover the negative "what ifs" then you'll have a far better chance at succeeding in whatever you choose. Stay focused, stay committed, and stay strong throughout the course of your journeys, both large and small. Don't just be married but stay in a marriage with whatever you choose to partake.

NOTES:____

DAY 188

Our entire lives, we've been pitted against each other, we've been told that competition is healthy....in life, in sports, in business, all over the world. And we have been forced to believe that this is the way to get "the best" out of everyone. The Blacks against whites, old against young, nation against nation, rich against poor. The lists never end, the powers that be will constantly find ways and reasons to divide us. The more divided we are against each other, the less of a chance we have of coming together to form a strong cohesive unit. The best way to grow, learn, and dominate, is through collaboration.... working together, in unity.

The strongest corporations are that way because the employees work together, the strongest, wealthiest families, work together. Anywhere, in any field, on any part of this planet, across any species, if you find success, you will find things that work together for a common goal. Even in families that hate each other, the common goal of cohesiveness, money, and power, outweigh their hate, and they continue to work together because if they don't, they KNOW they will fail. Even when families were at war killing each other, they would set up arranged marriages, to broker peace, and usher in eras of prosperity and longevity.

Every gas station around the country has the exact same gas prices, at the exact same time, it doesn't matter which company it is. They all go up at the same time, in the same amounts, and go down at the same time, in the same amounts. They've learned that they can charge whatever they want, as long as they do it TOGETHER, and this way everyone gets rich, and you don't have to fight anyone in the process. Don't look to be in competition with ANYONE about ANYTHING, look to collaborate. Look for ways to build, strengthen, and multiply, not divide, and tear down.

NOTES:____

DAY 189

People with addictions live a hard lifestyle. They are controlled by their habit(s), and do not live a life of sustainability. Many addicts lie, cheat, steal, and even do harm to themselves, to get to the next hit. The sad part is, that I'm not only talking about substance abusers. I am speaking about people who are addicted to all sorts of ills that you may not even think about. Those who are addicted to sex, porn, smoking, drinking, lying, stealing, gossip, hate, malice, ill contention, strife, greed, jealousy, envy, and I can go on and on all day with this list. Have any of the things listed hit close to home for you? Addictions aren't always so easy to see, and those are the hardest to fix because we hide them so well, that we even hide them from ourselves. We don't believe that we are on these "negative" lists, but can point out every flaw in everyone else effortlessly.

What are the addictions you need to work on, are you willing to take a deep look inside, are you ready to start the process, of breaking your bad habits and addictions, are you willing to open yourself up to others' scrutiny, so that they could point out the problems they see in you???? Self-reformation is one of the hardest things that you will ever attempt to tackle, but it's also one of the most uplifting, and worthwhile as well.

NOTES:____

DAY 190

This is a message that was sent to me seconds after id sent the previous one, showing me, that I'm on the right path.

I ground and clenched my teeth so hard against each other that I eventually broke one of my molars, which I had to replace. The technical term for tooth grinding is "bruxism." Bruxism can be the result of multiple things. Sleep apnea, anxiety, pain, and frustration are a few causes of teeth grinding. It also affects people with anger issues and aggressive, hurried, or overly competitive tendencies. After dealing with my sleep apnea and pain [which were part of a physical condition], I was left with anxiety, anger, aggression, hurried [feeling of being in a rush], and my competitive nature. Those tendencies align themselves with the soul, which includes the "mind, emotions, and the will" of a person. These issues have to be acknowledged, addressed and traced back to the origin of why they were formed in our hearts. I've been learning why I'm the way that I am and understanding how to unravel all of the hidden hurts that I've been reluctant to acknowledge.

Recently I watched a man trying to untangle two bucks [male deer] whose horns were entwined together with barbed wire. They would have died if this guy didn't intervene. At first, they struggled to get away from the man, but they kept pulling in opposite directions. After being exhausted, the deer stopped struggling, and the guy was able to free them. You see, we must stop struggling with the issues that have us stuck! Ask the Holy Spirit to reveal your own struggles and allow yourself to be helped by whomever God sends to set you free!

"But now is the time to get rid of anger, rage, malicious behavior, slander, and dirty language. Don't lie to each other, for you have stripped off your old sinful nature and all its wicked deeds. Put on your new nature and be renewed as you learn to know your Creator and become like him." (Colossians 2:8-10 AMP).

NOTES:____

____

DAY 191

Sometimes when we give, we think of the amount of money we've given to people, churches, and organizations. But when we give, there are so many more avenues of giving that we cover. Giving consists of our time, our effort, our energy, giving of our knowledge, and wisdom, our sweat, and our influence. Giving goes way deeper than monetary. When you give, you are giving a piece of yourself away, and hopefully like a Begonia plant, that small piece of you will grow in someone else. Planting a piece of yourself in someone else is like planting a seed to be carried away with someone else, a miniature copy, if u will. Plant seeds throughout your day. One seed can produce 1000 other offspring that can all produce seeds.

NOTES:____

DAY 192

No matter what, you're going to change in life, and even in death comes change. When you're buried in the ground, your body is decomposing....that's a change. So, the question isn't, *am I changing?* The real question is, *am I improving?* Every second you take a breath, you're changing....getting older, fatter, slimmer, taller, shorter....but are you completing anything? Are you on a purposeful journey to complete anything? Have u set goals, and standards to reach, do you have something driving you, pushing you, is there a fire inside of you raging for your escape????? If not, then maybe you're just living, or simply surviving. And if you are, that's ok, but try to find what will light that fire inside of you. A simple beginner's guide....think of everything you want, and a quick 10-minute thought process of how to accomplish that. This can start your journey of living, thriving, and succeeding.

YOU are the captain in your life, YOU control its course. Take the time to calm yourself and set yourself on the desired path. Live each day intentionally, knowing that you're working towards your ultimate goals. Push through the day with purpose, understanding that each step you take, each dollar you save, each thought you think, is in somehow, and some way, getting you that much closer to your ultimate goal.

NOTES:____

DAY 193

A man gave his son, an iron brick, and asked him how much he would pay for it. The son said, "Nothing." The man then told his son to take it to the horse trainer, the seamstress, the auto dealer, and the clockmaker. the trainer told him he could make horseshoes and sell them for $20, the seamstress could turn them into needles, and sell them for $1000, the auto dealer said he could use it for his cars, and add $5000 to his cars, the clockmaker said, he could use it and make gears, and springs, and sell his watches for $100,000. It's not about what you have in life; it's about what you have in life, but IF you know what to do with what you have. Can you take what you have and cultivate it into something beautiful? Every farmer is only given a seed, it's up to that farmer to clear their land, plow the field, plant the seed, keep the weeds and bugs away, harvest the field, and then cook, and/or sell the crop. It's up to you to figure out what it is that you have and build with that. If the farmer says he doesn't want to till the ground that day, he won't be able to put seed in the ground or reap the harvest.

If you consistently turn down options, and opportunities in your life, you're turning down seeds of blessings that can grow into many other opportunities. Every seed that makes it through to harvest, produces 100 times what went onto the ground. Are you going to eat your seeds (savings, OT, study time), or are you going to plant them, and allow them to bring even more seeds back??? What seeds can you plant, and cultivate, how can you begin to nurture and feed the things in your life you already have? Every day opportunities cross your path, but you don't see them or don't want them, and complain that there are no opportunities. Push through that veil of obscurity and begin to see the chances you're passing up.

NOTES:____

DAY 194

We have all been broken in our lives. We've been beaten up, tattered, torn, and left alone. At times I'm sure we've all felt as though we were the only person walking our paths, and we were too scared to talk to anyone about what we were going through, KNOWING that we were the only ones to go through this, so we suffer in silence. Let me tell you, that You are NOT the only one to have gone through what you've gone through or are going through, and you are NOT alone. There is someone in your circle who has been through something similar, if not that very same thing. There are people around you who not only can help you through, but help you get there faster, and with far fewer headaches. So, reach out to a select few, who you feel won't betray your trust. I can hear you now, "But I can't trust anyone around me with my innermost secrets".... Then should you really be keeping them around at all???? You will make it through whatever you're going through, the only question is, how long will it take you, and how beat up will you be? If you reach out to others, the time will be far less, and the beatings will be much less.

Your trials will build and strengthen you, but they are not simply for you, they are for you to be a mentor to someone else going through the same thing later, just as you found someone to help you. We are here to help, build, and support each other. Don't suffer unnecessarily, swallow your pride, and ask for help, far more people are willing to help than u think.

NOTES:____

DAY 195

I was watching a video on an NBA player, Patrick Beverly from Chicago. When he was in high school he averaged some insane number of points, I think it was like 35 points per game. So, of course, when you get to the league, you may not be thinking 35, but 15-20 hopefully, 10 at the worst. He said off the top of his head, he thinks the most he ever scored was about 10 points in a game. In order for him to get to the NBA and stay there, he had to become a defensive player. Everything he knew throughout his entire game was not only predicated on being an offensive player but a top scorer at that. When he finally reached his goal of making it to the league, what he'd done, wasn't good enough to keep him there. He had to reinvent himself, he had to go back to the basics and polish his defensive skills if he wanted to continue living his dream. He hasn't had the best, most prolific career, but he's living his dream. He won't make the Hall of Fame, but he's been in the league for quite some time and is living a relatively comfortable life.

Are you willing to give up on everything you THOUGHT you should be, to reach your goals and dreams, are you willing to break yourself down, and change your entire philosophy to get where you say you want to be? Will you continue to follow the same path everyone else has followed, and continue to say, "I've seen them do it, I know I can" and fall into obscurity, or change your lifestyle, your training, and your routines so that you can stay in the game? Do you have it in you to reinvent yourself, or are you stuck on one track? What GOT the job, won't keep the job, what got the husband/wife, won't keep them. If everyone took the highway to the beach, then that's why there's so much traffic. Yes, others who left before you made it with no problem, but now you're stuck in traffic. Will you get off and take a chance at side streets, or keep waiting in traffic, shortening your time at the beach....if you ever make it? Learn to adjust, adapt, and be willing to change.

NOTES:____

____

____

DAY 196

Let go of what you THINK your work has gotten you. If you pivot, and reassess, you just may come out better in the long run.

NOTES:

DAY 197

In slavery days, we used to cultivate and harvest crops for someone else's profit, now WE are the crops that are cultivated and harvested for profit. We are given under-funded, substandard education (which was only ever intended to make you a good worker), hoarded Into poverty-stricken neighborhoods, (red-lining still exists) given low-paying wages, over-priced homes and food, and over-policed, being streamlined into the people-for-profit penal system, where slavery was NEVER ABOLISHED, and fortune 500 companies literally get slavery labor....right back to the beginning, and everything comes full circle.

We must first educate ourselves and our children, and instill business-building and investing mindsets, not "hard work and saving" ones. We can build ourselves out of this modern-day crop sharing, and into true freedom. Don't be a willing participant in this modern-day slavery, be more diligent, more purposeful, and more determined with your, and your future seeds' lives.

NOTES:

DAY 198

Once you've decided that you will grow, there's nothing on this planet, other than death, that can stop that growth. When you become dedicated, steadfast, and unwavering in your determination, you are an unstoppable object. This is not to say that you won't face adversities, setbacks, trials, and tribulations, but to say that you can face every single one of your problems, and walk away from it a victor, instead of a victim. Continue, persevere, and continue putting one foot in front of the other. YOU are the only one who can stop your dreams.....everything else is simply a distraction.

NOTES:

DAY 199

You can do more when u have more. When you make that million dollars you can give to those charities, you've wanted to give to, when you get out of debt, you'll be freer to help others and start on the path to things you've always wanted to do. All of these are sayings we generally tell ourselves, to give us reason NOT to do something, and generally, it's false. If you can't find time to give up 2 hours on a Saturday now, to feed the homeless, where do you think it will come from when your dreams come true, and you'll be even busier???? If you can't find $10 to give to someone now, where will the money come from when you finally get those million dollars, and get the bigger house, more car notes, and even bigger bills? Whatever you want to do when "you've made it" begin to do it now. You can't say, "'ll work out when I make it to the NBA," you have to work out to get there, or you never will make it. And if you somehow miraculously did make it, you wouldn't be ready, or equipped, to handle what you were about to go through; you also wouldn't know how to handle it, because you hadn't prepared yourself.

Begin to intentionally carve out small notches of time and money, to put towards what it is you want to do in the future. You can start with as little as 15 minutes or 1 single dollar. It seems like nothing now, but over time, it begins to change your mindset, until you begin to see that you can not only do more....but so much more. The pyramids weren't built in a day, neither will your dreams. Learn to manage your time and money now, so that when it finally shows up, it's already second nature, what to do, and how to do it. You can't wait for your dreams to happen to work on them, you must work on them, in order for them to happen. Work on your dreams by doing the baby steps that will lead to the big steps.

NOTES:____

DAY 200

I was listening to an interview by a rapper named T-pain. In the music business, if you sample someone's music, you're supposed to get their permission, and the owner dictates how much they will charge you. They are usually pretty steep, like 70, 80, and I know in Michael Jackson's case, 100% of the royalties. T-pain didn't care about the royalties, he wouldn't fight if they asked for large royalties or even 100%. His mindset was that he would make the song so good, and so popular, that he could tour off of it, for the next year or two, collecting tens of thousands of dollars at every show for appearances, merchandise, pictures, and special venues, like after-parties. The old adage of "there's more than 1 way to skin a cat, never rang so true. We've been taught our entire lives, that ownership is of the utmost importance, but in actuality, it's about control, and where the money flows. T-pain doesn't "own" the rights to those songs, if he gives up 100% of the royalties, and he doesn't get paid every time it gets played on the radio or put in a movie, but he accepted that and turned it into something he can control and make even more money with.

Would you rather be the owner of a house or the renter??? The owner gets the rent every month, but the renter has control, and in many states, the law is on their side; with permission from the owner, the renter could sublet the property out to a business, Airbnb, or for large sporting events, and make 10 times more than the owner. If what you're doing isn't working, look up other ways of doing it, talk to others, find mentors, and think outside the box. There are more ways to do something than you can shake a stick at, but are you willing to do them, and are you willing to accept, that things hadn't gone the way you planned?

NOTES:____

DAY 201

There was a point in time, when I was going through a divorce, had no job, no prospects, and there was miniscule money coming in. I paid a $10 membership fee at a gym to shower there and take 2 gallons of water home with me every day to drink, so I wouldn't add to my water bill. I'd cut grass, and hair on the side, and that gave me just enough to pay most of my bills. Popeye's had a $2 Tuesday deal, for $2.22 you could get a 2 piece and a biscuit. On a good week, I'd get 14 deals. That would be 2 meals a day, to last me the whole week. The entire time, I was putting in applications everywhere, I'd go to the library, and if it said electrician, I sent a resume. Most people thought I was lying at the time, they all said, "How could you be doing that all the time, and nobody calls you back???" I didn't have an answer, I just knew something had to give. Well, one day I got a call asking if I wanted a temporary job in Texas. I told them yes, IMMEDIATELY. I didn't even remember putting an application in with this company, but to get to the job, I had to borrow money, overdraft my account for 3 weeks, skip a car payment, and drive with no insurance. This was a rough time in my life, but that time was a seed-planting time, that led me to where I am today.

That Texas job was the first of my traveling career. We don't think of it as much when we are doing good, but you have to plant seeds everywhere all the time because you never know what's going to sprout where, or when. That rough time in my life has led me to businesses, endurance, faith, a job I love, property, and so much more. Continue to do the right things, and your time will come. Never give up, and always push forward. You may be in a massive storm right now, but remind yourself, the best trees require the most water. You're being strengthened for what's coming later. The storms will subside, and you will still be standing. You only lose when you quit.

NOTES:____

____

____

DAY 202

What we WANT, and what we NEED, we usually see as being on the opposite ends of the spectrum; but in actuality, they are 2 peas in a pod. Nobody wants to deal with the rain and storms, but that's the very thing that gives most of the vegetation its water supply on the planet, which in turn feeds everything on the planet. If there's never any rain, nothing grows, and nothing is fed. The rain also shows you where the leaks and weaknesses are in your home's structure. The tough times in life are like the rain. The tough times are what feed your mentality and your soul; they strengthen you (if you allow them to), or they can drive you into darkness and depression. Understand that the tough times are there to build you just like the rain is there to water and quench the plants. When times get tough, and you feel things closing in around you, those are the leaks in your roof. They are simply telling you what needs to be fixed... what needs to be worked on. And just like most anything else, it's best to get to it sooner than later, or even more, maybe even catastrophic damage may occur.

Allow the tough times to build and nourish your soul. Look into the tough times, and find the lessons for you to learn, the growth that's there for the taking, and the opportunities that are at your fingertips. We want blessings without the rain, not understanding that the rain and the storms ARE the blessings. Everyone that you're going to go to, that can help you out of that bad situation, can help you, because they've most likely been through it, which means in order for them to help you is a blessing, so had they not gone through it already, they couldn't bless you with the help. Now, you're being blessed to be able to help someone else. " A smooth sea never made a skilled sailor." Allow your personal storms to build you up to your personal triumphs, and not tear you down into your personal hell. Continue to grow through all adversity and stand on the other side ready to help.

NOTES:____

DAY 203

There are many things that adults of any age should be working on in today's society; but 2 very important ones that will last throughout time, are credit and character. They are one and the same, but different, at different times. Credit is simply your word, written down, and tracked. Your character is simply your words put into action. Credit is your word written down. You said you would pay for these things, and it was written down, and tracked, to see if you kept your word. Sometimes we shoot ourselves in the foot and over-extend ourselves, we only plan for the best-case scenarios, forgetting that life is going to drive us into corners. We find ourselves in a ditch, and instead of stopping, we borrow even more to pay off our already deep debts, digging that hole even deeper. We've all been there; the only difference is....learning when to stop digging. That time to stop is today. How you do one thing, is how you do most things. If you're over-extended on credit, I'd bet a month of paychecks, that you're over-extended in your relationships, and at church, and most other places, where you just can't seem to find the time.

Slow down and begin to work on your word (credit). Begin to work on handling only the things that you KNOW you will be able to do in the good times and not-so-good times. Focus on the small things and begin to rebuild yourself. Some things will have to be let go, but it will help in the long run. Build your credit report and your personal credit with those around you. Keep your word as best you can, and don't put your word out there if it's not absolutely necessary. There are other avenues to helping you, than the general ones that you are aware of, but the final decision lies in your hands. You can get all the help in the world, but if you continue to make bad decisions, you will be stuck in the same ditch. Use your help, and information wisely.

NOTES:____

DAY 204

There was a funny video of a mother holding a hot pot with oven mitts. she wanted her daughter to come and take it from her, so the girl jumped up and went to grab the pot bare-handed. Mom says, "Don't do that, the pot's hot!" The daughter looks at her strangely and attempts to grab the pot again. The mom pulls the pot away and speaks slowly and loudly. "THE POT....IS....HOT!" The daughter, of course, looks at her mom bewildered, and yet once again tries to grab the hot pot bare-handed. This time, the mother had to holler and curse her daughter out. "I told you the mother-flipping pot is hot!" Then the daughter finally understood.

We don't all think alike, and we are not all on the same page at the same time.....we may NEVER be on the same pages at all in life. People are shrouded with, and looking through glasses stained with fear, hate, jealousy, envy, pain, and hurt. Sometimes the information you try to convey, can't be heard because of all these filters they are trying to listen through. Learn about the people you deal with the most and try to maneuver around one or two of their personal obstacles. It may make it a little easier for them to hear you. All we can do is supply the information to the best of our abilities and hope that we are heard. It may take some reiterating, and maybe some unconventional things to get through, but it can be done. And always remember, don't get offended if they choose not to listen, they simply may not see your way as the best option for their life. That's ok, wish them the best, and continue on with your day. Your life is its own path, and so is theirs, and we all must take our own steps.

NOTES:____

DAY 205

We always look at our goals, and how far away they are, how much more work we have to do, and how much energy it would take to finish the job. A lot of times, just those thoughts alone make us give up on our dreams. Not actually putting in the work, being burnt out, sweating till no end, going broke, losing friends....nope, just simply the THOUGHT of it all makes us give up. Sometimes it's ok to look back and see just how far you've come. Quite often, when I look back over my life and the things I've accomplished, I see that I'm not anywhere near where I want to be, but I also see that I am so much further from where I started and that stopping or turning around now would be ludacris, and asinine.

Look back, see the moves you've made, see the progress, see all of the gains, and see all you've accomplished. Allow those things to be fuel for your journey. In a long road trip, there comes a time when you're just tired of being in the car, and you're ready to get out. My road trips are usually about 12-15 hours, and I start reaching my breaking point at about hour 6 or so. Up until then, I'm coasting along; but after that, I've got to talk to myself, listen to audiobooks, and make phone calls; but I don't think about turning around, because I would not reach my intended goal. I would have done all of this planning, booking rooms, and gas for nothing....it would all be a waste. Don't allow all of your progress to be a waste by stopping now. If you stop now, you'll just have to start from the beginning again later, so just keep pressing on. You'll find things throughout your journey that will aid you along the way and begin to subtly make things easier for you. Your journey is not a waste, and you are making marvelous strides. DONT....TURN.... BACK. There's nothing back there but old habits you fought to get out of and to get this far.

NOTES:____

DAY 206

I was watching a television show, where a Doctor is given a new position as head of the hospital. He comes in firing an entire department, making new rules, and turning everything in the hospital on its head. Everyone there is telling him to slow down before he burns out, they tell him it's a marathon and not a race. All this Doctor does, is ask people to open up and come up with ideas, and how to make their department, their groups, and their lives better. What they don't know, is that the Doctor has cancer, and he may not have time to run the marathon. We have all lived long enough to see those younger than us die, those who we feel weren't supposed to go. We also know that the older we get, the faster that clock seems to wind down.

The truth is, we all always think that we have more time to do the things we want to do, but we never really know when our last day is. Take the time today, tomorrow, and every day after, to get what you want done. Sprint to the finish line, and you can rest when you're tired. If you have the right people around you, you can hand off the job, until you catch your second wind. Run like there's no tomorrow because one day... there won't be. Don't live a life of regret. Far more people are upset that they never tried than there are those who gave it their all, and things didn't pan out the way they thought. Don't be afraid to ask the question, because if you don't, your answer is already no; take the chance, shoot your shot, and go for the gold. Don't sit back and think you have more time or wish that you would have.

NOTES:

DAY 207

We like to be the first one to finish the problem, get the answer, and reach the goal. In our society, we focus on and are even pressured into being the first to do something or get the right answer. Less of an emphasis is placed on actually being "right" when we do get our answers. Being slow and right outweighs being fast and wrong by metric tons. Whatever it takes to get the right answers you're looking for is what it takes. In my last message, I said sprint for your goals, but that simply means to start now, and never stop until you've reached them. Don't take time off or push them to the back burner for other things.

When I say take your time to get to the right answers, I mean, make sure it's right when u get it. Check your answers, talk to other people, and see if this will fit in with your life, the way you really want it to. Being precise takes more time, but it's well worth it. Stay strong, stay focused, stay vigilant, and stay the course. Accuracy is more important than quantity. 1 shot to the heart, is better than 10 in the foot.

NOTES:____

DAY 208

Part of the reason Napoleon was at war, was because he didn't want his country, borrowing money, and owing the real true leaders (the bankers). When Napoleon was at war, the powers that be, as they do now, funded both sides of every war, so no matter who won, the lenders made money hand over fist. In one of Napoleon's earlier battles, he refused to borrow money to fight his war. The lenders were of course upset over this, but they decided to let him hang himself. For surely, without borrowing money, he couldn't afford to feed his troops, advance them, or do too much of anything very long... he had to have money. So, the lenders sat back and overfunded his opposition. At that time, he needed about 10 million dollars. France owned Louisiana, so they sold it to America for about 15 million. He funded all he needed for the time, and he didn't have to borrow from anyone, he sold off some of his assets, and lived to fight another day. We MUST build ourselves financially before we begin to try to live the life we want.

Everything that you hear about, life insurance policies, retirement accounts, the stock market, etc. are not bad ideas, but first, we need to get our financial houses in order. All of these are places where you put your EXTRA money. Get out of debt, build an emergency fund, and THEN begin to invest. The only reason Napoleon was saved, was because he had no debt and owned assets. We go purchase a car that has a monthly note and believe it to be an asset.

Pay down your debt first, yes that means you may have to cut back on other things first, but in the long run, it will greatly pay off. You were not made to go to work, pay bills, make someone else rich your entire life, and then die broke. The borrower is a slave to the lender...so STOP BORROWING. The deeper you're in debt, the longer you'll be working for someone else. Pay your debts, and eventually you'll be debt-free. There's no greater feeling in the world than financial freedom. Begin the journey to financial freedom today.

NOTES:____

DAY 209

Be a better YOU every single day. I don't care who is doing better than me, I'm doing better than I was yesterday.

NOTES:

DAY 210

Just because you're in the same place, doesn't mean you're in the same position. Don't look at where you are today and feel dismayed, even though it may be the same as last year. You can be in the same space, and in completely different positions. Even though you may be living in the same place as last year, if you've saved more money, worked on your credit, thought about business ideas, paid off debt, etc. you are in a completely different position than you were a year ago.

It's not always about where you are, but the trajectory you've set yourself upon. Look deeper than where you currently are, see your potential, and KNOW you may be in the same place, but not the same position. Continue to work on yourself and your goals, build your knowledge base, strengthen your mind, and body, and you will never be in the same position, and soon you'll see that you won't even be in the same place. Big things are built on smaller things.

NOTES:

DAY 211

Do you have someone in your life who listens to you, someone who truly listens, who listens without looking to interrupt, or interject, someone who you feel has YOUR best interest at heart? Is there anyone that you really listen to, that you actually communicate with? Actual listening has become a lost art. Nowadays people listen just to interject, to give their own viewpoint to your story. They call themselves listening while being on the phone, doing other things, and thinking of someplace else that they could be. Learn to intently focus on people and conversations.

Take the time to really listen, put your phone away, and listen to things said, and also those things unsaid. Pay attention to body movements, and posture. Some of the best, and most memorable conversations you will have will come from you paying the most attention to others. Everyone seems to be so separated, so alone now. They are so focused on projecting their words, and who they are, who they want to be, that we forget to pay attention to the needs of others, and how to truly help. Unplug every now and again, write a handwritten letter to someone, let them know what they mean to u, and then listen to what they have to say. Instead of always being heard, try hearing. You have 2 ears, and one mouth for a reason.... listen more than you speak, and your life can change in an instant. Your words can never be misunderstood or taken out of context when they're not spoken.

NOTES:____

DAY 212

Very rarely do large life-changing events alter our lives, usually, they're smaller, seemingly nonchalant, even non-noticeable events, much like drops of water in a cup....one drop at a time… and you never notice the cup is filling up. So, too, should you be intent on making small, positive strides in your life. You won't hardly notice them, but they are adding up in your ledger.

Every purposeful step, every time you intentionally make a move towards your goal, you're filling that cup, you're adding one more step to the other side of the scales, either tipping them in your favor or adding to the security in your favor. Big goals are made of smaller goals, and smaller goals are fulfilled by small steps. Keep pressing, moving, stepping, and striving daily toward your goals. The more steps you add, the closer you get, and the further you distance yourself from everything else u don't want.

NOTES:

DAY 213

The world is not only full of distractions nowadays, but it is built on them. Distractions keep us and our minds occupied, but not nurtured and truly cared for. The powers that be continually come up with shiny objects for us to chase.... but just like the fish to the shiny object, there's a hook in these distractions given by the world. The hook is a distraction, and we can't even see it. The distraction, whatever it is, whether it be TV, Facebook, Twitter, alcohol, drugs, men, women.... WHATEVER keeps you occupied, and unable to reach your goals. The longer they can keep you distracted, the longer they have power over you, and you can't see the real plays happening.

Set a goal, and stay focused, set a specific amount of time apart each day, for you to focus on your goals. No TV, phones, or radios, just you and your goals. The more you focus, the more power you have, soon it will be, where you don't even want the distractions anymore. You can unhook yourself from the addictions of distractions, and simply ask yourself, "Is this getting me any closer to where I truly want to be?" If it doesn't line up with your goals, it needs to go. The only thing more powerful than a focused person is multiple people all focused on the same thing. Set your goals, focus on them, and if you can, get others who are focused on that same goal, and watch the winds change in your direction.

NOTES:

DAY 214

Once a piece of Wood has been set on fire, it's easier to burn again. The hardest work is getting it to burn the first time, that's when it's at its best. That's when the wood has the most moisture and has its internals at its strongest. Every time heat is added, the wood gets worse, it gets drier, and further broken down until it's singed, burned, or turned to ash. If it's simply a piece of wood, cut off from the tree, there is no recovery, the best you can do is hope the damage doesn't get worse.

You can take the wood out of the heat, and the environment, and soak it in water to hydrate it, but the damage is done. People are the same way. Sometimes we wonder why we can pour so much into people and get very little in return.... they've been singed, scorched, or burned by life's trials and tribulations. You have to figure out how burned they are and learn to traverse around the damage. Don't forget, that you too have been burned, and must learn to navigate your own damage as well. At all times be open, be honest, and be willing to put in the work on yourself.

NOTES:

DAY 215

A lot of times in life, we give so much of ourselves to people, places, jobs, or situations, so that we feel empty, or maybe even possibly abused. We usually feel this way, because we don't feel as though we are either getting what we want in return, or at least an equal trade in energy. To give every ounce of everything you have to help someone else, and not feel reciprocated is tough, but are we expecting too much? Many times, we cause our own headaches, and cause our own problems, when we EXPECT things to be done in a certain way, or at a certain time, or even by a certain person. You can tell people what you want, what you expect, and how you'd like it....and the rest of the story (as Paul Harvey would say) is left up to the other people. Maybe they didn't have the time, ability, structure, strength, knowledge, or....enough give a damn to do what you wanted/needed done. Either way, it's who they are, and what they've done. Your only option is to continue dealing with them, and adjust YOUR expectations, continue on the same path, and keep frustrating yourself, or cut them off.

Our problems come from trying to control others and MAKE them bend to our will. Control yourself and make adjustments for whatever it is you need. Do your best to put yourself around people who believe in reciprocity, and who at least TRY to give you what it is you're looking to get. You can be giving someone all the love you have, but if your idea of love is giving diamonds and gold, and all they wanted was a hug and conversation, you're not going to go very far. Understand those around you and make your needs and wants as clear and precise as possible.

NOTES:____

DAY 216

Growing up, I remember reading the Bible, and it said, "Ye shall know them by their fruits." (Matt 7:16) I always thought that meant you'd know people by their offspring, and how they acted, or what they did... And while this is partially true, I've learned over the years, that it's more of a totality, a culmination of a person's life that's the fruit they are speaking of. When you speak Micheal Jordan's name you automatically know his fruit is basketball, or business, or shoes, Hitler's is hateful, holocaust, murderer. Martin Luther King, Jr's is peace, equality, and intelligence. These are just a few who most would know by their fruits.

When I call your name, in a room full of people, or on a quiet bench in the park, what will your fruits tell me, how are you known, what are you projecting to others? YOU control that narrative of your fruits by the way that you live. Some will see the good, and some may focus on the bad, but the bad is still what YOU produced. They couldn't have it to focus on if you hadn't done it. Focus on producing better fruits, focus on doing more of the things you want people to praise you for, and less of the things you don't. Begin to build a better you, and slowly, but surely your fruit will get sweeter and sweeter. Be the change you want to see.

NOTES:____

DAY 217

Many times, you hear people saying, "This is your harvest season;" and we get all excited, we get giddy, happy, and joyous because we believe that it's time to sit back, relax, and allow all of God's blessings that we KNOW we've put the work in for to come to us. Yes, harvest time is the time to collect the things you've been working on, but what very few of us understand is that Harvest season is the hardest time of the year. This is when your blessing is at its peak, so not only do you want it, but everyone else sees its ripeness and is ready to get at it too. Your neighbors can see it, the passersby, the bugs, the animals, and anything else in the vicinity with eyes and a nose, know that it's harvest time, and they can collect on the work that YOU put in.

You must first KNOW what harvest time looks like, so you know when to harvest, and then comes the work. You have to go to every stalk, every tree, every vine and get to pulling everything down; also, you have to have a place to store your belongings while u preserve them, eat them, or sell them. And remember, all of these skills, are individual lessons on their own. Without just 1 of these skills, your harvest season can possibly be wasted. You can harvest all you want, but if you don't know how to preserve what you've got, you'll have to make do for 11 more months... If you don't plant seeds for the future, you'll never have another harvest. So, when you hear harvest season, and you KNOW it's your time to shine, be ready to sweat more than you have all year.

NOTES:____

DAY 218

Everyone wants to be happy.... and in general people want to make others around them happy. Often, we forego our own wants, needs, desires, and happiness to try to bring happiness into others' lives. Seeing happiness in others, joy in others, peace, and a smile on someone else's face is a joyous thing, but not at the cost of your own happiness. You must first find happiness, peace, and joy in your own life, and find out what that means to you. The old adage...."You can't pour from an empty cup" rings so true. Fill yourself first, and KNOW what that means, so you can constantly, and consistently keep yourself filled so that you can pour into others' lives.

Once your bank account is empty, you can stop giving, or blow right past the goose egg, and go into overdraft fees, so u now owe what you took out, plus the overdraft fees. Instead of a cash account, we're withdrawing from an emotional account, and we've been taught that it's normal to "overdraft" our emotional accounts. This is partly where depression begins to deep root itself. We must learn to work on ourselves in all aspects, before reaching out to help others. It's perfectly fine to tell people NO. It's ok to say, "I'm not in the position to help you." If your legs were broken, you wouldn't add more weight on your back to carry, you'd heal first; so, take the time to emotionally heal. THEN and only then should you attempt to help others.

NOTES:____

DAY 219

Your standards are YOUR standards, and you can be whatever you choose. The higher the standard we keep, the more likely we are to succeed. Standards work on teams, as well as in your personal life. If your standards are too low, anyone can join the team. If all you require is a heartbeat, that hits just about anybody. The lazy, the lonely, the shiftless, irritating, miserable, and unhappy, all fit your bill. They probably won't add anything of substance, but hey.... you've got somebody on the team… right? What many of us don't realize until we get older, is how to build a standard, or a measuring stick to measure things to. It's about what you want and focusing on that.

Don't say what you don't want, just focus on what you do. If you don't want someone who uses drugs, say, "I want someone who is health-conscious, and values their health and fitness." Every desire you have for someone to be on your team is one more brick added to your wall. The more bricks you add, the harder it is for others to get over it, and the less you have to deal with it. Those who value being on the team will work to meet those standards, and they will value those standards even more because they know how difficult it is to attain them. Stop lowering your standards to accommodate everyone, you were made for a select few. There's a reason a Porsche costs far more than a Honda. Also be careful not to have standards so high, that no one will be able to reach them. There is a fine line between standards and loneliness.

NOTES:____

DAY 220

No matter what trade you're in, when you are working in construction, things must be put up straight, level, and plum. Everything must be aesthetically pleasing to the eye. Sometimes these two things contradict each other, and you must decide what to do. There are times when things have already been installed that may not be quite level, or even, or plum. Maybe there was a reason, or maybe the person who came before you just wasn't as proficient or didn't care and said, "It's good enough" either way. It's up to you to decide, will you match the subpar work and look like everything else? Most people possibly never notice any difference because everything matches.... or will you put your equipment up the right way, straight and true, causing others' inadequate work to show? These are the choices that we must make in our everyday lives. Do we follow what we know to be wrong, but it's "good enough" and everyone else is doing it anyway, or do we do what we know to be right, and go against the grain because it's the right thing to do?

Other people will tell you to do it their way because if you are doing it the right way, it will shine a light on them doing it the wrong way. Don't allow someone else's subpar work to be your guide. Do what you know to be right, no matter what came before you. If those before you are just a little off, and you're a little off, and the ones behind you are a little off, soon nothing will be level or even, and when you stand back and look at the big picture, it will all be a disaster, and unrecognizable.

NOTES:____

DAY 221

When we want to change our bodies, we at least have some small semblance of what we need to do to get the desired effect. At our core, we know if we want to lose weight, we should eat less, eat more nutritious foods, and do more exercise, whether that be walking, running, weights, etc. Now whether we do this or not.... hey, it is what it is, but at least we know. We have a plan, a guideline for our body, and if you were ever to begin working on it, you'd find the more you do it, the more you'll learn.

Many of our life's problems come from our lack of planning and implementation. When we don't plan and implement our diet and exercise, our health, and weight suffer; when we don't properly plan our money, our finances, credit, health, and future suffering; and when we don't plan some sort of continuing education, whether it be schooling, courses, certifications, business-related, or simply reading more books, our mental capacity, and knowledge are severely hampered.

Proper Planning, and implementation, are paramount cornerstones of any successful venture. Are you planning and implementing the things you want to succeed in, in life or are you winging it.... hoping, and praying everything will work itself out???? That's probably not the best plan to make it to your destination. Do you just get on the road and drive, and HOPE you'll make it someplace....no you use a map, and plot out a course, then you follow that plan. If I told you I wanted to drive from New York to California, and I'd never done it, but I had no maps, no plans, no navigation, and no help. You'd think I was absolutely insane. But this is how many of us live our daily lives, and constantly wonder why we are lost, stagnant, and can't find our way.

Take the time to build a plan for something in your life, implement it, and see if it doesn't go a lot smoother, than just hoping it comes true one day. Then you can begin to plan more and more until you are seeing the better benefits from planning, and implementation.

NOTES:____

DAY 222

In the Olympics in the middle to long-distance races, they use what's called a "rabbit". This "rabbit" is a person who picks up the pace of the race for a while, and then after a certain distance, simply exits the race, leaving the runners at their picked-up pace. This is part of the job of a mentor. A mentor sees your potential and tries to pick up your pace in your given field. They will push you and guide you along the way trying to ensure you're up to the task and not slacking.

I remember being in the gym and being on the elliptical. I like to try and keep a certain pace, but sometimes my mind just wanders, and I'm not 100% focused on my speed, so ''ll slow down, until I realize I'm not breathing as heavily, or sweating as I should; and I look down, and sure enough, my strides have dropped by 25 strides a minute. Then I have to pick back up and try to stay focused. On the few occasions when there are others in the gym, on the other ellipticals, I try to match, or exceed their pace, it gives me something to focus on, something to attain. When I have my "rabbit" in the gym, even if they don't know it, they keep me motivated and paced. Find a mentor or someone in the gym of life you can pace yourself off of. Even with the best of intentions, we can find ourselves slowing down, and not even noticing it. Get with a group a friend, a family member...ANYBODY so they can help you stay strong, motivated, and on the right path.

NOTES:____

DAY 223

I speak a lot on mentorship, and about how valuable I believe it is. Finding a mentor can help guide you, help you avoid many of life's pitfalls, and make your journey far shorter than it would be without them. Life is also about trying to BECOME a mentor. You may be thinking that you couldn't teach anyone anything, or nobody would want your advice, but someone's life out there mirrors yours exactly. There are also those out there who may only need help through one or two situations that you've already had to fight to get out of, and a few well-placed words of wisdom from you could be the keys to unlock weeks, months, or even years of ease that they otherwise might have had to fight through. There is an old African proverb that says, "When an elder dies, a library dies along with them, and a school is burned to the ground." Don't let your library die, not having lent out any books or knowledge.

There have been studies showing that you actually learn more when you teach a subject. Finding a mentor is immeasurable, and incalculable in the amount it can help your life, and propel you forward, but actually BEING a mentor, makes immeasurable calculations, in so many other people's lives. If you could only help 3 people in your life, who helped only 3 other people, that's a total of 12 other people you've helped build to become a better person in some fashion. Find several mentors and become a mentor to several others.... the seeds you eat can only feed you, but the seeds you plant can feed thousands.

NOTES:____

DAY 224

I was reading the book "You're Not Listening" and it has a passage that says, that when we get angry during conversations, the parts of the brain that activate listening decrease, and when we actively listen the parts of the brain that activate anger decrease more. So, when you're having conversations, if you feel yourself getting agitated, or upset, try to sit back, and listen a little more Intently. Listen, not to find fault, or poke holes, or even respond, but listen to understand, listen with the mindset of accepting change.

When your emotions begin to overtake you, it becomes more, and more difficult to truly listen, and have a conversation. When your emotions begin to get out of check, you're getting closer, and closer to a shouting match, or an argument, and nobody wins with that. Sit back, put yourself in check, and see what you can learn. Listening is a superpower that can get you everything you've ever wanted.

NOTES:____

DAY 225

It is difficult to become that which first you have not seen. Open yourself to new ventures, and new opportunities, because the more you see, the more you hear, and the more you open yourself to, the more chances you give yourself. It's like the branches on a tree, the more branches it has, the more leaves it can produce, and the more leaves it produces, the easier, and the more it gets fed. Make yourself easier to feed by giving yourself more opportunities. Make getting out of your comfort zone a daily activity. Our comforts keep us caged like a captive lion. Every day we have the chance to open the cages and allow our animals to roam free. The cages are opened, and for fear of the unknown, we refuse to venture outside of the cage. What we don't understand is that no matter how bad it gets out there, the cage will ALWAYS be there, and we can go back at any time.

Step outside of your comfort zone and see what else the world has to offer you. Grow more branches in your life. Look at the life others are living, and allow that desire to propel you forward, to push you out of that cage. Allow your dreams and desires to be stronger than your fears. There are far more people around you, far more people around the world who wish they would have taken the chance than those who wished they hadn't. Don't be the latter....step a step outside of your cage of comfort zone today.

NOTES:____

DAY 226

Our lives are built on action but run on muscle memory. When a boxer, a basketball player, a football player, and even soldiers go through specialized training not only do they learn the basics of what they need to excel, but they learn in-depth and also obtain muscle memory. When a boxer gets in the ring his excitement and endorphins can carry him through the first few rounds; for the good ones, conditioning can take them through the next few rounds; but to get through the last few rounds, it takes muscle memory.

Muscle memory is attained from continuously doing the same things over and over, and getting to the point where you can unconsciously complete tasks, to the point where you don't even have to think because your body automatically reacts. Every day you are training yourself into muscle memory, but are you training yourself into a successful muscle memory, by going to the gym, reading books, looking up something about your goals and dreams, writing down a game plan, or are you training your muscle memory, to sit on the couch, watch TV, eat junk food, sleep, and do very little of the things you know would help your future self.

Begin to train for the positive you today, so when the time comes that you really need to use it, the muscle memory is already there, and it's automatic to do because it's second nature. The average person says they don't make enough to invest, the successful person knows they can't afford NOT to invest. What would $5 per check hurt to put away???? You'll be training yourself to do bigger things when you make more. If you can't find a way to make it happen when you're at your lowest, it's exponentially harder on the way up. No matter what, you're training yourself, but will it be to your betterment, or to your demise....only you get to decide on that.

NOTES:____

DAY 227

It’s ok to ask for help, it isn't a sin. If you're stuck, if you're down, if you're having troubles, you SHOULD ask for help. You may not necessarily get that help, but ask, ask, and ask again. Don't allow anyone to dissuade you, or make you feel bad for needing help. We have all been there and needed help at one point in time or another. Reach out, and see what hands reach back to help elevate you. Even those who you believe did it "on their own" had plenty of help from others, there is no such thing as a "self-made" person. Believe in yourself, have faith, and reach out when things begin to go wrong. It’s easier to fix 1 problem than it is to fix 20 problems because you didn't want to ask for help earlier.

NOTES:

DAY 228

In life, you are given according to what you can handle, and what you're capable of, NOT what you want. In the Bible, there's a parable about a man giving his servants talents (money), he gave one of them 5, another 2, and the last 1. The Bible states that man gave to each servant ACCORDING TO HIS ABILITY. So, it wasn't about what they wanted or needed, it was about what he knew they could reasonably handle. The servant he gave 1 talent to (again, he knew he wasn't too capable) buried it in a hole, and when the man returned all he did was give him his money back. The other 2 servants doubled their money and showed what they could do.

Are you capable of handling and multiplying what you're asking for? Are you a good incubator, a "safe bet" or are you prone to fumble the ball when it's given to you? At work, there are certain people you refuse to give certain jobs to, or even if they do get it, they are heavily supervised, and scrutinized. We don't trust them because they haven't shown that they are capable of handling the task given to them. They must go through the process to learn the new skill. They must be taught by someone (mentor), then they have to practice the skill they learn, and yet still must prove to at least one person, but usually a few people that they know what they're doing before they are given a project on their own.

The way we better prepare ourselves and become more capable is to LISTEN, study, practice, and seek out mentorships. seeing yourself in the same position, means you're not learning the lessons being thrown your way, you're letting the same things beat you over and over. In high school, my football coach had a saying "Run it till they stop it." It's up to YOU to stop the things in your life you don't want to happen, and it's also up to you, to learn what you need to learn, and implement it to get where you feel you need to be.

NOTES:____

____

____

DAY 229

When we are learning anything new, we look at it as an immense problem that we have to solve. Take math for instance, many people struggled to learn addition, they tried to memorize 1+1, or 8+37, or 6+4....and although route memorization can solve your problem, there's a better way to get the answer to your current, AND future problems. It's figuring out HOW to solve the problem. In math, much like in life, HOW to solve your problem doesn't change much, until there's an immense change. Basic math (addition, subtraction, multiplication, division, parenthesis, and exponents) will get the average person through most of their days; and in most cases, the actual problems don't change, it's only the numbers that change, but you solve it the same way. Once a few basic tenets are established, and you have some basic tools (paper, pencil, eraser, maybe calculator) it's like clockwork, you just plug in the different numbers. Your biggest problems will come from advancing....like when going from basic math concepts to geometry, then to trigonometry, and so on. But the further you advance, it is still built on basic principles.

Our lives are the same way. We must first learn some basic principles, like controlling our temper, listening intently, keeping the peace, not interrupting, and not always being greedy or selfish. Once you master these basic tenets, your problem-solving becomes much easier, and just like the math problems, it doesn't matter who, or what problem is in front of you, you can use the same basic problem-solving skills to solve most disputes. Keep calm, don't get upset, try to keep the peace, listen to what someone is actually saying and truly wants, and don't interrupt them when they're speaking (it angers people even more). Solving your problems in life is built around simple basic equations, and the only thing that's different is the people. Build your basic skillset and watch how many of your problems become so much easier to handle.

NOTES:____

DAY 230

We all look to be helpful to others, especially those closest to us. Oftentimes, our friends and families go through trying times and situations, and we look to lend a helping hand or two or try to help them get themselves out of a hole they've dug into. But it is not our job, to get people out of situations that they have gotten themselves into. Sometimes people need a listening ear, sometimes people need a shoulder to cry on, and sometimes people need a pat on the back, or a swift kick in the pants (my personal favorite) but at all times, they need to put in the work necessary to get on their feet.

I'm not saying people should never be helped, I'm simply stating that if you're not asked, do not interject. If asked, that's up to you, but too much help is worse than not enough help. Many times, people need to stumble through situations to learn how to do it on their own. If help is always given, they can never learn how to fix their problems, and they will always be looking for assistance, until the day it doesn't come. If you pick up a baby every time it stumbles and carry them, they will never learn how to walk; and if you continue to do it, those muscles will never develop; and given enough time, they will never be able to use those muscles again.

NOTES:

DAY 231

There was a man in prison, who would write to his wife often, and she always wrote back. Now when you're in prison, any letter you write is read by a guard, so there really is no privacy. The couple was pretty poor and had a garden to ease some of the financial burden of groceries. His wife wrote to him one day and said that she couldn't plant because the ground around the house was too hard for her to break through. He quickly wrote back and said, "Don't dig around the house, because that's where I buried all of the guns and drugs. A few days later, he got another letter from his wife; and she told him that the police showed up and dug up the entire yard. He wrote her back and said, "Good, now you can plant the garden."

Even when you are in bad situations, there are still ways out. They may not be the easiest, the most convenient, or the most accessible, but a way is there. We have to begin to teach ourselves how to think outside of the box. If one way doesn't work, try another, and another until it can be accomplished.

His wife's problem was simply an everyday conversation for her, and her husband feeling her pain and desperation on a piece of paper knew what to do. He thought outside the box, something most people would have never thought of or even attempted; but an uncommon problem has needs for an uncommon solution. Find a problem you've had issues solving and ask a random person what they would do about it. Listen to the answer, and now you have another way of attacking the issue and you have begun to teach yourself how to think outside the box.

NOTES:____

DAY 232

You should truly learn those in your "inner circle." Just like on a debate team, you have to study both sides of an argument equally, not only because you never know what side you will be given to argue, but also because you will have a better understanding of the argument as a whole, and you will have a better understanding of the tactics and arguments they may use against you. If you're going to do anything, you should already know how those closest to you should respond. There should be a closeness, a bond.

Have you ever noticed, there are people who instinctively know when something is wrong with you, whether it be in person, through a call, or even a text, and you've told them nothing?? You should have this same type of intuition when it comes to others. Those that you speak to and deal with the most, those you see and hear from the most, those who you can touch and truly feel.... those are the ones you should be most intimate with… not in a sexual manner, but an emotional one. Don't try to "win" disagreements, but rather listen to what they say, how they feel, and WHY they think that way. This is one of the best ways to learn about not only the ones around you but people with differing opinions. The more you know about those around you, the closer your relationships will be.

NOTES:

DAY 233

When playing any sports, or the game of life, we look at it, as though we have to win. If you want to win, you must know how the game is played. Sports and life are team sports, where the better your team, the further you can go, and the more you can accomplish. What many of us have to focus on is "spreading the wealth." We believe that we have to do everything to get anything done. If that's the case, you need to find a new team. Those in power and many of those ahead of you have a team, and everyone on the team is doing different things so that nobody is overwhelmed. It's not about ME scoring, it's about US scoring. It's about who has the highest probability of scoring or making positive progress. Not only will one person doing everything, wear that person down and make them feel resentful, but their doing too much work overshadows everyone else's capabilities and talents.

Michael Jordan was a great individual player, and he and his teams got beat every year in the first round of the playoffs. All the points he scored amounted to nothing, but when he built his TEAM up, and they began being a cohesive unit, he began winning championships. Build your team up and find out everyone's strengths and weaknesses in your circle. Learn to delegate.... if you're not good at a task, give it to someone who is. If you try to carry too many tasks, you'll get weighted down, and/or begin to drop things. Pass the ball and allow your team to advance. When they win, you win too. Build your team, so that they can build you in return.

NOTES:______________________________

DAY 234

It is perfectly okay to take some time off. The human body was made with the idea of rest built into it. We weren't made to go on and on and on without any rest. Rest was built into everything on this planet, including the soil. GOD said to plant in the ground for 6 days, and on the 7th don't plant anything, and let the soil rest. GOD himself took 6 days to create existence, then even he rested for a day. Resting isn't the problem, it's stopping and/or quitting. Resting is brief, it's temporary, it's only meant to catch your breath and recuperate. We take the rest and get back to the tasks at hand.

There will be time to rest once you've completed your tasks; but until then, continue to work. The longer you wait to get started again, the longer it takes to reach your final destination. Once you do reach your destination, you'll ask yourself, *Why was I procrastinating?* You will probably begin to show others how you did it, and how easily they can do it too. It seems easier to quit now, until the pain of regret begins to set in, and you see someone who started with you flourishing, making progress in the very thing you started together. You can be there too, you can achieve the very same goals, just get back up and begin to press forward again. The only thing stopping your progress is YOU.

NOTES:

DAY 235

Keep the right circle of people around you at all times. The right people aren't necessarily the ones you get along with all of the time or the ones with whom you agree most often. These are the people that can shine in places that you can't; the people who will tell you you're wrong and give advice on how to correct things; the people who know their roles and positions and do them without poking and prodding. If you had the greatest desire to open a restaurant, but couldn't cook, you can either take the months and years it takes to go to culinary school and become proficient, or you can get someone on the team who is already proficient at running a kitchen, and you can run the business side of things within 6 months to a year.

There's a large margin of people who believe that they will get a great team together when they become successful, not realizing that they are putting the cart before the horse. If you don't have a good team to begin with, your journey is exceedingly more difficult. Find out who the leaders are around you, who the good workers are, who the salesmen are, and those who can speak to anyone. Who has the skills to accomplish your goals that you yourself don't have? It's not about doing the work; it's about getting the job done. When you finish a task at work, you turn it into your supervisor, who then turns it into their supervisor, and they praise your supervisor for getting the job done. He didn't turn one screw, type one word, attend one meeting, but the job was completed. Take notes and run your circle the same way. Everything doesn't have to be on your shoulders. Find the success around you, and that will catapult you to even greater success, and even greater people to add to your inner circle.

NOTES:____

____

____

____

____

____

DAY 236

Every time you turn on a television, or a radio, get on social media, or even listen to a conversation on the bus, you can hear just about anyone saying what they don't like, what they are against, what upsets or angers them, and even what turns them off. There is so much negativity out there, and it's growing daily. Knowing what you don't like or are against is a good thing, but what's even better is knowing what you are for. The list of things that you don't like is never-ending, I could build that list and probably work on it until I die.

You could stay so focused and continually come up with new "don't like" things so much so, that you wouldn't have any time to focus on anything worthwhile. Begin and end conversations with things that made you smile today, what made you laugh, what made your heart skip a beat. Did speaking to someone give you butterflies? What are you thankful for? Tell me what your dream life, job, or home looks like. Begin to be the change you want to see. There's far more than enough negativity and hate out there. Put some sunshine out there, no matter how brief. With only 15 minutes of sunshine, many plants can go days, and in some cases even weeks until it needs sun again.... Be those 15 minutes of sunshine and positivity in someone's life today.

NOTES:

DAY 237

Never look at ANYTHING anyone has to determine your life, unless it's to make it better, and you're using it as a marker or a goal post. We tend to look at the worst in people and say, "If that's what's going on, I don't want it." We take the worst relationships, the worst preachers, the worst politicians, and the worst coworkers, and structure our lives off of them.

If a relationship is what you want, then search out GOOD ones, and see how they got where they are. If I wanted to be in a professional sport, I wouldn't emulate someone who never made it. I'd go to the ones who did make it and study them. Study the successful business owners, NOT the ones who went bankrupt. If you focus on and look for good, that's what you'll find. Look for the positive things in life, and they will show themselves to you, they are already all around you, you're just not focused on seeing them. It's like a pair of binoculars... When you first put them on, they will probably be out of focus, but with a few small adjustments, you can see the things that were right in front of your face the entire time. Learn to make small adjustments to see what's already in front of you. Look at the good grass, not the weeds; focus on the happy relationships, not the ones that break up. To be better you have to see better; to see better, you have to think better.

NOTES:____

DAY 238

Quite often, we say “It takes a village,” which is meant to be said about raising children. But it also goes for adults. It takes a village to help each other, keep each other uplifted and motivated to help pull us out of our muck and mire. We need each other for encouragement and support, and to also help guide us through difficult situations. We need each other's wisdom and love. Keep the faith, I believe in you, you can do it, you are strong, and you are a beautiful person inside and out. You have goals, dreams, and aspirations, and You are driven towards these things. You are motivated to accomplish them, and you think outside of the normal boxes that you were taught and ascribed to.

I am a home of love, peace, and solitude in your village. I will also jump down your neck and beat u unmercifully about the head and shoulders with a blunt object, repeatedly, when you doubt yourself, and speak negatively. The Bible says, “…and the word became flesh.” Your words will become your life; so, speak positively, speak encouragingly, speak unflinching abundance, and speak love.

NOTES:____

DAY 239

Learn to say when enough is enough. For most people, we've all held onto things far past the point we should have let go.... pain, hurt, relationships, jobs, homes, etc. There is a point at which you have to let go to save yourself. I am reminded of something Dave Chappelle said his father told him. "Name your price in the BEGINNING, and if it ever gets more expensive than that, get out." Most of our problems are, that we name our price in the middle, then change it, and change it, and change it again, and sometimes we may NEVER set a price. We tell ourselves if we hold on just a bit longer, maybe things will change; but what we're really doing is training that thing that is causing us the pain, to give us even more pain; you're teaching that thing, that person, that job that you will accept what they're giving you.

We've been conditioned through movies, television, music, religion, and schooling to accept our circumstances and hold on for better days because a savior is coming to save us; or put everything on the line and a last-ditch effort will get you the notoriety you seek. Rarely do any of these things pan out, and you're left worse off than when you started. Had you set your price in the beginning there's no way you would have done those things or held on that long. Don't stand in the boxing ring of life, and let it beat you to death. Tap out, recoup, and start over. It's better to start over now than to let life beat you until you HAVE to start over, but with something that's unrecoverable. Set your price today, and when it comes up, walk away.

NOTES:____

DAY 240

He who has will be given more, which means, “if you want more of anything, you better get started on getting something.” Some people see this as a negative thing...."Why should the one who has more, get more, don't they already have enough? It should be spread out amongst the ones who are less fortunate." Some of you may agree with this statement, I, however, do not. You don't get more simply because you have more. I believe you get more because once you get something, you know what it takes to get it, you know the struggles, you know the legwork, you know the hurdles; and what you also know, is how to get around a hurdle or two, making the trip that much shorter to the next thing to get.

Successful investors know where to put their money, and when to take it out. They are familiar with the rules and laws, so they know how to maneuver when it comes to taxes, lawyers, loans, livestock, etc., all of which make their money grow even faster. Those who don't have, don't know any of those things; so, the little money they do have, doesn't grow. You are given, according to your understanding and ability to handle. 70% of lottery winners are broke again in a matter of a few years, which means it's not the money, it's the lack of understanding. If you want more money, love, happiness, understanding, or whatever, first you have to learn how to obtain a small amount; then find out what it takes to protect that amount; after that, you need to learn how to keep and grow that small amount. If you can figure these out, you can have an abundance of whatever you wish, then soon you'll be the one who has and will be receiving more.

NOTES:

DAY 241

The best way to get your point across in life is to live it. People are more apt to follow someone when they see them practicing what they preach. Even if the words someone is saying are valid, they will have a much smaller following if they aren't doing the very thing that they're telling you to do. An athlete who doesn't eat properly, a depressed motivational speaker, and a preacher who openly sins are all prime examples. You can give the best words and push people to the limits, but the minute they find out you're not living the life you profess; you lose the majority of credibility you had with them. The message is still the same, but now the messenger is tainted. Weight loss gurus, who've had surgery aren't trusted in the general public's eye, because we don't believe they have the drive, passion, persistence, or determination to lose weight the same way I'm trying to do it. If you can't believe your own words, why should I? People see us in the same way. How can you expect someone to take your relationship advice, if you are in a horrendous relationship, or listen to you telling them to save when you're robbing Peter to pay Paul?

Be the change you speak about to others so that they can see that not only does it work....but also that it can change someone for the better because it changed you. If you want better people around you, activate your better life by speaking about a better life and living a better life. You WILL be the catalyst to change 1000 lives. Will you be the catalyst that warms the building and brings comfort to thousands or the catalyst that brings heat and burns the building down? The choice is yours.

NOTES:

DAY 242

Never chase anything or anybody. If you're chasing it, it's running from you; and if it's running from you, it doesn't want to be with you. You can put energy into trying to acquire something/someone, but a chase is different. If you make a plan, act on said plan; give yourself a deadline and a price tag. If it goes out of any of these ranges, then you're chasing; and when you chase, you can lose far more than you ever thought possible. If you're chasing after an animal and not paying very close attention to your surroundings, not only can you get turned around and lost, but you can fall prey to something else. When you chase people and things, you begin to lose your sense of self, and lose direction; and you can look up, and not know who or where you are because you are so focused on the chase. Set your game plan and stick to it. If you find yourself outside of your preset parameters, stop and reevaluate yourself, and your situation, it may be time to cut your losses.

NOTES:

DAY 243

There is a study that shows 63% of American employees can't handle a $500 emergency. We've been taught and bred to become nothing more than consumers in America. We must get back to becoming producers, savers, investors, and business owners. This country was built on small businesses, and everything from slavery to the modern-day stock market was funded by the average citizen. Now, the average citizen can't afford to fund even the smallest of inconveniences. We put our funds towards everything to look more successful rather than to actually be successful. If you're one who can't afford a $500 emergency, look for ways to cut $20 a week from your spending, and in 6 months you have your emergency fund. If you can only do $10 a week, you can have your funds in a year. It may sound like a long time, but what were you doing 6 months to a year ago????

$20 a week in America is 1 meal a week for 1 person at a restaurant, 2 cups of coffee a week at Starbucks, or even extra snacks you buy while grocery shopping or when you're at work. We must begin to PLAN better and make better decisions with our money instead of buying things that keep us indebted to someone else for years. Begin small and you'll be amazed how quickly those small steps turn into giant leaps and bounds. If you purchase something and it causes you to not be able to save... it costs too much, so put it back. Financially plan for the bad days when you'll be sick and miss a week of work, if you can still afford it, then you can truly afford it.

NOTES:____

DAY 244

Because we don't see the immediate consequences of our decisions and haven't been taught how to look down the road to the future, we tend to continue down our negative paths until it's too late to miss the consequences. We don't see the heart attack, so we continue to eat bad foods, we don't see the financial emergency, so we continue to buy expensive things and not save, we don't see the many things we miss out on due to our lack of knowledge, so we continue to not read and fill our minds with valuable knowledge. The signs are all around us, but we refuse to see how we are marching to our own demise.

We want to feel good now, believing that we can feel just as good later, but not fully understanding the price that must be paid for that feeling. If you don't have a proper budget outlining your finances, your education, your time, and your rest, then you're surely planning to fail. We cannot continue to run through life wildly, not having plans laid out and written down for our futures, continually doing things we see others do, because we think we are capable but have refused to lay out a foundation of planning and preparation. We keep setting traps for ourselves and wonder why we continually fall into them. Begin to feed your mind, with better financial planning, and time management material, and it will guide you to better, longer-lasting decisions.

NOTES:____

DAY 245

When I moved into my current residence, there was a tree in the easement of the property, it was overgrown, the leaves and branches covered the sidewalk leading from the street to the house, and it had enough overhang that rodents could come and go as they pleased. All the leaves and branches also blocked the street view from myself and my security system. Shortly after moving in, I decided to purchase a chainsaw and chop down the tree. I chopped it into pieces, and the city hauled it away.... problem solved, or so I thought. Over time, the tree began to grow new branches and leaves, beginning to slowly block the street view again; but as more of a big bush, and not a tree anymore. I chopped them off, drilled holes in the stump, and filled it with salt, which didn't work; then with poison, which didn't work; and finally, I let many of the leaves grow back and sprayed them with a generous amount of weed killer, which seems to have worked.

Your problems aren't your problems, your problems, are SYMPTOMS of a major problem that you probably can't even see, or don't know about. You're battling side effects, and not the root causes. Stop chopping off branches that keep growing back; either chop the tree down, pull it up by the roots, grind the stump, or burn it. We keep thinking about the answer to our problems, which is trimming the branches off the house when we need to completely get rid of the entire tree. Put more energy into finding the root of the problem, so you can spend less time and effort chopping away at the branches.

NOTES:____

____

____

____

____

____

____

____

DAY 246

We tend to look at things in life as right and wrong, black or white; yet there are so many varying shades, and hues, and simply seeing things from a different viewpoint. We will argue each other down, demanding others see our viewpoint and agree with us, instead of listening. This brings a cartoon to mind that I saw some time ago. Two men were standing a few feet apart, and there was a number drawn on the ground. To one man it appeared to be a six, to the other, a nine. This, like so many situations in life, is indicative of how we tend to only see things from our own point of view. If we took the time to listen to each other and step across the line to look at things as others see them, we may have a different point of view, we would at least cut down on wasted energy, and unnecessary arguments. Through our upbringing, training, different life circumstances, and chance encounters, we've all been programmed to believe in our own unwavering rigid belief systems.

You'll never know what the world has to offer if you don't open yourself to other possibilities. A person who doesn't want to listen to other options and opinions is like a person who has never left the city they were raised in. There's so much more of the world to see than the town where you were raised; but many carry that as a badge of honor, just as those who only see from their viewpoint and refuse to see another carry their ignorance as a badge. Being open to LISTENING to another point of view opens up so many other avenues in life. If you're not 100% where you want to be in life, there's probably another way to do the things you've been doing. Open yourself to other opportunities, and you're opening yourself to better possibilities in life. Take the time to see what someone else has to say; you don't have to agree; if you just listen, you never know what may come of it.

NOTES:____

DAY 247

I recently read a story about a young lady, who had very little money. Nobody she knew had money, and she knew nothing much about how to get more money, but she started with what she had and what little she knew. She knew she had to save for her future goals. Having little money to save, she cut out getting her hair done, getting her nails done, and going out. She started writing a check to an account, and on the check, she would write something to the effect of "to my future goals." She knew she had to put as much in the account as possible, so she made a goal to add 5% more every month. The funny part is, that she had absolutely no idea how to calculate 5%, but that didn't stop her, she just added more. Who knows what the percentages were, but she just did more. Her family and friends had actually gotten to the point where they thought she was on drugs because she wasn't coming around anymore, her hair and nails weren't done, and she kept to herself, but none of that stopped her either.

She wanted better and kept plugging away. Again, she didn't take any classes, or seminars, didn't know anything about money, but what little she did know she used it. For 3 and a half years she did this and walked into the bank one day to see how much she'd had. When she showed them, her ID, everyone knew who she was, because they had been seeing these checks for all this time, and everyone wanted to know what the dream was. She told them she didn't know, but whatever it was had to be funded. They showed her, her balance, and she thought it was someone else's account. She had 65k in her account. This was more money than she could ever even imagine, more than anyone she'd ever known had.... all because she started with what she knew and chose sacrifice over fun and looks for a period of time. Imagine what you could do if you started today with what you knew, and sacrificed small things like alcohol, going out, hair, and snacks for a time. Is 3 and a half years really too much to give up?

NOTES:____

DAY 248

Leadership is a driving force in success. Whenever a company is taken over, new management and leadership are usually installed to bring a new mindset, new vigor, new ideas, and new work ethics. When new sports coaches take over teams, it's not just a new head coach, but an entire new coaching staff that comes with them. There are new leaders at every level and in every department. Not only because these are the ones who know the overall scheme of the new management, but they have generally shown an aptitude for success.

If you want to succeed in your goals, you either must be a good leader, become a good leader, or be under a good leader. Either way, good leadership is mandatory. Find a good mentor, so that you can become a good mentor to others. Even if you don't see yourself as someone who can mentor, you can. Your story can and will help others, not only the "today" you, but every day you grow, and become better, so the "tomorrow" you will leap years ahead. Anyone you can think of as a mentor today, was at one point down in the dirt, possibly broke, sick, broken, hurt, in an abusive relationship, etc. but they overcame it, and you can too. Be the leader that your future self needs you to be.

NOTES:

DAY 249

There was a TD Jakes sermon, where he said, "Be careful that you don't wear people out, constantly bringing them all of your problems, never bringing them a blessing." Even the strongest people get tired, and even the largest cup eventually needs to be refilled from time to time. It's okay to go to others with your problems but bring something every once in a while. You can't continue to order steak dinners, and pay McDonald's prices, or worse yet, don't pay at all. You're stealing people's time, energy, and overall life force. No matter how much a person gives, they love to be given to as well, they love to be filled, and they love to be taken care of, as well.

Many continue to give because they know what it feels like to be in a bad situation and have nobody there to help; so, they help to prevent someone else from feeling that pain. That doesn't mean taking advantage of them and never reciprocating, or taking them for granted, thinking they owe you something. Giving back helps build the relationship, and it also takes a load off of the person who's usually giving. If all you ever do is take in life you will eventually find yourself in a position needing help, and others won't be there to help you, because you've taken so much. Support those who support you, and you will find that you have meshed with someone and built a support system, which is stronger than either of you could have ever done alone.

NOTES:____

DAY 250

We often look at things in life as problematic and are very ungrateful for the "bad" things that happen to us, not realizing that they are actually blessings in disguise. I had a good friend whose car died on her, and it cost her nearly $400, which, she really didn't have to spare. I personally still see this as a blessing, but you may ask how. The way I see it, she'd broken down in town and was able to get the car to a mechanic, got the car back the next day, and although it was money that wasn't slated for a repair, she had the money saved. Not to mention she'd just come from an out-of-town trip and planned another for next weekend. She wasn't stranded on the side of the road, stuck out of town, missing work, dealing with some shade tree who'd run the bill up on her because they saw she was in a bind. Even in our bad times, we can still be truly blessed, it's all based on your perspective, and how you see things.

If you always see unforeseen things happening as negative, you'll go down the rabbit hole of negativity, and only see bad things; or you can CHOOSE to find the good in every situation, and begin to open, and broaden your horizons. If you choose negativity, there's only darkness, positivity is light. There's absolutely no difference between a dark room and a lit room, except the fact that you can see. When you choose to see only the negative, you're stumbling around life in the dark, bumping, fumbling, and falling over things, but the light will help. Not to say that you won't still trip, fall, and occasionally stub a toe, but that happens far less, and you can do things in the light you couldn't imagine doing in the dark. Look for the positive, embrace the light, and search for the good in a situation. Sometimes you may not see the good for years down the road, but it will come. Find the good in everything else around you.

NOTES:____

____

____

____

____

DAY 251

I was with a coworker, who was looking for a charger (he'd left his at home). I had an extra block, but his cord couldn't fit it. I recently purchased a charger that allows you to plug 7 things up at once, with multiple connections, so I let him use mine. He made a statement "We work at a power plant, and I can't get a charge." Then the thought instantly popped into my mind. The power we need is everywhere, and all around us, we just have to know how to tap into it. All of the groundwork has been laid, the time put in, the power generator, the transformers, the outlets, and all of the safety bells and whistles you can think of. He even had a charging cord but was missing the charging block.

In life, we take so much for granted and complain that things don't go our way. In your life, the power you want, the answers you seek, and the revelations you ask for are sitting in your face; and you know how to tap into it, you just choose not to bring your charging block and cord. To lose weight, you gotta consistently exercise, and eat better, to save money you have to spend less and cut some things out. You want to know how to start a business, but won't take courses, read books, or find mentors. We have the internet literally at our fingertips, but we're spending our time looking at cars and social media. We have libraries full of any book you can name but won't spend 2 hours in one. The power is there, you just refuse to tap into it. Once you learn to tap into the available power, you begin to learn about other types of available power to tap into.... bigger, stronger power. But you first must tap into the small power source you are aware of, and soon instead of siphoning power, you may become a power distributor yourself.

NOTES:____

DAY 252

You don't know who a person really is in your life, until you've seen them not get their way with you, not get what they want out of you, even though you are giving them everything they've ever wanted. As long as you're giving to others, you are their best friend, you're family, you're a confidante, and you can do no wrong. But when the time comes when you either cannot or will not do for them, you will begin to see their true colors. Many people will switch on you when they aren't receiving what they want out of you, whether it be your time, your money, your gifts, or even your conversation. Because you've given so freely, certain people believe they are owed the things you possess and will get angry when you don't give it to them.

Test the waters... Begin to ask for reciprocity, tell them you are unable to help them the next time they ask for help, don't be so accessible, and be unavailable at times. Ask yourself, *If I were in the same position they were in, would they do for me, what I have done for them?* For 95% of the people you know, it's a CHOICE not to help or do for others. They CHOOSE to spend all of their money, they CHOOSE to not save, they CHOOSE to buy expensive things, they CHOOSE to live for today, and not think about tomorrow, and they CHOOSE not to educate themselves and use more discipline in life. You chose to make different decisions and are better off because of it. Be cautious of those who are around because you mesh, and those who are around because you're a giver. Everyone loves the fruit tree when it's feeding them, but how many will stick around and feed and protect the tree in the fall and winter?

NOTES:____

DAY 253

Your present position is probably not your final destination. You can be where you're at and be grateful that you're there, but still be hopeful for and also wanting more. Where you're currently at in life is a weigh station, a pit stop; and you can choose to stop and spend your life there or continue on your journey. Even though you may be somewhere that you feel safe, your life, whether it be a job, a relationship, a home.... whatever, if you desire more, if you long for more, if you feel you want to reach higher levels, then make those moves. If I'm traveling from New York to California as a final destination, I have to stop to eat, refuel, and rest during the journey, and I may even have some car trouble. Some places I stop will be in small nowhere towns, and other places I stop will be bustling, thriving cities.

You can choose to spend more time in any of these places. You may even say, "I need more rest, so I'll stay here longer," but the longer you stay, the longer you'll take to get to your final destination of California. As good as these stops may be, they are not your destination, they are merely rest stations, which aid you in getting to your destination. Is the place where you are now your final destination or is it a rest stop? If it's a rest stop, amass all you can hold to continue your journey. Amass all the knowledge, finances, strength, wisdom, energy, and rest, because it will all be needed until you reach the next pit stop. Don't think you're obligated to stay where you are, you are not a rooted tree, you can pick up and move at any point you choose. Don't turn your pit stops into destinations.

NOTES:____

DAY 254

Culture is what you think, how you think, what you do, and how you do it. Its definition is the attitudes, and behavior characteristics of a particular social group. What is the culture of your different social circles? Are they attitudes and behaviors of winners, successful people, business owners, and entrepreneurs; do they push each other to accomplish goals and become better; do their attitudes and behaviors inspire you to be and do better, or are their attitudes and behaviors more lackadaisical, a live- for-today attitude, don't plan for the future, don't pre-plan, and don't pull the trigger on the things they want attitude? Is there a culture of saving and investing, or a culture of smoking, drinking, and partying? If you can't change the people around you.... change the people around you. A new culture changes everything.

NOTES:____

DAY 255

All of the things you need to survive this life are right on the surface for you to get to. The trees grow freely to produce oxygen and shelter, and the animals and plants grow abundantly to feed you. To get wine, grapes have to be crushed; to get oil, olives must be pressed; to become a diamond, immense pressure must be applied. Seeds must be covered in dirt and buried in the darkness and begin their growth cycle all on their own. Gold, silver platinum, cobalt, and any other precious things are made and buried deep in the dark earth. Most of the things for basic survival are easy to get to on the planet. But air, food, shelter, and love. ..those things which are considered "valuable", are much harder not only to get to, but also to refine, and make presentable.

For you to make it through this life, it doesn't take much… a job at any fast-food restaurant and a cheap room… and you can survive. But if you want to do better, if you want to be considered "valuable", if you want to thrive, you have to dig deeper in yourself, past the surface, into the dark places. You've got to go to the places you've been hurt, to heal them, and turn them into springs of healing, nurture, and love. You've got to dig into the areas that have been crushed under the pressures of life and learn to make them places of support and building for others; find the caverns that have been wrecked inside of you and rebuild them, making them havens of protection. By digging past your surface facade, you can become so much more. Do more than live and survive...THRIVE and become valuable. Put in the work, and buy the equipment needed to unearth all the treasures that are within you.... the books, the seminars, the counseling sessions, the mentors. It's well worth what you'll dig up.

NOTES:____

DAY 256

We have to begin to think as a people as WE and us, not I or me. There is power in we, but not in "I". Together, we can stand back-to-back, and see almost anything coming, 4 of us standing together, back-to-back, can see it all. Not only can we see it, but we can take on the onslaught of enemies coming our way. When one is sick, weak, or tired, they can rest, while the others continue the fight. One ant, even if it bites you, is nothing more than a nuisance, but when an entire colony attacks, it can eat a human down to the bone in about 3 weeks. One dollar can't do much of anything, but if we collectively pool our resources, and work together, we can start our own businesses, have our own insurance policies, our own accounts, and our own communities. The old saying rings loud and true... "If you want to go fast go alone, but if you want to go far, go together."

A one-man basketball team will never win because everyone else is playing as a team. Those who play as a team get further faster, and the better your team, the more dominant you will become. Strategically build your "we". Find those who are strong where you are weak, and who are willing to fight together, even in tough times. Everything around you was built by a team… your house, your car, your job, your clothes, your food… but we've been programmed to believe we should do it by ourselves. The powers that be want us in this position, to take advantage of us, with their teams, and take all of our resources. A slap hurts, but when you bring all the fingers together and they work collectively as a punch, they can knock a person unconscious, and even kill them.

NOTES:____

DAY 257

Do u know where you're headed, do you know your destination, do you have your goals set in your mind????? If you know the answer to these questions, it makes it so much easier to complete your daily tasks. If it doesn't align with your goals, then you know that you shouldn't be doing it, taking it, or giving it your energy. Does what you're about to do today, get you closer to your goals, or do you know? If you don't know where you're going, any road can take you there. But if you know where you're going, there are only a few key ways to get there, and you'll know everything that definitely WON'T take you there. If I'm headed east, it doesn't matter how free, or how wide open the west road is, it can be the best-lit road, with free gas and guaranteed no traffic, and some will take it because it's the easier path, but you will still be driving forever, never reaching your destination. When people ask where you're going, you'll say, "I don't know, but I'm getting there free and fast."

Quite often you'll run into roadblocks, traffic, accidents, stalled vehicles, and run-down roads with no lights for hours, but you have to know what your goal is and have it mapped out, or you can get turned around, and the slightest thing can get you off course. Get your goals and keep them in the forefront. Map out your trip and stay the course; your destination is coming.

NOTES:

DAY 258

Every bad thing that happens in your life isn't the devil, karma, or the universe. Most things that happen to us are CONSEQUENCES of our own actions. The devil ain't working because you can't pay your bills. YOU get that house you couldn't afford, YOU got an expensive car note, YOU purchased those things online that you KNEW you didn't need; and you're the one who is constantly trying to impress people around you, who don't pay your bills, help you when you're down, and most assuredly don't look out for you in times of need. We must be better stewards of our time, our money, and our self-discipline. If we want better results out of life, we have to start putting better into life.

Better ideas, better study habits, better nutrition, better exercise, better business ideas, and better discipline. With better ingredients, you get a better pie. It's never too late to change course. Make better decisions today, so that they translate into better living tomorrow. 1 consistent mile today is 1-pound next week; 1 consistent healthy meal today is less heart disease and diabetes in 5 years; 1 consistent dollar saved and invested is a comfortable retirement in 30 years. Better choices today lead to a better life tomorrow.

NOTES:

DAY 259

What motivates you and pushes you past your comfort zone? What do you tell yourself to keep going once you hit the briar patches in life? What is your why? When you begin a process, you've got to find a strong reason to keep going. It's easy to start something, and it's easy to keep it going until adversity hits. Can you keep going those days that you're tired, those days that you had to work a double, when the children acted a fool, if the house ain't clean, if you still got to cook, and when you got a flat tire? Will you still put in the work on your dream? Are you doing it just because, is this a bunch of lip service to you, or does it mean something? Do you want to become a Doctor because you think they make a lot of money, or did you see your grandmother die slowly from a disease nobody could figure out, and you're going to make sure nobody has to do that again?

If you can get up every day, and go to a job you don't like, when you're sick, tired, hungry, depressed hurting, etc. because you have bills to pay, then you can put in an extra hour into your dreams every day so that you don't HAVE to go to work to pay bills. Come up with a strong enough WHY, to keep you motivated. Legacy, health, healing, rest, generational wealth, happiness, peace. It doesn't matter, as long as it drives and pushes you on the bad days. Figure out your reasons to push through and let nothing stop you.

NOTES:

DAY 260

This is why I'm considered a troublemaker and rebel by many. I question the reason we do things, especially the ones that make no sense to me. I'll question the direction, and if I'm not given a satisfactory answer, I refuse the task. We are told to question everything, and when we do, we're called troublemakers, or instigators, because you don't "fall in line."

The systems want sheep to blindly follow and never question. They want you to be a cog in a system so that they can literally drain your life force. They want you to work for 50 years, pay every tax they give you, give them bailout after bailout, making them richer and richer, never saying a word, complaining, or causing a fuss, and then... die. I CANNOT go down without a fight, never questioning the status quo. I will never be pushed to the side or quietly relegated to the dark corners of society.

https://www.facebook.com/reel/604222718271743?mibextid=fGINcQ&s=yWDuG2&fs=e

NOTES:____

DAY 261

You don't have to be who everyone expects you to be. Your life is based on what makes YOU happy. Many times, the choices that make YOU happy will make others upset, but it is your life to live. We can take others' feelings and concerns into consideration; but at the end of the day, you have to do what best fits your life and your future. You must set the boundaries for your life. Many will be uncomfortable with these new boundaries because they benefit from your lack of boundaries; but they will adjust, or you won't have to deal with them, because they will excuse themselves from your life. Why would you want people in your life who don't respect your boundaries anyway????

Being who YOU want to be and setting boundaries gives you peace of mind. Initially, you may have some anxieties, but they will soon dissipate once you enforce your new boundaries. Be the person YOU expect you to be, be the person you wished someone would have been for you. Be the person who puts a smile on your face and laughter in your heart, you deserve that.

NOTES:____

DAY 262

An object in motion stays in motion, and an object at rest stays at rest unless acted upon by an outside force. Wealth in motion stays wealthy, and poverty at rest stays broke. You will continue to be broke unless that brokenness is acted upon by an outside force. If you want to do better, you've got to be better, you have to ACT on things. The only way that your body will burn fat, is if you get up and move, or burn off more calories than you consume. So, you can eat less or move more, but either way, you must act. If u do nothing, you'll either stay the same or get worse.

You've got to start moving, spiritually, mentally, physically, emotionally, or you'll find yourself getting worse. Many are scared to make a move for fear of making a wrong move, but even if it's not the right move, you're now more informed and have more knowledge, which is NEVER a wrong move. Being stuck in indecision is the worst move possible because you're neither moving forward nor backward, which are both learning opportunities. You are the outside force that you need. You have the ability to change your trajectory and your future. You can make the choices to go faster, or slower, to the right or the left. Stoke your fires and become an object in motion. The faster you go, the harder you are to stop.

NOTES:

DAY 263

I saw a meme, that said to ignore anything that can get you out of character or lose your focus; and initially, I thought that was really good, and agreed with it, until I began to think about it. The more I thought about it, the more I disagreed with it. To me, this is something that "sounds good" and many people will agree, kind of like the saying, "Happy wife happy life," when in actuality, this saying disregards the husband's happiness altogether and makes happiness only about 1 person. What SHOULD be said is happy spouse, happy house. If you avoid the things that distract you or cause you to lose focus, you are avoiding the things in life that will make you stronger.

You can't get physically stronger by avoiding any type of resistance training, and the same applies with your focus and attention. Don't avoid distractions, but embrace them, only to a point. Just like you can only lift so much weight, you can only take on so many distractions. If you avoid distractions, every little thing will pull you away, and in the long run, you will have no focus and no attention span; and people and situations will always pull you out of character. If you allow a few in at a time, you learn how to deal with different things; you become stronger, more resilient, and more powerful.

Those people you see who are calm under pressure, who keep their heads and are poised no matter the situation, aren't that way, because they've never seen adversity; they are that way because they HAVE seen adversity.... many times, and they've learned to overcome it. They don't shy away, or cower in fear, they accept it, and in some cases run toward it. Learning to deal with adversity, is learning to master one's self; and once the self is mastered, NOTHING is an adversity again, only a small hindrance.

NOTES:____

DAY 264

Be prepared for your time to shine, you may only get one chance. Most success stories come from preparation. Recently, I was leaving work at 4 am. My alternator went out on me. It was working well enough as long as I kept driving, and I could keep driving at about 20mph, but the problem was, I couldn't use any other power... no lights, no radio....nothing. I almost stopped at a stop sign and the car rolled. I had just enough momentum to roll into someone's yard. It was too early to knock on a door, and I was blocking their driveway.

I decided to use a jump box that I had to jump the car, then thought I'd leave it on there, as I only had about 10 miles to go. I drove the 10 miles with the hood opened about a foot, with no lights on, just using a flashlight as my headlights, and running off a jump box. It wasn't pretty, but I made it, not from luck or skill, but because I was properly prepared. I'd been in similar situations over the years, which allowed me to amass different needed tools; but as time progressed, I became better at handling situations, because every time, I added another tool to my arsenal.

Don't take tough times in your life as a slight or negative thing. Instead, use this time to build your arsenal, so that each time something happens, you are that much more prepared to handle it. It is a building process, not an overnight one. To run a marathon (which is what life is) you start by running a mile and building on that. Take each and every circumstance and situation and continue to build upon those.

NOTES:____

DAY 265

What makes a man great isn't never failing, but failing repeatedly and getting back up again, and again until he gets it right. Persistence is the sign of a good man. When you fail the first, second, or even the 19th time and continue to get up again and continue to strive forward, you not only strengthen your resolve, but you also learn new and other ways to do things. You can find answers to questions that you haven't even asked yet.

NOTES:____

DAY 266

We are all here to be an inspiration and motivating factor for those around us. The things that we go through are here not only to STRENGTHEN us but to BUILD those coming up behind us. We should be a stepping stone for those behind us, just as those who came before us were stepping stones for us. The pain, heartache, lessons learned, blessings, and overall knowledge we've picked up along the way should be passed on, so those behind us won't have to fall into the same pits we did. Be a bridge over the pitfall for those behind you; and one day, they may be a bridge for you, so that you may get to the next level of life.

NOTES:

DAY 267

If there is something you want from a person, sometimes, it can take nothing more than opening your mouth and asking for it; and at other times, you may have to beg, borrow, or steal to get what you're looking for from someone. There is a better way to approach a person u want something from. Show them what they plan to gain. Banks don't loan money simply because you need it, they do it to get the interest off the top. Doctors don't heal you because they're good people; a large portion of it is the money, notoriety, and societal status they gain. If you can show someone something they can gain or achieve by helping you, then you will have a much better chance of getting what you are looking for.

On any professional team, players listen to the coach, even when they don't personally get the glory, because they desire something else.....a championship. Even when you are in need, you still have the ability to build others up. If you're borrowing money, offer interest; if you need someone's time, offer some of yours. Are you in need of advice??? Show them that you will put what they say into action, and they're not just wasting oxygen and time giving you advice you won't use. There are billions of people on the planet in need of the same help as you. Show them why you deserve to be the one they help, and show them how u can build each other, instead of simply them building and servicing you. Reciprocity helps to ensure that you have a strong team behind you.

NOTES:____

DAY 268

Everyone who touches you doesn't touch you in the same way. Everyone around you in life, whether it be a co-worker, family member, a church member, or some stranger at a store, touches you. Most touch you physically, and some will greet you with a handshake, a pat on the back, or maybe even a hug. There are even fewer who touch you mentally. There are those who add mental value to you, who bring knowledge and wisdom, who can teach understanding and bring wisdom; and there are those who can touch your inner man, your heart, and your soul....they can bring you peace in the storm. Then there are those special people in the world who can touch you in every way. Those people in your life are like a garden for your soul. Keep those people in your life, and water them, so that they can continue to feed you. Begin to touch others in ways you haven't thought about, be a garden to someone else today.

NOTES:

DAY 269

The old saying is "What you don't know won't hurt you." But What you don't know WILL hurt u; it can literally kill you. This is why we need to learn as much as possible, as soon as possible. What we don't know within the realm of the financial sector is not only hurting us by limiting our funds today and the possibility of a brighter future and retirement, but it is also hurting the futures of our bloodlines and descendants that follow us, by strapping them to the same chains of poverty that have been strapped to us.

We don't even understand how much of what we don't know is destroying us, in all aspects of our lives. Math, communication, history, sciences, current affairs, banking, social studies, economics, and relationships. The lists go on and on. We MUST learn more so that we are able to do more. What you don't know is hurting you the MOST. The larger and stronger the base, the higher you can build. The deeper the roots, the longer a tree will stand.

NOTES:

DAY 270

More often than not, the more successful a person is, the more open they are, and the more willing they are to share their knowledge. Successful people like to see others succeed, as well. Many successful people love being mentors to others. Successful people aren't just those who make a lot of money or have a lot of followers. Successful people are those who make a choice to accomplish their goals and get it done. The ones who made a plan to save $1000, the ones who made it out of their poverty-stricken neighborhoods, the ones who were the first to get their diplomas, or the ones who opened their own small businesses.

A saying amongst the Freemasons is "To be one, ask one". All that means is, "To get where you want to be, ask someone who's already been there." Find someone who was already successful at that thing and follow their leads. When you've gotten the information, don't forget to reach back, and show others the very same things you're learning. Each one teach some. Look for mentors who are ahead of you, while being a mentor to those behind you. Don't break the chain.

NOTES:

DAY 271

Our lives are a constant fall, then we try building again. We are a living game of Jenga, and oftentimes, we take blocks and pieces of ourselves, to build someone else's tower. We forget that we must keep our tower strong and stable. We struggle financially but continue to give to other individuals and organizations....the blocks removed from our tower. We are emotionally, and mentally spent, but we try to help others through their problems....the blocks removed from our tower. We struggle with the funds to put groceries in our own homes, but we give them out when someone asks....the blocks removed from our towers. Then when our tower comes crumbling down because it is unstable we are mortified and wonder how God could do this to us.

It was not God, but YOU. You must first secure your own tower before you can hand blocks to others. If you can't miss a paycheck without something going unpaid, you can't afford to give someone else money. Use that very same money to build your savings. Put a $10 check into an account until you reach your savings goal, and you can't give any money away until your goal is reached....you literally can't afford it. We MUST secure ourselves before we build someone else up. Build yourself up today, so that you can help build someone else up tomorrow. If I give you the tire off of my car, now I'm stranded. Get your tires and your spare together, and THEN you can purchase them a tire. Until then, all you do is put yourself in jeopardy.

NOTES:____

DAY 272

What we see as failure, is probably not failure. We simply have to find our niche in life. Just because you didn't make it as a professional athlete, doesn't mean you failed; it just may not have been your area. Following and failing in the footsteps that have been pushed and forced on you shouldn't deter you. Find YOUR path put your energy into that, and THEN see where you fall. If you tell a goldfish to throw a football, he's not going to be able to do it, but is that what you would really consider failure???

Many times, we haven't figured out what it is that WE really want out of life, we're so busy chasing someone else's dream that we believe it to be ours, and we can't see it until we bottom out and have no chance of making it; or we do the opposite and actually get what we're aiming for, and find out that obtaining it still leaves us empty and hollow....unfulfilled. Where you find peace, happiness, joy, and contentment is probably the place for you. If you can't see what you're doing bringing you peace any time soon, or EVER, that's probably not a path that you should be on for too long. To find YOUR path, talk to others, try new things, and open yourself up to new possibilities. Your dream life is probably wrapped inside something that you would have never taken a second look at.

NOTES:____

DAY 273

Recently, Norma Gibson, the wife of the actor Tyrese Gibson, left their marriage and filed for divorce. Before they got married, she'd signed an ironclad prenuptial agreement, where everyone who read it was surprised he'd actually gotten her to sign it, because It was so stringent. Initially, Norma told him that she wasn't there for his money or fame, and that's why she signed the paperwork. Tyrese (from the outside looking in) hadn't been in the best mental space, as of late. He'd been doing interviews, and recording videos where he was seen crying, arguing, and flipping out. Norma saw this, as well as her friends; and her friends persuaded her to leave Tyrese, and file for divorce. Not only file for divorce but attempt to take him to court for monthly payments. Now Norma has said that she's made a mistake and wants to reconcile with her husband, and Tyrese has told her no.

This is not a message of divorce, fighting it out, or sticking together. It's simply about whom you keep around you and who you let into your ear. The people around her persuaded her to not only leave her husband but to go against her initial mindset of not taking Tyrese to court to get money out of him. She's admitted, that if she had different people in her ear, she would not have made the choices she made. Be careful of the people you keep around you, and the ones you take advice from. Many people are steering you in a direction, that best works for THEM, not you. Solid people help you build a solid foundation and look out for YOUR best interests. Keep solid people in your corner, not those who steer you down dark roads.

NOTES:____

DAY 274

I went to the gym the other day, and got on the elliptical, as I always do, and I put my weight in (which I normally don't do). I usually just get on and set my 45-minute time and the resistance. I usually burn about 500-550 calories in that workout. This time I did a 30-minute workout, and the machine said I'd burned 562 calories. Nothing had changed, I put in the same amount of energy, the same amount of strides, same, same, same. The only difference was that I put in my actual weight and got a proper reading. People look at others and see that they are doing what appears to be the same thing, in the same timeframe; they are doing the same motions, and they are upset that someone else seems to be progressing more.

You may be progressing at the same rate; it just looks different. The actual calories I burned never changed, the display readout is what actually changed. My body burned the same amount of calories in the same amount of time. If you're doing the best you can do, the results will come. Just because it LOOKS like someone is advancing, doesn't mean they necessarily are. If someone built the frame of a house and put Siding on it, that house would look further along than yours, but you've dug and done the basement, framed the house, laid everything out, and ran the plumbing and electrical; theirs just LOOKS further along. As long as you're putting in the work, you'll eventually get there. Keep your blinders on, and focus on YOUR goal, not someone else's.

NOTES:____

____

____

____

____

____

____

____

____

DAY 275

When you start out running, you're fresh, you're strong, and you start out fast. As u tire, your strides get shorter and you slow down, your breathing becomes more labored, your muscles ache, your lungs feel like collapsing, and u bend over in agony. Everything that we've done in this case has made that very situation even worse. When you tire, your body is looking for more oxygen to feed the muscles, but we bend over and compress our lungs, allowing LESS oxygen into the body. The more we tire, the shorter our steps become; but we actually use MORE energy taking smaller steps, because it takes almost the same amount of energy to take a small step as a big one. Now you're taking 2 or 3 small steps instead of 1 big one, we take shorter breaths, not allowing our lungs to fully inflate and transfer oxygen throughout the body. If you keep the proper form and keep the strict mindset to watch your breathing and stride length, you'll still be tired, you'll still be hurting, but you'll get to your destination so much faster.

Many of us live our lives the same way. We find ourselves hurting in life situations and make it harder on ourselves. Bad day...we break our diet, unexpected car repair....may as well spend what little I have left over on an outfit anyway. A decision didn't go your way, my plan didn't work, so I'm not planning anymore. Keep your form in life, as well. Stick to your plans, make adjustments if need be, and keep saving that money. Yes, you may have taken a hit, but you're still further along than if you stop now and dig yourself deeper into a hole. Stay true to what you planned initially. The mishaps that come are only building your strength and endurance, to make you a better person, and to help reach your goals faster.

NOTES:____

DAY 276

A lot of times people are chosen based on certain criteria, and if you aren't in the know, you often feel this criterion is unfair. One certain criterion is your credit score. I've often heard people say, "How can they base your entire life on 3 little numbers? That doesn't tell you who I really am at my core." But in most cases, it does. Credit scores aren't just about paying bills on time; it's about knowing the basics of how money and credit really work. People with bad credit scores usually don't budget, plan financially, save money, pay their bills off, or have excess money available for emergencies. They don't know about life insurance policies, annuities, or even CDs. Most couldn't tell you where a good place would be to put money for an investment, or what rate of return on that money is considered good. In all aspects, what seem to be trivial criteria, are actually well-thought-out rules that gauge the average person in that field. If you dress me in scrubs and sit me in a room full of doctors, it won't take long before they figure out I'm a fraud. I just simply don't belong; I don't know the first thing about the basics of being a doctor But even though you don't belong TODAY, that shouldn't stop you.

At some point in their lives, those doctors were at the very same point as you and knew probably less, but they made a change and decided to stick with that change. They learned, and worked, they studied and passed tests, and state boards. You have the ability to grow into anything you choose and prove the numbers to be a liar. Get knocked down, then get back up. If you miss a payment, make the next 10 on time. Keep kicking, scratching, and clawing to prove you belong. The criteria hold true to the ordinary person, so you have to make yourself EXTRAordinary, to beat them. Be the one to push through the adversity, the guilt, and the shame; and fight for your spot like you're the third lion getting on Noah's ark.

NOTES:____

DAY 277

No matter who you think the greatest person is in any given situation; whether it be business, sports, teaching, entertainment, etc....they have all had mentors and trainers. Kings, queens, presidents monarchs, and country leaders; Michael Jordan, Donald Trump, and Bill Gates, all have had people telling them what to do, where to be, when to work out, what to eat, what to say, and what not to say. No man (or woman) is an island unto themselves. Athletes have shooting coaches who tell them how to shoot; weight training coaches, who tell them how much weight to do and how much to run; and dieticians who tell them exactly what to eat, and when. All business people and leaders have advisors and mentors they look up to, to get advice in different tough situations.

Stop believing that nobody can tell you anything and that you can do it all on your own. The most successful people in the world are told what to do, which is why they are successful. They surround themselves with suitable, competent, and capable personnel. If you want to go fast, go alone; if u want to go far, go together. Being told what to do is only a bad thing if you're listening to the wrong people, who don't have YOUR best interest at heart. Be teachable (or tellable), have an ear, and heart for correction.

NOTES:____

DAY 278

For most of us, our great great grandparents, and on down the line, didn't have much of anything to pass on to the next generations. Many did all they could and all they knew. They knew to get you away from where they were, to get us an education, and to teach us to work hard and save. These are great starting points, but we keep teaching every generation the exact same things; and every generation continues to be stuck at the starting line, while everyone else races off. Each generation is to add to what they've been taught and search out new ways to grow.

We have to build something for the generations coming up behind us, other than working hard and saving. You save to invest in something that will bring forth its own flow of money. We need to purchase life insurance policies for our family members and friends. We must begin to teach our generations how to pass wealth between generations with Insurance policies, homes, businesses, art, and other things of value. If someone close to you were to pass today, and you would be asked to help with the burial, because they didn't have enough, then at a minimum, you should have a burial policy for them. We've got to stop having fish frys to bury our people. A little discipline and sacrifice to pay for a small policy would put us leap years ahead of where we are. The time for passing down prayers, well wishes and financial problems is over. It's our time to mobilize and push the envelope. Our children MUST not live the same struggles we have.

NOTES:____

DAY 279

Negativity is CANCER, and you need to keep it as far away from you as possible. It will eat you from the inside out. Being negative, and/or hanging around negative people, begins to get into your inner being, and it changes you without you even knowing it. The negativity seeps into your mind, which permeates into every piece of your being. Negativity brings you down emotionally, mentally, and physically. The more Negativity you're around, the more you notice; and the more negativity you notice, the less positivity you will see. We have been programmed to see negativity, which makes it harder to see, and therefore reach our goals in life. Don't allow the negative things in your life to grab hold; brush them off and keep moving. Force as much positivity into your life as you can stand… positive books, positive TV, positive MUSIC, positive living, positive words, and positive beliefs.

NOTES:

DAY 280

In a properly working family structure, grandparents play a vital role in the family's core strength. While the parents are just gaining their footing in life, starting their careers, beginning savings, and starting with the rest life throws at us, the grandparents can be there to step in, and not only help with the raising of the children, but also impart their knowledge, wisdom, and life experiences onto the next generation, giving them a good solid base to build off of.

The young children are like sponges and will begin to soak up much of the elder's wisdom. They can keep the family from becoming unhinged with anger in certain situations and be a guide and beacon for everyone. They also have the ability to absorb a few mistakes the parents make, making the effects not nearly as harsh. Grandparents can pass on peace, joy, and solitude, along with the persona of slowing down to smell the roses and enjoying every minute while you're in it. They can bring forth a calm in the midst of a storm, that the parent hasn't even recognized yet. A grandparent's wisdom can be a crown of gold to their heirs.

NOTES:

DAY 281

When we see great people, we often say how strong they are for all they've done, or all they had to endure. You may see a Barrack Obama and think how strong he must be because of everything he had to do, and how much he had to fight; or a successful businessman who made it to the pinnacle of his company; or even many of the great orators of our times. Although all of these people are considered to be strong... the strength of might, is not the only strength there us. Oftentimes overlooked is the simplest, but yet still the strongest of all strengths, and that is the ability to hold oneself without reacting. Inner strength to deny oneself is often overlooked, but the man who can control his own desires is the strongest of them all.

Whether it be, holding your tongue from a vile lashing towards someone, denying yourself sexual pleasures, pushing back the plate, or something as mundane as turning off the television. When you can control your inner-man, that is the strength you should be seeking. That strength is unmatched. If you focus on strengthening the inner-man, the inner-man will strengthen the outer one. Begin small, turn off the TV for an hour, then two, then 3. Then slowly build your stamina until your confidence and your lifestyle are beyond reproach.

NOTES:____

DAY 282

Most people have a social media page, and on that social media page, they use an algorithm that focuses on the things you watch, like, and comment on the most. They have different types of ads, different posts about a variety of subjects, and pretty much any category you'd want to indulge in. And every once in a while, new things will come up, that you're really not interested in, so you just scroll right on past them; but if you ever do click on it, you'll see more things like that for a short time, unless you don't click on them anymore. Real Life is the exact same way. What you focus on, and send your energy to, what you choose to interact with is what will continue to show up in your life. Opportunities will show up in your life all the time, but because you don't often associate yourself with them, they aren't noticed; and just like the algorithm, they soon return to the backdrop of life.

Try something new and different from time to time, it will open up an entirely new algorithm in your life. It will open you to new areas, new ideas, and new opportunities. If what you're doing isn't getting you where you want to be, then why keep doing it? Reset your algorithms by interacting with new things, watching something else, and listening to something new. It won't always be a positive experience, but you've learned something new, and it gets you closer to finding what best works for you. You can change your algorithms, you can change what you see, and what you hear, and reprogram yourself to be better. You can easily start by taking a different route home today or go to a different gas station.... maybe walk in and pay, instead of paying at the pump. Fill up at half a tank instead of when the light comes on. Do a few small different things, and you'll be able to make a few bigger changes. You have the power to change your life for the good, or the bad.

NOTES:____

____

____

____

DAY 283

Growing up in church, I've often heard about the struggles of those in the Bible… the downtrodden, the hopeless, and the poor. But for some reason, very rarely do I remember preachers preaching about prosperity. Ecclesiastics chapter 10 verse 19 says "A feast is made for laughter, and wine maketh merry, but money answereth all things." This tells me that any questions, any problems, any issues, and just about anything can be answered with money. People will say you shouldn't focus on money; but I say, whatever you're looking for can be made far easier with a pocket full of money. If you want to give out food for free every day, someone has to pay for the food, the labor, the material, and the transport of it. If the streets of heaven are lined with gold, then why would GOD want us to live in poverty on earth?

If you've never had a thing, you usually don't know how to treat it or respect it, so how are we supposed to live as royalty on this planet? Be willing to sacrifice comfort for 5 years to live the way you want for the rest of your, AND your children's lives. 5 years ago, most people weren't living the life they wanted, with no look at doing better in the next 5; some have even regressed, so why not be intentional about your moves, and make them count towards something? The people you look at as a success story sacrificed, and continue to sacrifice, BUT once you make it to a higher level, you find out that it wasn't a sacrifice at all. Most who lost 100 pounds or more will tell you that not only is it worth what they had to give up, but that they really don't miss their old ways that much. Make the money moves to prosper today, it'll be well worth what you THINK you have to give up.

NOTES:______________________________

____

____

____

____

____

DAY 284

We all have things we'd love to accomplish and things we are working towards; and while working towards those things, other things come up, life happens, and we may go down another path, focus on the today issues, and forget some of the things we initially set out to do. We focus on buying a house, and forget we promised ourselves to save a certain percentage of our income. We get a new position at work, which requires more time, and we forget we promised ourselves we were going to dedicate more time to our health and fitness; or we get lonely, and forget that we told ourselves, we wouldn't go back to a certain person who wasn't a good fit for us. During these times, it's good to have people around who will remind us of the things we initially set out to do. People who not only remind us of our beginnings but those who will feed us as well. It's ok to CHANGE a goal or plan, but that requires a thought-out process.

What we don't want to do is rationalize our current circumstances and forget about our initial plans. We have a way of slowly moving the goalposts over time, and slowly but surely pushing our needs, wants, desires, and goals further and further off, until we no longer are even working on them.

Remember where you started, and what you were initially getting into it to do. Have those people around you who won't let you forget. Keep written notes at every stage so you can review and bring things back to your remembrance. Don't rely strictly on memory, because life will happen and throw you off kilter, and into survival mode....by the time you get your bearings back and begin to reassess your situation things get lost in the sauce; so, stay focused, and leave people and notes around to keep you grounded at all times.

NOTES:____

DAY 285

Stop being so understanding and forgiving. Make these people understand that you are not their plaything. Step forward with an erect spine, and let your voice be heard. If you don't voice your dislikes and displeasure, they'll beat you, take everything you have, and tell everyone you're OK with it. Don't let that man, that woman, that organization, or even that job believe that they can treat you any kind of way. Peace of mind, pride, and dignity are better than anything ANY of them have to offer.

The repercussions may sting for a moment, but I assure you that the sting will surely fade; and there are far more men, women, organizations, and jobs out there, that are far better for you. Even if it's the best you've ever seen, there is better and more to be had. Your respect is worth far more than they have to offer. Draw your line in the sand, and fight ANYONE back who doesn't respect your boundaries.... mother, father, sister, brother, son, or daughter. You train people how to treat you by how much respect you demand, and how much disrespect you allow.

NOTES:

DAY 286

No matter what you may think, everyone endures trauma. The definition of trauma is "a deeply distressing or disturbing experience." Usually in life, our traumas can be directly traced back to a decision we've personally made; and had we made another decision, things would have turned out differently. There were also times when the trauma was completely on someone else. Either way, whether you had a part in the trauma or not, it's up to YOU to heal that trauma. Yes, what happened to you was horrible, it was painful, and it broke you into a million pieces, but that doesn't mean that's where you're supposed to stay. You can either stay broken or you can begin to rebuild yourself, one piece at a time. The bank doesn't care WHY there's no money in your account, they just care that there isn't any. Just like society as a whole doesn't care WHY you're not functioning properly, they just see that you aren't, and are ready to punish you when you don't meet their standards.

Find what it takes to begin your own healing process and start the journey. It can be counseling, working out, finding a confidante to open up to, yoga, religion, or any number of other extracurricular activities; but you have to begin the healing process in your life. Now is the time to quail our innermost demons, and learn to control them, instead of allowing them to control us. The first step is to believe that you can be better, that you can do better, and that you deserve better. Even if your trauma was your fault, it's OK...today you reset and begin anew. What happened can't be undone, but you can start fixing it or begin the atonement process today. The sooner you start the healing process, the sooner your trauma will be handled. We go through things in life to build us up, make us stronger and help so many more behind us get through the same things. You are not alone, you're not the only one going through this hell. Others have made it out. Mentors aren't just for business, but they're personal too.

NOTES:____

DAY 287

Patience and timing are skills that nearly everyone could improve upon. Even when things are destined to be, they still take time to grow and mature. During the growth and maturity time, there will be some of the most difficult and trying times that you will see. When the seed is planted, it's covered by dirt and has to fight, just to get to the daylight. Even after sprouting, it is still weak as it grows. The now sapling must fight off animals, and keep growing, through its puberty and full growth. This time varies with every seed. Some seeds are flowers and grow in a matter of weeks, some seeds are redwood trees, and take many years just to get to puberty. How much you grow is completely up to you; but regardless, it's still a process that takes a lifetime. If I give a child a car, they may destroy it, and possibly kill themselves and others; but if I take the time to properly train them, they have the skill to avoid many pitfalls, but they would still need more time to mature to make better decisions.

In the Bible, God told David he would be king...it still took another 15 years of running for his life. Joseph was shown that he would be ruler over his brothers. It took about 16 years of being a slave, and a prisoner before that happened. Every situation takes time to grow and mature. The only thing we can do is keep a positive attitude and continue to follow the plan we have laid out (which means you need to lay out a plan before you begin things). When you begin your journey, you believe that your goal is the destination. The more you grow on your journey, the more you realize, it's more about who you're becoming, and who you can help along the way to your goals.

The fastest way to get where you're going is to go slow. Even as the tree grows, it will have to endure storms, that knock its leaves and fruit to the ground, and have to grow them back, but even this storm is a blessing in disguise because now the tree is spreading its seeds through the fruit that was knocked down. And during the dry season when the tree hasn't gotten any rain, it grows its roots even deeper into the earth to look for water. This not only allows it to drink from a different source than what it's used to, but it also strengthens its position, because the deeper the roots, the stronger the base, which makes it even more difficult to knock over in a storm. Focus on your goals and understand they will take time. Know that storms will come and go and knock your fruit down; but as long as you don't stop, you will come back better, stronger, and more resilient. The process takes time.... how much time, is all up to you. You'll continue to go through your obstacles until you've learned them and adapted to overcome them, and part of that adaptation is reaching back and helping others miss the pitfalls that you fell into.

NOTES:

DAY 288

There are necessary pains and necessary evils that we must endure in life. Because we can't always see the final results, we think that every pain we endure is a negative thing. Sometimes the pains we endure in life are to move us from where we currently are because something better is coming, and if we don't move, we'll miss our opportunity. Sometimes the pain we feel is necessary to prevent us from an even bigger pain. The heartache you received from the breakup allowed you to go into solitude, to work on yourself, and to find an even better mate.

The pain you felt from not being able to pay your bills, being distraught, and destroying your credit, was the opportunity for you to learn, build, and grow....to repair your financial situation and start saving, and investing. If you can remember the pain, you have a better chance at change. Pain is a motivator. Will you allow it to push you into the greatness it's meant to do, or will you cower and buckle under the pressure? You have the ability to stand tall and make the necessary changes in your life in order to avoid the same pain. You can study your pains and learn from them, hoping to have less pain in the future; or you can allow the pains to overtake you, and break you down repeatedly. Learn, do better, be better, and allow the pain to teach you a better way. How many times must you touch that hot stove before you find another way?

NOTES:

DAY 289

Everyone needs to work on themselves. Some need a lot of work, and everyone else needs even more work than that. We all need work at some level. Take whatever time, energy, and money it takes to do the work needed for yourself. Self-revelation, opening up, even unto yourself can be a very dark, stressful, and painful time; but it is necessary pain that must be endured to heal. To help the body fight cancer, cutting it out can be a great help, but that also injures the surrounding area, and many times the entire body. Finding the help you need, and working towards being better, is like cutting out the cancers in your life.

As you begin to do the work, self-hurt, self-doubt, and even self-sabotage may begin to show; and instead of running from it and shutting down.... face the fears, face the horrors, and become a better you… you'll thank yourself in the future. Just like in any time-travel novel, or movie, they've always said, "Be careful if you go back in time, because if you change the smallest things, they could lead to the biggest changes in the present day." Well, just like a time travel movie, the little things you do today can lead to monstrous changes to your own future. The work you do today will put your life on an entirely new trajectory, and possibly light years ahead of where it is currently slated to be.

NOTES:____

DAY 290

Your time simply may not be today. I knew a man who was in good financial standing, had a high credit score, money in the bank, bills paid up, and an emergency fund, and his bills were low compared to what his salary was. Multiple times he tried to refinance his house and pull his equity out to make business moves. Each time he tried, he was denied for one reason or another, usually small trivial things. He never got upset, instead he just worked to fix those things and tried again. Over 2 years he got denied until he spoke to someone who said he shouldn't try to refinance, but get a home equity line of credit. He could pull more money out, have a lower interest rate, do everything he wanted to do, and if he set it up properly, have it paid off in literally half the time.

Had he gotten any of those refinances in those 2 years, although he may have never even known it, he would have been in a worse financial situation. So even though we can't always see the end, sometimes what we want isn't always what's best for us, even if what we want isn't a bad thing. There is always something bigger, better, and more tangible out there for us, we just don't know how to get to it yet. Patience, and persistence during the patience are key. It's not simply about waiting for something to happen or show up in your life, it's also about training while you wait, so you're prepared when your dream and the opportunity finally come knocking at your doorstep. Hoping, wishing, and praying, without proper planning, preparation, and strategy is a recipe for disaster, shame, and hopelessness.

NOTES:____

DAY 291

Sometimes proximity is mistaken for hereditary. The meaning of Heredity is "determined by genetic factors, therefore being able to be passed from parent to offspring." We see many things as hereditary that are really due to our proximity to our kin. Many sicknesses, diseases, obesity, and learning deficiencies stem from being around the same people, eating the same things, in the same situations, and doing the same things. If you change a person's diet, and they exercise regularly, many "hereditary" things disappear. Too much lead like that of Flint, Michigan, can cause learning deficiencies, as can too much sugar in your diet, as can lack of exercise; and if the same meals are cooked, and the same pattern of minimal exercise is exerted, your problems can compound very quickly.

Many of your personal problems, also arise from your proximity to others in your circle. If you continue to eat the horrible diet of gossip, arguing, greed, lying, cheating, etc., you can easily find your life spinning out of control; but if you change the people who are in your proximity, see how your attitude, conversations, and lifestyle begin to change. Reading, positivity, love, trust, truth, giving, peace, and happiness are just a few of the things that should be added to your daily social diet. What are you in proximity to, that you need to change? Who/what should you be getting in closer proximity to, to further yourself? How does your physical diet need to change, and what about your "social diet"?

NOTES:____

DAY 292

Stop blocking your blessings by not allowing people to pour into you. You think we are being modest or showing humility by turning down offers of help, or handouts, but what you're actually doing is crippling yourself and blocking your blessings. When we ask for help out of a tight situation, we expect the clouds to open up, music to play, and lightning to flash; then someone appears and hands us a bag of money or opens our accounts and magically there's way more money in there than it should be. When you ask for help, more often than not people are sent to help you, or you are put in a position to help yourself by doing some extra tasks that you don't normally do. If you turn down the helping hand stretched out to you, you have just said you don't need the help you asked for. I can guarantee the help won't be sent for long if you continue to turn it down.

When asked what you want, or what you need, open your mouth, speak up, and say what it is you want. If you constantly say you want/need nothing, why are you so surprised when you're not given anything or progressing in your field...? You've stated you didn't want or need anything. Accept the things that are given to you freely, and listen to those trying to feed knowledge, understanding, and wisdom into your life. You may not see the $5 being offered to you as the answer to the $300 you needed; but it's still more than you had, so take it, apply it, and build on that small momentum. You can't get to your bigger blessings if you continue to discard the smaller building block blessings. One big house is built from individual smaller bricks. Build with your blessings, don't block them!

NOTES:____

DAY 293

There aren't too many things in life worse than having a poor mindset. A poor mindset is a defeatist attitude, one where you feel "wo is me" and that everyone around you owes you something. You are an adult, and nobody owes you anything, no one should be doing any more for you than what it is they CHOOSE to do. You are able-bodied and have the ability to put in the necessary work to change your own circumstances. With a poor mindset, you've already defeated yourself, and blame everyone else for YOUR circumstances. With a poor mindset, there is nothing but a bleak, and limited future. Unlimit yourself, by challenging the limitations you put on yourself, and set goals for yourself, slightly past what you think are possible.

Believe you can be better, then work towards it. Your mindset is what's holding you back, and you have the ability to change that. It's not too late....it's NEVER too late. If you start today think where you can be 1, 3, 5 years from now. THINK, you can be better, ACT, on those thoughts, and BECOME anything it is that you desire.

NOTES:____

DAY 294

Sometimes our traumas have forged our minds to make us believe that the trauma we have experienced is normal and that it is the norm in everyone else's life as well. We base our lives on the rights and wrongs of situations that we FEEL should be. Our emotions, our feelings, and our thoughts all fit into our own personal box. Everyone has this box. Some are bigger, smaller, more elaborate, etc. But we focus on OUR feelings, and OUR own box when we are dealing with other people. We forget that they have their own viewpoint on things, their own emotions, feelings, and trauma-colored lenses, and that things look a little different from their box, with their upbringing, and their thoughts. Learn to get different points of view from people you trust in your circle.

Have general conversations about varying topics with a multitude of people, just to see not only how they see different situations, but why they feel that way. Even if you don't agree, you can at least seek to understand. Our traumas have caused us to grow in a defensive state of survival and have skewed our vision to believe the entirety of society lives as we do, and that our viewpoint is what MUST be the guidelines; but if you've lived their trauma, you may understand why they act as they do. Having a conversation with a man, allows you to walk a few blocks in their shoes, and take a slight glimpse into their life. Open up to others and take the time to listen before making a judgment. You will probably learn a thing or two, and who knows.... you may have a different opinion at the end of the day.

NOTES:____

DAY 295

Love isn't about finding someone who makes you feel special, love is about BEING the person you need to be to attract and share a loved life with. When you love something, you build it, you should care for it, protect it, and add value to it. You constantly and consistently put work into it, for years, and sometimes a lifetime. When you build a home, you pay for it, add amenities to it, maybe even add on to it, paint, re-paint, clean, scrub, put insurance on it, protect it with locks, lights, cameras, security systems, and fix things as they break. The house doesn't supply anything that YOU haven't given it. It only protects you from the elements because you paid for the supplies and builders, it provides protection, because YOU paid for the locks, and security, and comforts you because YOU paid for the beds. You love the home because of what YOU have done for it. Even a home that is already built, you're constantly paying for it.

Finding love is more about finding who YOU are as a person and seeing how much you're willing to put into yourself, to get what you want out of another person, job, home.... whatever. The more you put into yourself, work on yourself, and build yourself, the more you can work on finding that "better home" for you. Every book you read, every class you take, and every seminar you attend, adds another stream of income to your "love account". How can you ask someone to be the security system for your heart, if you yourself don't know how many doors, and windows, you have that need protecting? The contractor will only fix what you tell them is wrong, and what you pay to get done. If you don't put the work in on YOU to figure out where you're broken, where you're vulnerable, what it takes to fix these things, and you have the time, energy, and patience to fix these things, nobody will be able to help you. Love isn't about finding someone else; it's really about finding YOU.

NOTES:____

____

____

____

DAY 296

The Bible says, "Train up a child in the way they SHOULD go, and when they are old, they won't go away from it." It doesn't say they will listen when they're young, it specifically says when they are old. But the bigger, and more important issue is the TRAINING of your child(ren). Feeding, clothing, and sending your child to school is only training them to listen to someone else. To train anyone at anything, but especially young impressionable children, requires time, effort, energy, frustration, and repetitive actions. We have to train our children about how to talk to elders, supervision, manners, and law enforcement. They have to be trained in law, business, investing, savings, life insurance, wills, trusts, credit, and taxes. This means they have to be consistently shown these things, taught what they mean, and how to use them properly. Some may say "But I don't even know these things;" and if that's the case that's OK, you should be learning as well; and in the meantime, look for classes or seminars given at the library or through your city.

You can ask your friends or coworkers what they know about any of these and spend a Friday evening with them to get a beginner's crash course, then continue with books (they're free at any library). Just as we train our children in sports, we need to train them in life skills. Every day they go to practice and are pushed to their physical limits, as we too should be pushing them to their mental limits daily. This is how we should properly train them. Our children are drastically falling behind. The Bible says that they will not depart from their training because it becomes muscle memory and an automatic reflex when done properly. It's just instilled in you to revert back to what you know. What are/have you trained your children, AND yourself to do on a daily basis? That's what will show. We all want the next generation to be better than us, so that means we have to actually take the time to BUILD a better generation.

NOTES:____

DAY 297

We often give ourselves undue and unnecessary stress and heartache. We take on others' problems, as though they are our own. Sometimes the ones we love tell us about their lives and plans, and we feel the need to interject, with our views and thoughts. We say we are helping them through their situations, and our way is the best for them to go. But are we really helping, if we haven't been asked our opinion, or what to do??? Even though we believe we are truly helping, you may be doing more harm than good. If you weren't asked your opinion, you're simply trying to force your way of thinking, and belief systems on someone else, and when they don't listen or do it another way, we get upset. I've had to learn this in my personal life. If I am not specifically asked my opinion, I listen, say ok, then continue on about my day. I no longer have the time, energy, or money, to make everyone else's problems, MY problems.

If you are not an underage child, I will let you live your best life. Carrying everyone else's baggage weighs you down and makes your personal journey longer and more arduous. The more you interject, usually the harder they will fight against you, and the more they fight.... you get the picture. Let nature run its course and teach them what you were racking your brain over. So much peace comes over your life when you learn to let go of everyone else's problems and burdens and focus on yourself. When I was younger, I was a lifeguard, the first thing they taught me was to approach a drowning person from the rear because they are so full of fear, that they will drown, and take you with them in the process. Injecting yourself into someone else's problems without being asked is like approaching a drowning victim head-on, they have the ability to take you down with them.

NOTES:____

____

____

____

____

DAY 298

Trying to change a habit is difficult. It's like shooting a rocket into space. There's more energy, more fuel, and more power used during the first few minutes lifting off, getting to the upper atmosphere, than there is the rest of the journey combined. Your habits are made over years of repetitive behavior; and every time you do something, those habits anchor themselves a little bit deeper into your psyche. If you are looking to change any habit that you have, just like that rocket ship, you're going to have to intentionally put maximum effort, and maximal energy into changing. Although the effort is very important, you also need accessory things like someone to steer you in the right direction, because what good would it be to apply all this energy, just to steer yourself into the ocean, and never make it anywhere?

In the beginning, the process is tough, you're fighting against familiarity, fondness, comfort, and even reassurances; the toughest part though is getting going and continuing to keep moving. If you can keep that consistency, and stay focused, you can change your habits. If you fail, that's ok. NASA didn't make it to the moon on their first try either, but the goal is to never give up. You have the strength and ability to change your habits into better ones if you so choose to do so. Make your mind up to change, do research, so you not only know what you're changing into, but also how to go about doing it, and keep people around you who will remind you of the goal you wanted, and who will push and assist you along your journey. It will not be an easy road that you're about to travel, but it will be worth it.

Whether you are Black, white, rich, or poor, there are two things that will affect your life more than anything else… that's health, and wealth (or lack thereof). We live our lives, working, and toiling, hardly ever giving thought to either of these, unless something goes wrong with one of them, but by that time you're already behind the 8ball. We go to work every day, to acquire more money, but most of us have no idea what to do with it, other than pay bills, rack up more debt, and die, leaving bills and debt for others to pay off. If there are two things that we need to focus on, they are health and wealth. Your health affects your wealth, and your wealth affects your health; and when one of them begins to go off-kilter, it can be a spiraling circle downward, until you hit rock bottom or die.

The more we study these two subjects, the better chance we have of having strong, fulfilling lives. Many say money just isn't that important to them, but ANYTHING you want to do needs money to operate. If you want to feed the homeless, help starving children in Europe, replant a forest, or save animals in the wild….it all costs money, and your health is at risk. The more health and wealth you have, the better your life will be, and the better you can make others' lives. Focus on your health and wealth above all other priorities, and many other things will fall into place.

NOTES:

DAY 299

Our entire life, from the day we are born, we are taught how to be independent. How to do everything on your own, walk, talk, get your own place, and pay your own bills. All of these things are great and wonderful, and they should be done, but it is only the first step towards true power…the power of interdependence. More money and more power have been amassed; more buildings have been built; more wars have been won on interdependence than anything else. When you work together, your powers are amplified and multiplied. Just about anything successful that you can think of has people working together to accomplish the success.

Building with each other, trusting each other, and working together, are cornerstones to success. There is almost NOTHING that can be done if you don't work with someone. You didn't sew your own clothes, build your own house, make your own car, harvest your own crops, or for those who see themselves as successful entrepreneurs.... you didn't buy your own products; someone, somewhere has done something for you. If you were more open-minded, you'd find even more people to build with to broaden your base, and the bigger your base, the higher you can go. Working together these days is a lost art, but for those special few who still use it, it is a resource and tool that is unmatched. Learn how to build strong relationships that rely on others, and also learn how to be relied on. There is so much out there for you if you learn to have interdependent relationships.

NOTES:____

DAY 300

The Bible says (Ecclesiastics 10:10) that if the axe is dull and one does not sharpen it, then he must use more strength. This is a true statement, but it goes further than an axe and a tree. If you do not prepare properly for your endeavors, you will waste so much energy. Abraham Lincoln said, "If you give me 6 hours to chop a tree, I'll spend the first four sharpening my axe." Proper preparation prevents piss-poor performances. Whether you're at work, going over your finances, working out at the gym, or anything else, your plan is more important than the work, because the plan is what tells you not only WHAT work to do, but how much of it needs to be done. If all you know to do is pour water into a cup and never stop, you'll end up overfilling the cup and wasting all the excess water.

This is how many approach their everyday lives. They jump in headfirst to situations, with very little forward-thinking or planning, then spend 80% of their time in turmoil, and agony because situations that they didn't see continue to arise. Instead, we should be using that same time to plan, calculate, ask a few questions, get more people involved, and get different perspectives. That's sharpening your mental axe. Some people are so unprepared, that it's like trying to chop down a tree with a baseball bat. An ounce of prevention is better than a pound of cure. A little forethought, a little bit of planning, and a few questions will go further for you than just about anything. Sharpen your axe daily.

NOTES:

DAY 301

When you hear the word addiction, you may see flashes in your mind of people strung out, needles, pills, dirty clothing, or any number of other things at once. But addictions are even more subtle, and far-reaching than that. there are sexual addictions, electronic addictions, lying addictions, and even shopping addictions, to name a small few, and one that we don't even think is an addiction.... eating. This isn't just for someone who you may think is overweight but for all of us. The human body wasn't meant to eat three meals a day. On average, depending on a number of factors, it usually takes from 1-3 days to completely digest a meal, so at best, we are only supposed to eat once a day, and the hunger we feel is more withdrawal than actual hunger.

So many diseases are associated with overeating.... heart attack, strokes (too much cholesterol), diabetes, cavities (too much sugar), liver diseases (too many fatty foods, and alcohol)… the lists go on and on. We were told to eat three meals a day to boost profits in someone else's pockets by consuming more food; and they make 1000 times more profit, by "curing" and operating on you when the side effects of overeating begin to show their ugly faces. The food pyramid we were taught as children, was strictly made for profit, it had nothing to do with health.

Begin to cut back, start by replacing 1 meal with a smaller one, and more water, then cutting a meal out altogether. Meal replacements or cutting out meals completely won't happen overnight; we are addicted to overeating, and it may take years to get to the ideal situation you want to get to, but you'll be slowly getting healthier along the way. The human body actually begins to heal itself when you fast. The longer you can go without eating, the more you can benefit. Your body uses more energy digesting food than it does on anything else, so when you stop eating, it has the ability to put that energy towards other things, like boosting your immune system, cell repair, body maintenance, and so many other benefits. Anyway....it's not like any of us are going to die if we miss a few meals, we all have a few pounds we can spare.

NOTES:____

DAY 302

Your "one true love" is not what most people think it is. We are told that there is one person out there who will know, understand, and accept us as we are and that we don't have to do much to sustain that love. That's a fairy tale, and if you believe that, I have some magic beans I want to sell you. First and foremost, YOU have to be a person who is giving, nurturing, protective, caring, knowledgeable, and all the things that you yourself are looking to attain. Even when you find the person you want to be with, you BOTH still must continue to work on each other and build each other, it's not only about you, but your partner needs as much happiness and love as you do.

ANY relationship constantly goes through ups and downs; they need daily, weekly, monthly, and annual maintenance, tough conversations, adjustments on everyone's part, relationship goals, rules, and consequences for breaking those rules. Relationships are not a found love, and then nothing else needs to be done. There will be times when life weighs heavily on one, or even both of you at the same time; and it's during that time when you find out, not only who your partner is, but who you truly are.

Can you still be that same giving, loving, caring, compassionate person in the relationship, or does your partner take a back seat to your anger, fears, frustrations, and misunderstandings??? Love is an action, it's what you CHOOSE to do on a daily basis. Can you be the proverbial "mailman" in your relationships, and continue to deliver love, in the rain, sleet, hail, and snow of the relationship???? These are the questions that you should be asking yourself, and your partner, these are the things that should be contemplated. Not "How do you feel about me?" because those feelings will come and go. What are you willing to continuously do is a far better question.

NOTES:____

____

____

DAY 303

You can't enter new places in life if you're using the same old thinking. You can't get yourself out of trouble with the same thinking that got you into that trouble. You have to change, grow, and expand your thought process if you want to reach new and different levels in life. If you are a consumer and want to become a banker, those are two totally different levels of thinking. If you use consumer mindsets in the banker world, your banks will be bankrupt within a year. It takes a different mentality and different discipline to be a banker. Most consumers are worried about what they are going to do today, or maybe within a year or two from now. Most bankers are thinking about how their decisions are affecting things a generation or two from now.

We have been trained our entire lives to think, believe, and live a certain way. I If you're happy with your life as it is, then continue to do what it is you've been doing; but if you're not satisfied….it's time to make a change. Your life trajectory is influenced by your habits, your habits are influenced by your routine, your routines are influenced by your behaviors, your behaviors are influenced by your thoughts, and your thoughts are influenced by your daily feeding of the mind, i.e. what you read, what/who you watch, and what/who you listen to.

If you want to move to different levels in life, it begins with who and what you surround yourself with on a daily basis. Different levels require different skills, different associations, and different patience levels. Are you ready, willing, and able to begin to make the mental changes needed for another level? Are you ready to distance yourself from people holding you back? Are you ready to let go of the very thing you think is saving you, or that you believe is your status symbol in life????

NOTES:____

DAY 304

During the holidays, many people feel as though it's a time for family to gather together. Not only is this not always possible, but oftentimes I would advise against it at all costs; and above all, I believe that you should keep peace and a positive mentality. Keeping the peace at all costs sometimes means that you don't deal with certain people and places. We should be seeking peace, prosperity, mental clarity, and solitude as well. If being around certain people in your life brings personal pain, anxiety, depression, and a generally unwell atmosphere in your life, then you should do all you can to avoid those people and situations. Just because someone is blood, doesn't make them "family".

Someone who does not have YOUR best interest at heart should not be considered family, no matter who they were born to. Keep your distance from those who bring you down, no matter the relation. You make a conscious CHOICE every day to be happy, or sad, and if you CHOOSE to continually go around, and mingle with people who bring you down, that's a decision you can only make yourself. When you stand in front of a judge, he will ask you about the choices YOU made.... not what your mother, father, cousins, or siblings made, but YOU. YOU have the ultimate power to change and uplift your situation. If you want peace and happiness, there are just places you can't go and people you can't associate with anymore. If it doesn't bring peace, prosperity, happiness, laughter, strength, or a paycheck, you should probably reevaluate its existence in your life. Go where you are celebrated, and not simply tolerated.

NOTES:

DAY 305

A garden is a plot of ground where fruit, herbs, vegetables, and/or flowers are grown. A garden is a place that life literally springs from. Not only is a garden full of life, but it is also life-sustaining. If you grow the proper things in your garden, that garden can sustain you for the rest of your life. Over time, even If a garden isn't kept up, it can still thrive. Plants that aren't eaten or picked, fall back to the ground, and the seeds go back into the earth to grow even more life-sustaining plants. As this process continues season after season, the garden can become an oasis. A desert is pretty much thought to be the opposite. It is dry desolate, and barren, and there is no life throughout its vastness. BUT there are seeds, flowers, and life-sustaining foliage lying just below the surface of the desert. All the desert needs is a constant supply of water, and it can produce just like any other garden.

Are you a garden, or a desert, do you surround yourself with gardens or deserts??? Yes, a garden can feed you, but a well-taken-care-of garden can feed you and your family forever. Take care of the gardens that feed you, feed the gardens that take care of you. The gardens need water, care, pruning, weeding, fertilizer, and tilling. It's not all about reaping an award, even the best garden needs to be maintained. Leave the deserts in your life, because even if you do water them, and they bring forth a meal, it doesn't have the natural resources to keep it up. You have to pour all of your effort, energy, and resources into it to make it viable.

NOTES:____

DAY 306

In order for us to know where we fall in life, we usually compare ourselves to other people. We look at others' positions in life, on the job, or on a team and use them as a benchmark; either as a higher standard, something that we should attain to be or be like, or as a subpar standard, an area to stay away from. But that's our biggest problem.... we focus on everyone else instead of focusing on ourselves. You can always find someone who is bigger, better, faster, stronger, smarter, or better-looking, so you will never feel good enough in your own eyes.

Conversely, you can always find someone who is slower, dumber, uglier, poorer, or worse than you in any given situation, which can leave you with an unnecessarily inflated ego. What we should be doing is challenging ourselves against ourselves. My personal best in the mile will never be what Usain Bolts will be, and if I ever choose to compare the two, I may possibly give up altogether, because I could never achieve his accomplishments. Instead, if I hold that up to MY personal achievements, and I see what I have done, I will see that time was a personal best, and it could give me more drive and energy to continue my regiment.

The only person we should be in competition with is ourselves, if you look at YOURSELF a year ago, and you're pleased with the progress, then fine; if not, what do you need to do to make better progress? Focus on YOUR own journey, and not that of someone else. Your journey may take you to places someone else has never gone. On a football field, how many yards you gain is measured from where the ball starts at the beginning of the play; and anything forward of that, where the ball stops at the end. If you run around in the backfield 100 yards evading the other team, none of that counts as yards gained, you have to go further forward than where the ball started. You're comparing your situation of evading depression, improper training, abuse, poverty, addiction, and sickness to someone who has none of these things, or who conquered them years ago.

It's OK to strive for better and look at someone else for motivation, but keep in mind, that we all have our own battles and demons to face along the way. Your journey probably won't be like someone else's, because you don't have the same background or mindset. Learn to be ok running YOUR race.

NOTES:

DAY 307

Be very careful who you give to. If you have the ability to give, and the inclination, then give; and if not, or it would put you in a tough position, then don't give. There are those out there who will take everything you are offering PLUS more, and when you have given till it hurts and stop giving, they will browbeat you, slander you, tell others how much better you believe yourself to be, and drag your name through the mud at all costs. They believe they are OWED your help, and that it is your responsibility to save, sacrifice, and work extra hours, while they play, frolic, and throw caution to the wind, knowing you will not let them fail. They will talk 10 times worse about you than the people who've never helped them or given them a dollar.

Ensure you're keeping company with those who are grateful for anything that is given, and who are appreciative of your time, and efforts. Remember.... only give what you can afford to never get back.

NOTES:______________________________

DAY 308

YOU are your biggest and best asset. Not your house, car, job, or any other investments, but....YOU; and everything that you need for a better you is within you, just waiting for you to make moves. Either you're going to make moves to intentionally better your life, or you're a pawn in someone else's game, being moved on. Success is built into each and every one of our DNAs, we just have to learn to tap into and unlock our endless potential. Your success depends on how much work YOU are willing to put into it. How much reading, how much, sweat, how many hours, how much planning YOU do, and the associations that you choose to keep around you. Your potential is screaming to be used and waiting for you to begin digging so it can show you its treasures.

Finding your potential is like digging for gold in the earth; you may have to dig a while, and if you have no clue where to start, just start where someone else found success. Soon you may find a small piece of potential, then another, and another, and hopefully, you find an entire area full of potential. The more you look for your potential, the better you'll become at finding it. You'll learn shortcuts, and you'll begin to streamline your processes. But none of these things can happen if all you do is sit on your potential and allow yourself to be used to make others happy. Promise yourself 1hr a day to work on yourself, to build yourself, to make a better life, the one that you've always envisioned yourself living. 1hr of reading, research, exercise, meditation, prayer... SOMETHING can get you one step closer to where you want to be. Your destination only seems extremely far because you haven't started the journey. If I told you there was a trillion dollars' worth of gold buried in your backyard, you'd start digging. Well, YOU are that yard, and the gold is your potential. Will you let that gold sit there, or are you still going to let someone else come by and dig in your yard, and rob you of all your assets?

NOTES:____

DAY 309

Prepare yourself for when your time comes; you may only get one shot, and it may take years to get there. Everyone knows the story of Joseph in the Bible. He was sold into slavery by his brothers, where he was sold again to an Egyptian, and became such a good slave that the owner didn't even check his stuff anymore under Joseph. The owner's wife lied about Joseph and got him thrown into jail, where he interpreted a dream, which eventually got him out of jail to interpret a dream for Pharaoh. Joseph did such a good job that Pharaoh gave him more power than everyone in the land but himself. Your position doesn't matter, your title doesn't matter, and your background and experience don't matter. Your knowledge is what matters most. Hebrews (Joseph) and Egyptians (Pharaoh) didn't do well together, they were like Blacks and whites in the 1800s, so he wasn't a person he would normally see; plus, Joseph came straight out of prison, so he actually had to be cleaned up and given a haircut, and clothes before he talked to Pharaoh. Joseph had no experience when it came to being in a political arena or running a country. But what he did have was knowledge of not only how to interpret a dream, how to run and manage people, and how to increase what he'd had.

If you train yourself on constant improvement, and you can hone your gifts, you can change your entire life with 1 conversation. When asked, Joseph was ready, not only to interpret, but he also gave steps on how the situation should be handled. When Pharaoh heard Joseph's suggestions, he knew he was the man to run the country and prepare them for what was coming. Nothing mattered but what he knew. It took him about 14 years of slavery, and building himself up, honing his skillset, leading everywhere he'd been, even as a slave, to be able to sit in front of Pharaoh ONE...TIME. Had he blown that, he may have suffered a lifetime of prison, or worse.... death. He was prepared and didn't fold under the pressure. Stop worrying about where you come from, what you look like, or what you've done in the past, focus on being the best you, that YOU can be, and honing your skills to the best of your ability.

You may not end up running a country or being the CEO of a Fortune 500 company, but you just may end up pulling yourself out of the situation you find yourself in today. Don't worry about the things you can't change and focus on the 1 thing you can.... YOU. Do whatever it takes to build your knowledge so that you can turn that knowledge into your working capital.

NOTES:

DAY 310

There is a quote that says something in the realm of "Evil men succeed when righteous men do nothing." This is a statement that I agree with but on multiple levels. It's not just evil men and righteous men, but it's bad and good all together. The only thing for your fat to succeed is for you to do nothing; the only thing for your poverty to succeed is for you to do nothing; the only thing for all the negative things to continue in your life is to do.... nothing. If you want positive things in your life, you have to do SOMETHING. The more you want, the more you have to do. The better quality you want, the more you have to PLAN. Success isn't some magical place, you find yourself one day, or a huge dollar amount, or even that dream job or house…. success is making your mind up to do a thing, and then…. doing it.

Huge successes, your big dreams, the job, the house, the car, that special relationship, are all made up of smaller, individual successes. If you can master making your bed when you get out of it every day, you can find another small success to conquer, and so on, and so on. The Great Wall of China is the longest wall in the world. It was actually a bunch of smaller walls for other cities, that were connected together, and each of those smaller walls was built from a bunch of smaller, individual bricks, that came together to make the complete wall. Everything is a process, learn to control the smaller things in your life. Even the biggest ship is controlled by a relatively small rutter.

NOTES:____

DAY 311

If you take a poll of the best people in any field, whether it's sports, politics, business, or even your own job or extracurricular activity, you'll find that the very best of them put in more work than just about everyone underneath them combined. They are the best businesspeople, doctors, lawyers, cooks.... whatever are there practicing their individual crafts when everyone else is gone. Kobe Bryant would be in the gym, already at a full sweat, when everyone else showed up; he'd do an entire practice with everyone else and when everybody would leave, he'd still be there putting in more work. Warren Buffet reads an average of about 5 hrs. a day.... every day. Reading about markets, other businesses, CEOs, and all things business-related.

Many of us envy those in the top positions but fail to realize the amount of work it took to get and stay there. Many would say "If I had the last shot, I could make it too," but you don't make the smaller shots you take daily. You don't read the business perspective the night before the big meeting; you show up late to work often; you aren't fluent in your own job description and tasks; and when something comes up that you don't know, you try to lie your way through it instead of simply saying "I don't know" and then going to do some actual studying to find the answers. The more you want out of your life, the more you should expect out of yourself. Your output is directly proportionate to your input. Put in more, and you can be anything you want to be, have anything you want, and move mountains in the process; but only if you have the determination to never stop putting more in.

NOTES:

DAY 312

When we think about the lion pride, most people think about the females hunting, and bringing the food home for the male lion to eat, and that the male lion is there for breeding and fights against other male lions. While these things are true, they are not the only thing the leader of the pack does. The male lions roam the plains of their territories for weeks at a time, by themselves, ensuring that the pride's "home territory" is safe and secure from other prides and other predators, and possibly scoping out new territory to add to his own. In some cases, this is done with another male in the pride, but usually, there aren't many male adult lions in the pride, so he goes it alone.

There is a fine balance between having other males around to help with the protection of the family and having to watch your back because they are looking to take over the pride themselves. But additional males are needed to help protect against other male attacks. These are some of the very narrow lines that the males in your life walk. At all costs, they are looking to protect the family, but they are juggling exactly how to get it done. The men in your life are walking the plains of life and are being attacked from all sides….it doesn't matter if you are a man or a woman, the men in your life need your support. If you are a man, then join up and help fight the world off together, it's harder to take out 2 soldiers than 1. If you're a woman, support the men in your life, encourage them, build them up, and make their lives easier in some way. It doesn't have to be your husband or boyfriend. Buying someone a lunch or getting them a card can change their outlook on the day. A small token of appreciation, showing you value them in your life. If the men aren't around, then who is there to protect and fight for the family?

NOTES:____

____

____

____

____

DAY 313

There are times when you're going through and being absolutely beaten by life at every turn you make. It's not that you've done anything wrong; it just needs to be this way, so that when you finally do come out, people see where you came from, what you've turned into, the effort you struggled with, and the determination you had. THIS will allow the people to come to you, and put you in rooms with leaders, and deal-makers. How you handle and come out of your tough times is telling people the kind of person you are, and IF they want to deal with you. When the children of Israel were in the process of gaining their freedom, GOD said He was going to not let Pharaoh say yes, just so that he could do all the wonders, and plagues he wanted to do; so that when the Israelites finally did get their freedom, EVERYONE would know who Israel was, and what they and their GOD was capable of. Show people who you are, and what you are capable of.

NOTES:

DAY 314

There is a sermon by Miles Munroe, where he speaks of a woman who came into his office crying. The woman had just gotten laid off, was on her last check, and didn't know what to do; she was hysterical. He calmed her down and asked if she had a stove and how many days it worked. Of course, she said she had one, and she cooked on Sundays. He remembered she'd made him some cookies once, so he told her, "Take part of your last check and go buy cookie materials. Then go back to where u just got fired and give them away for free. Begrudgingly she did it, and before she got home, she had orders for more cookies. He preached on utilizing what you have and changing your mindset, but what I saw was the importance and value of leadership and being able to follow.

Following someone who can not only see your talents and values but who can also guide you properly. This woman could have said, "He's crazy, this is my last check, and I'm not going to spend it just to give it away to others." But luckily for her, she chose to listen and allow herself to be led. She now has one of the largest cookie distribution chains in the area. Had she not listened to the leader in her life, she would have spent the last check on bills, and been broke the next week anyway, wondering where her next meal was going to come from. Why not spend it on materials and bet on YOU???? What skills are you overlooking in your life, and what leaders in your life are you not listening to? Learn to decipher those in your life who can properly lead, when things aren't going right in your life.

NOTES:____

DAY 315

Things happen little by little, one step at a time. Even though we may want them to happen immediately, or overnight. The best results usually take a little more time and a few more steps. Going from extreme to extreme can cause more problems than you already have. Growing up in Chicago, we were always told, that if you come in from a cold day and wash your hands, you do it in cold water. Warm or hot water will burn your hands because that's a drastic temperature change. If your engine has been running at operating temperature, and you spray it with cold water, you will probably crack the engine block and ruin it. Gradual increases in life, just like in temperatures, are needed, so that everything has time to find a new level and settle out.

Too much too fast can be worse than not getting a thing at all. Too much water at one time will kill you faster than not getting any water at all. Even though you strive for more out of life, enjoy where you are for now, and use the time to start building your base for the next level. You can't move up any higher if there's nothing for you to stand on.

NOTES:

DAY 316

There has been a lot of talk around the subject of Generational wealth lately. People are looking to pass something on to the next generation. This is a great idea, and I believe wholeheartedly that this is what everyone should be trying to do; but Generational wealth is far more than money, cars, clothes, and businesses. Those things are actually the results of true generational wealth. The things that we should be passing on to future generations are knowledge, wisdom, education, insurance policies, dedication, love, happiness, peace, manners, respect, determination, a solid work ethic, protection, sacrifice, collaboration, teamwork, and a host of other positive attributes.

If all we leave future generations is finances, they are doomed to fall into the pitfalls of life, and more than likely go broke because they haven't learned what to do with the finances when they get them. They don't have the discipline or structure to continue the growth of the money, and they don't know what to do to pass it along to the generations behind them. If we teach them to focus on the more positive attributes in life, the finances will follow. The school systems are babysitters, who are teaching our children nothing other than how to be a good subservient worker who gets a check, stays in debt, makes no waves, and dies unhappy. WE must teach our generations about the things we want them to know, and WE must allow the village to feed into the generations behind us. If we spend our time actually teaching future generations, we won't have to worry about passing down wealth, it will happen automatically.

NOTES:____

DAY 317

What are you doing in your free time? Daily steps lead to grandiose travels. The average person who wants to advance puts in an extra 2-3 hours a week… maybe. If you give simply 1 hour a day towards your goals, that's 365 hours of training that you're further ahead than where you were last year....3 times further than the average person who is putting in the extra work. The smallest daily steps will lead to the largest lifetime changes and shifts. The things you are doing are being watched, people are paying attention to you, and they are paying attention to not only what you're doing, but how you're doing it.

The harder you work, and the more you put in, not only gets you closer to your goals faster, but it also shows those who are watching you, what it will take to achieve their own goals. You can be the beacon for someone else's life. The times you have to make the changes you seek are everywhere. You can wake up an hour earlier, go to sleep an hour later, and use your breaks and lunches at work. Turn your phone scrolling time into life advancement movements and turn 1 television show into 1 chapter. 1 hour can be found anywhere, it doesn't even have to be all at one time. 4, 15-minute intervals can get the job done the same as a 1-hour shift. Find the time in your life to change your life.

NOTES:

DAY 318

Leadership is a multi-faceted position. Many people see leadership as being at the forefront, making great decisions, winning the game, or coming up with the solution that catapults the team to the next level. While these things may be true, it's only a very small percentage of what leadership actually consists of. The bulk of leadership consists of late nights, and early mornings, squashing inner-team problems, taking the heat, when things go wrong, teaching, and mentoring your subordinates, and not only allowing them to grow but also to make their own mistakes and not broadcasting it to the world. Leadership is about protecting those under your charge, it's about working, while others rest, it's about spotting the potential in those around you, and finding the best way to pull it out of them. Leadership is pushing those around you, to be greater than you.... greater than even they believe they can be.

Anyone can be a leader, it doesn't take a job, title, or pay rate. You can be a leader in your various circles of life. Look to see how you can better the people, and situations around you, that's all a leader really breaks down to.... making situations better. And we never have all the answers, which is why you look to others to help, different people react to different stimuli, so bring others in and learn different approaches, and different styles. Leadership is constant growth, self-evaluation, and self-discipline. Leadership is far more about working on self, than working on others. If you want to learn how to lead a team, first learn how to lead yourself.

NOTES:____

DAY 319

The definition of faith is, "complete trust, or confidence in someone, or something." The Bible says faith comes by hearing, so you believe in the things you hear the most. What are you filling your eardrums with????? What movies are you watching, what music are you listening to, what people are you allowing to speak to you? It's your audio diet. The more you allow things to feed your audio pallet, the more ways you open yourself to be pulled in multiple directions.

Stay focused, and consciously be aware of the things you allow into your body. Very few cities are ever overtaken strictly from the outside, they are usually weakened and helped internally. Keep as much negativity out of you as possible. Your body is fertile ground, and when you listen to obscene music, you're allowing those seeds to be planted, and sooner or later they will begin to grow. Don't allow yourself to be overtaken from the inside, watch, listen to, and eat a better choice of material.

NOTES:

DAY 320

When we think of doing something new or different in our lives, that usually requires us to do more, be more, or give more; in essence, we are turning into, or becoming a new person of sorts. Although you feel the same, and look the same, you are taking on new characteristics, ever so subtly, which makes you new. What we should be focusing on is intentional change. We should be planning and calculating our future and our next steps, and every step that we take should be a step closer to building the new you and killing the old one. Every step won't be easy, but every step should be calculated, and made in the direction of your new self. There will be times when you're being tested, and it looks like everything is pushing you back to your old self, but it's simply a detour, you're still on the best path.

NOTES:

DAY 321

Proper Translations are critical when translating. The wrong word here or there, can start wars. Translations don't just mean, from culture to culture, they can be between two people who speak the same language. There is a general difference in how most men see/understand things, and how most women see/understand things, so unless you make it a point to actually hear and understand where someone from the opposite sex is coming from, there is a good chance that you all will reach a misunderstanding because although your words may be the same, your meanings aren't. Even when it comes to people in your own home ... your siblings, your mates... everyone sees words differently.

Ask a few questions of those closest to you, just to see what they say. Ask them to explain what love is, happiness, peace, freedom, justice, equality, and just see what they say. See how close their definitions are to yours. You believe your mate doesn't love you, but they are loving you 100% that they know how.... according to their definition of the word. Begin to listen to more than people's words. Listen to body language, it can tell you more than anything, without ever saying a word. Listen to expressions, listen to how people interact with other people, and then ask questions to get clarity and understanding. The better understanding you have, the better your translations can be, and the fewer problems you'll have.

NOTES:____

DAY 322

We are always wanting different, new, and better things. We ask GOD, the universe, and anyone who will listen, for a better job, a mate that checks off so many boxes, a more luxurious vehicle or home, or any number of other things. We want so many more things that will presumably make our lives better, but we are forgetting to look within and see if we are actually ready for what it is we are asking for. Are you ready for the rigor of that new position, are you ready for the responsibilities it entails, will you show up early, or leave late, is your temperament able to handle the fluctuating emotions, and attitudes of subordinates? Can you be with the perfect mate, who pushes you to be a better you, and never allows you to quit, whose drive is insatiable; can you handle a mate who will not accept deterring off the chosen path, and can you accept a mate who is harder on the children than you would be to make them better, smarter, and stronger?

We only think of the things we want, but rarely ever think of the price that must ultimately be paid. The saying goes "Be the change you want to see." That simply means, if you want better, YOU have to be better, if you want more, YOU have to give more. You can't wait for others to make the situation better; YOU must step up to the plate. To make your, and your future generations' life easier in the future, you must work harder in the present. You may be wondering why you're going through what you're going through; it may be because you're being prepped to accept the very things you've asked for.

NOTES:____

DAY 323

No matter how good a situation is, no matter how well things are set up for you, or how paved the road is, if YOU don't believe in yourself, you'll never have anything. If I buy you a house, walk you into it, give you the keys, and tell you it's yours, but you never believe it, you think you're being set up, and you believe it to be a scam....you'll walk away from the house, leave the keys, and go back to your life you've been living.

YOU have to know that you are worthy, YOU have to know you deserve more, YOU have to believe in yourself. No matter what others do to you, or for you, you are the one who makes the largest impact in your life. Whether you believe you can, or you believe you can't, you're right either way. Your beliefs and your work ethic are the only things keeping you from what you want. Believe it, work for it, and let nothing stand in your way.

NOTES:

DAY 324

You don't get the gift, then manage it, you have to manage, and then the gift is grown. If you get the money, then figure out what to do with it. If you get the perfect mate, before you know how to handle them, and feed into them, you'll push them away. You go through trials and tribulations in life, to prepare you for the very things you're asking for, and you see the same trials because you have yet to learn the lesson. This is not the "no child left behind" life. If you don't pass the tests, you don't move on. For those who are given the gift ahead of the management, and have not learned discipline, they don't keep what was given to them for very long, because they have no idea how to keep it and grow it. So, like an unkempt plant, it withers and dies.

Look at your struggles with lessons, look for growth opportunities, and don't look at them as bad things happening to you. Bills overdue???? The lessons are, to learn how to budget, save, spend less, and make more. You may say, "But I saved, and it took even more than I had." All that means is, to save even more, and spend less. Save to invest, so that the money can grow outside of your work. Learn to manage your time, your health, your finances, and your emotions better, and things in your life will magically start falling into place. Good management in any life, on any job, or any aspect of life will raise any entity to the stratosphere or bury it in a grave. Good managers can take the best employees, and turn them into useless shells of themselves, or they can take a willing person, and turn them into the best employee. You are the manager of your life, your health, your finances. Are you ready to manage your life into the stratosphere????? Then start today.

NOTES:____

DAY 325

There is a scripture in the Bible (Numbers 30:13 but read the entire chapter to get context) that says if a woman makes a vow to GOD, and her husband hears it, he can void that vow, and GOD will say "Okay, I won't keep her to that vow." BUT, if the husband hears it, and simply doesn't say anything, whatever she said will stand. We have been taught that if you simply turn a blind eye, that's better for you; and if you ignore the issues around you, that's safer for you. Not only has time shown us this is wrong, but this verse tells us that if you don't say anything you agree to it.

What are you agreeing to in your life, that shouldn't be? Are u accepting abuse, disrespect, and lack of promotions? If you don't speak up about how you truly feel about situations, people will continually walk all over you and will tell anyone who will listen that you love it. Don't be silent about your pain. Broadcast it to those involved with doling out the punishment. Initially, they may blame you, but stand on what is right, and refuse to accept that treatment. You will be called a villain, the bad guy, and a host of other names, but you must be able to live with YOURSELF. Never let it be said that "I never knew you felt that way." Remember, if you don't say anything, it's the same thing as saying, "I'm okay with it." You're already NOT okay with it, you just have to let THEM know, you're not okay with it.

NOTES:

DAY 326

When we watch movies dealing with witches and warlocks, we hear them casting spells, and performing rituals in the dark, under the cover of darkness, robes, and candles. They are usually speaking some unknown language and sitting inside a pentagram. We think this is what casting spells look like. In reality, it's actually much, much simpler. It's simply the spoken word. Any negative word is a curse, and often we put curses on ourselves without even noticing or recognizing it. When we sing along to songs or repeat movie quotes about negativity, these things get into the subconscious and are spread throughout the universe. We curse our youth by telling them, they are slow, lazy, stupid, will never amount to anything, or they are just like such and such. It's just as easy to bless yourself, your seed, and others, as it is to curse.

Speak life and positivity over yourself. Find a song that uplifts, builds, and makes you want to do and be better. I used to listen to a song by NAS named "I Know I Can." Every once in a while, I still pull it up and listen to it. It uplifts, empowers, and feeds into me. Bless your children, and tell them how smart they are, how much you love them, and how good they are. When you say that you'll never get it, or learn it, maybe you'll always be broke, or how you can never catch a break, all you're doing is piling more negative curses over your head. Start blocking those curses, by speaking positive blessings over yourself and others. You will begin to open yourself up to a new world, and new opportunities.

NOTES:

DAY 327

A budget isn't scary.... the lack of one is. A budget is simply telling yourself what to do, and when to do it instead of waiting for something to happen to you, and reacting to it, and more than likely NOT being to handle what comes your way. A budget isn't just for finances; you can budget your time, how much time you want to spend in certain places, doing certain things. You can budget your sleep, exercise, extracurricular activities, reading, learning, and time to start a business.... you can budget almost anything. You're only telling yourself what you want to put where. If it's a financial budget you need to start with every bill you have, then go through your accounts for the last 3 months, and see where you're spending your money, see where you cannot spend as much, then open up separate accounts for your expenses that you can send money to out of every check. Mortgage acct, savings acct, car note, utilities, insurance, savings, emergency fund, etc.... whatever you need an account for. And if you have more going out than coming in, focus on one bill to pay off at a time, work overtime, get a 2nd job, and sacrifice until you can get to a manageable place.

It's difficult to get more if you can't handle what you have now. When you budget your time, you'll find you can do far more in a day, when you're not wasting time on your phone, in front of the TV, or any number of other things that waste time. The better your budget, the more you'll find you can acquire. A junky room has little space, but if things are neatly put away, you'll have more space than you thought.

NOTES:____

DAY 328

You will find what it is you're looking for, and you will change things that are anywhere close to your thought process to match your beliefs. If you believe your spouse is cheating, you will find things that align with your beliefs. Every message, every call, every minute out of step, is a sign of infidelity. Take a minute to Look around your current area and find anything that is blue. Now don't look around anymore and tell me how many black items you saw. I'll bet you can't answer that. It's because you were looking for the blue. When you're looking for something, that's what you focus on, and you usually block most other things out. Learn to pull back and be more objective. Broaden your horizons and don't focus only on the thing that you want, but more possibilities. Sometimes you bring a thing into reality by focusing so intently on it.

NOTES:

DAY 329

If all you ever focus on is the destination.... the final goal... you'll miss the journey it takes to get to the goal. On a road trip, we all want to make it to where we're going, but taking in the scenery along the way is breathtaking at times. Imagine the pristine freshly fallen snow over the valley and trees, the warm autumn colors as the seasons change, the plush green growth of summer bustling with life. You may even decide to come back and visit someplace during your journey.

Life is exactly like that car ride; about the lessons you learn and pass along on the way to your ultimate goal. It's not simply about reaching your ultimate goals, but who you've helped and pushed towards their goals along the way, those whose eyes have been opened to a new reality because you helped get them there. Even the places you'd like to go back and revisit sometime later. Sit back and smell the roses every once in a while and make a new friend or two. A ride with good companions, and laughter, no matter how long, is always half the trip of one by yourself.

NOTES:____

DAY 330

Sometimes it's difficult to track your own gains. If all you do is look for the mile markers or the big gains, you can be sorely disappointed. If your goal is to save $1000, and you aren't satisfied until you hit it, then you'll miss the fact that although you aren't there, and an unexpected bill took $350, you actually had the $350 saved to pay the bill. You'll miss the fact that the $400 you have in there, is more money than you've had saved in 1, 2, 5, years, or EVER. The large $1000 goal can be broken down into small incremental goals that you can track better. Keep track of the smaller wins in your life. Every large gain was built with several smaller gains. The better you get at tracking your smaller increments and noticing smaller wins, the better you'll be at focusing on the larger wins. Even though they are harder to see, the smaller gains are the most pivotal, and crucial. Focus in on the small goals and the larger ones will fall into place automatically.

NOTES:

DAY 331

The court jester was one of the most pivotal roles in history. Often thought of as nothing more than a fool and a side note, the jester saved more lives than can be counted. The jester was the modern-day stand-up comic, but his purpose wasn't to get a chuckle from a crowded bar or brothel.... instead, he had a very particular audience. His audience was mainly the king, and royalty. Laughter would hopefully put the king in a good mood, and when he was in a good mood, his sentence would hopefully be lightened. If the jester didn't do a very good job that day, not only could a person or a group of people lose their lives, but the jester himself was in danger of death.

Keep the mood around yourself as light as possible and surround yourself with Joy and laughter. When you're in a better mindset, there can be far less collateral damage. Keep your moods light, as much as possible, and stay away from those whose nature is just one of fear, hate, anger, destruction, or anything negative; they only bring even more destruction with them, whether they do it intentionally or not.

NOTES:

DAY 332

When people think of the worst thing against doing right, most will say "to do wrong.," It makes perfect sense. But in actuality, the worst things against right are good and better. Many people do a "good job" at things, but it's not the "right" thing to do. When you were young, and your parents told you to clean the kitchen and you cleaned the living room to the best of your ability, you did a very good job, but you didn't do the right job. When you're on the job site, and your boss gives you a task to write a synopsis of the meeting, double-spaced college rule, done in a certain timeframe, and you give it to them word for word, embodying all the sentiment of every individual, but it's single-spaced and late. You've done a good job, but again.... not the right job. Another thing that jeopardizes right is "better."

Comparing ourselves to others, and doing "better" than someone else, can cause a lot of loss. If you abuse your spouse, but in their last relationship, they were abused AND their partner didn't pay bills, you may think to yourself, *They should really love me;*" but in all actuality, you still aren't doing the "right" job. Comparing ourselves to others' actions, and not doing fully what we know to be right, continually skew and blur the path, not only for ourselves, but for others coming behind us as well. Keep "right" in the forefront of your minds, and push, "good," and "better" further back.

NOTES:

DAY 333

Everyone is raised differently. Even those raised in the same house by the same parents are raised differently because every single person is different; and everyone has different temperaments, different attitudes, and different frustration levels. No matter how you may receive, or accept things, understand that many things people do are acts of love, and not torture, or an attack. If I am pushing you to be a better you, it's out of love. I see you have more potential; I know some of the pitfalls on your journey, and I'm trying to help you avoid them.

Those who push you hardest, usually do so out of love. Don't take it as an attack, look at it from a different viewpoint, and allow yourself to be taught, even if it's not what you are used to. Sometimes people are harsher, or more abrasive than you'd like, or are used to; but get past HOW they are speaking and listen to WHAT they are speaking, WHAT it is they are truly trying to convey, and the point they are trying to get across to you. In many cases, people are only trying to make you better, the best they know how.

NOTES:____

DAY 334

Sometimes you have to give them what they're asking for. We usually try to look out for people's best interests, and many times that requires making tough calls. We know that nobody likes making the tough calls, and even fewer people like having to live through the tough calls. Even though nobody likes them, the tough calls still have to be made. Often the very people you are trying to help grow and protect are the ones who will fight you the hardest. You may tell them and show them that you're not giving them all the money they are owed because you're saving it for them in the future; or when you scold them for a mistake; or when you don't purchase the exact thing they are looking for because you KNOW it's going to cause problems in the very near future. When these things happen, and you've explained your viewpoint, people will still kick and scream, and absolutely demand what it is they want. And at this point.... let them have what they're looking for. If they won't listen, then let life teach them.

No matter how good your intentions are, sometimes people have to learn lessons the hard way. Give them what they're asking for, and allow them to see what you were trying to warn them against; but if you truly want them to learn the lesson, and not make the mistake again, don't give in when reality slaps them in the face and they want your help getting out of the hole they've put themselves in. When they've gone through, AND figured a way out on their own, then they will have a greater appreciation for your words.

NOTES:

DAY 335

Everyone, including ourselves, is not always in a place to receive what is being offered. Whether it be a child, a coworker, a friend, or a loved one, everyone is not fertile ground for what is being given to them. We must understand that it is not our job to make anyone "listen" to us, or "make" anyone actually "do" anything. It is our job to get the information to them, and that is it. A quote from Malcolm X "We can't be quick to condemn someone for not doing what we do, or believing what we believe, because there was a time when you were given the same information, and didn't believe, or do anything with it." It takes time, but we must learn to pass on whatever information we believe is vital, allow them to process it in their way, and their time, and then, let go, and move on.

On a farm, under the best conditions, where the land is fertile and has been tilled properly, and seeds are planted and harvested at the optimal time, every seed still will not grow; and even more so, every one that does grow will not give a good harvest. Some are simply good for putting back into the earth and fertilizing for the next season. Everything you give to others won't take hold, they may be planted in non-fertile ground, or maybe they aren't being properly watered, or given enough sunlight. Stop allowing anyone else's inefficiencies to trouble YOUR life. Their ability to not listen, should not cause you to lose any sleep.

NOTES:____

DAY 336

When you allow the small problems in your life to persist without working on them, they become far greater than you could have imagined. A small leak in your roof unchecked can lead to the loss of the entire house if left unchecked long enough. 1 drop a minute, turns to 2 drops a minute, then 4 drops a minute, and soon you will have a steady stream, followed by mold and rot, which can destroy the base of the house.

Don't let the small problems in your life fester and turn into even larger ones, which can damage, every area of your life. Once you find a problem, do everything that you can to attack it, and get it out of your life. A little blood pressure unchecked long enough turns into a stroke, and a little debt turns into sickness, foreclosure, and bankruptcy. A little cholesterol unchecked turns into a heart attack. Little problems unchecked, lead to major problems that have the potential for catastrophic endings. Don't stick your head in the sand like an ostrich because the wolf will still attack. Fix the problems the best you can when you find them, because an ounce of prevention, is worth a pound of cure.

NOTES:

DAY 337

1 Samuel 25 shows the importance of not only having the right spouse, but overall, just the right people around you and in your circle. David met some herdsmen, took care of them, looked out for them, and helped keep them safe in their time together; when they left, and made their way back home, David sent his servants to their master and asked if the master could feed his men, he told the master how well he and his men were to the herdsmen, and the master said no. When David heard this, he got his men together, ready to go to war and kill EVERY man in the master's house. One of the herdsmen knew his master, was a hard-headed stubborn mule and decided to talk to the master's wife and let her know how well they were treated.

It was Jewish law that you took care of your Jewish brethren, ESPECIALLY if you had extra to spare AND your people were already taken care of. The master's wife IMMEDIATELY gathered food, and wine, didn't tell her husband anything, and sent her servants out to take the food to David and his men. The wife followed behind them, and when they met David he told her it was a good thing she did that, because he, and the 400 men with him, were coming to destroy that house. This is the value of not only a good spouse but good, smart, wise, people around you. Those closest to you can uplift you or destroy you. Keep your circle tight and filled with those who have proven themselves to make good, and wise decisions. Otherwise, they just may be leading you to a path of certain destruction.

NOTES:____

DAY 338

We have to be careful of the words that we speak. All words have meanings and definitions. One of the popular words of the day is narcissist. Most believe this is a negative word, making someone seem like a villain, but have you ever actually looked the word up, and broken it down? Narcissism definition: thinking very highly of oneself, needing admiration, believing others are inferior, and lacking empathy for others. If we break down admiration, it simply means respect and warm approval. So, so far, a narcissist is someone who thinks highly of themselves, who needs respect and warm approval, believes others are inferior, and lacks empathy.

Now, no matter what you believe, some people are higher than others in life. You don't give the same reverence to a king, that you do to a crackhead. Those who have shown and proven their worth are put on a higher pedestal. If I've sacrificed, put in the extra hours, struggled, taken the hard road, showed up early, stayed late, missed the parties to hone myself and my craft, studied, read books, paid for seminars, taken classes, then yes, I feel as though I'm higher than the person who sits around on their phone all day, who refuses to do any extra, and waits for something to be handed to them. And lack of empathy is the lack to sense others' emotions or imagine what someone else may be feeling. To a degree, most of us fit there, because unless you've been through the same exact situation, it's very difficult to understand how a person feels or understand their mindset. The point is, after reading the definition, and actually looking up the words, a narcissist probably takes on a little different meaning than what you thought it was yesterday. Start looking up the words you're using, and you'll find many of them don't even line up, with the intent you're trying to convey. Be careful of what you say, the wrong words, meanings, or translations, can start wars.

NOTES:____

DAY 339

In order to move forward, in order to progress, you have to leave where you are. You can't do greater things by staying in the same spot. Whether you take the stairs the elevator, or the window-washing scaffold, if you try to straddle floors, you're stuck in limbo. The next level in your life requires you to let go of some things, some people, and some places. It requires you to add some things to your repertoire.... certain skills, different abilities, and traits. You have to begin to set yourself apart. The people you're hanging around obviously aren't getting you where you want to be, and the places you spend your time, haven't produced the fruit you're looking for, but you stay in the same spot, with the same people, and the same thought processes, looking for different outcomes. Begin to set yourself apart from your present space if you want more. Begin to look for more people who are where you want to be. If you believe there is a physical place you need to be, go there, and just hang around, something is bound to pop up sooner or later. There's an old saying, "Hang around the barbershop long enough, and you're bound to get a haircut sooner or later."

What things are you shooting for? What things are you willing to let go of? What things will have to be pried from your grip? The key to your better future is in the daily habits you are avoiding, like studying, reading, exercise, better meals, daily prayer, the budget, or the meetings. It's a scary step, but you have to let go of your comfort zone to reach your goals. Get out of that comfort zone, switch things up, change your routine, and stick to it. What three things can you do tomorrow, that can put you on the path to your goals? Write them down, then start tomorrow; if at all possible, start TODAY, and make a promise to yourself to keep it up.

NOTES:____

DAY 340

Your environment plays a very large role in how your life ultimately turns out. Your environment can be the epicenter and catalyst of change in your life, or it can be the fire extinguisher that doused your flames. If I take an apple seed, it doesn't matter where I plant it, when it grows, it's going to be an apple tree. If it's planted in a rainforest, or a desert, in my backyard, or in the king's castle, it's still an apple tree. But the environment depends on how these different seeds turn out. In the desert, the seed is sure to be dead the second it hits the sand. There's no dirt, no nutrition in the sand, too little water, and temperatures are too high.

One would think that in the rain forest, around all of the fullness, and bustling with life, an apple tree could thrive. On the contrary, the tree can grow, but due to high rains during pollinating months, it's difficult for it to produce any fruit. In my backyard, it would probably begin to grow, and then I'd forget it was there and cut it down every other week when I cut the grass, thinking it was a weed. In the king's garden, you're protected by knowledgeable people, who know exactly what you need, how much of it you need, and when you need it.

What environments do you keep yourself in? Are you keeping yourself in a desert, around people who don't even give you a chance to begin to sprout; are you in an area where you're doing good enough to grow, but can't bear any fruit, like a job that's just good enough to pay bills, but with no savings or emergency funds, no investing, or trips. Or you could be in someone's backyard, who runs you over every time you begin to grow. Maybe intentionally, because they are scared you will outgrow them, and cast your shadow over them; or unknowingly, they just don't know that you can give them shade on a warm day and feed them if you're taken care of properly. Take the time to find the right place to plant yourself. Part of life is planting yourself in the wrong areas, learning to pull your roots up, and replanting yourself. It's all part of the process. Where you are planted is completely up to you. You have the ability to stay or go, in almost any situation.

NOTES:____

DAY 341

There are many things in life that we all want, but sometimes because of our circumstances and situations, we may not be able to. If your goal is to build a house, there are a lot of areas to be covered before you start building. Money needs to be saved, plans need to be drawn up, and approved by the local government, and land needs to be researched, surveyed, and purchased. A contractor would probably be next, then material purchased.... all before the first shovel goes into the ground. And if you've never done this, or are doing it on your own, this can be a daunting time-consuming process.

King David wanted to build a house for GOD to dwell in, but he couldn't because all of his time was spent at war with other countries. What he did do though, was acquire all the land needed, all the funds, the right relationships, and brought peace. Then when the kingdom was turned over to his son Solomon, he had peace to think, plan, and build; he had all the money he needed; and he had the right relationships with the producers and distributors of the material needed. The beginnings and foundations of a thing are far more than we can imagine, and maybe that's all we have time for. You may be getting things ready for those coming up behind you. Maybe your job is to lay the groundwork so that others can build the house. Life is a relay race, and we all should be sprinting to hand off to the next in line.

NOTES:____

DAY 342

Sometimes it's not worth getting on the ground. When I was younger, I HAD to do many things myself; I simply couldn't afford to pay to take it someplace, especially when it came to my car. I had to change spares, plug small air leaks, change the oil, and any other thing I could possibly do. We didn't have YouTube and videos, so I had to go buy a Chilton manual for my vehicles from the auto parts store, read that, and go from there, for every repair needed. One day I came across some older gentlemen who paid to get their oil change done. I said, "You can do that yourself for half the price," and they all said almost in sync "Yea, we can, but it just isn't worth getting down on that ground anymore." Now that I'm older, I get it.

Although I know how to do certain things, it's just not worth me getting on the ground anymore. Your life is the same way. Certain things shouldn't bother you the way they used to, you should have grown and evolved beyond some things. Some people you shouldn't be running behind because they just aren't worth getting on the ground and getting dirty for. As you mature and begin gaining more "emotional funds" you shouldn't still be acting and operating on the same scale you were 3 5, or 10 years ago. The wiser you get, the more you learn that some things, and some people really just aren't worth the dirt, energy, and effort of getting down on that ground with them.

NOTES:____

DAY 343

We are all out here trying to make a living. We are doing the best we can to support and build ourselves and our families, but we are going about it backward. We go to work to get money to pay our bills and do the things we want to do. We are working for money when the money should be working for us. We should be teaching our children about businesses, finances, and investing. If we put our energy into these investment avenues, they can bring back more money, without much work, if it's done properly. We are told that it's crazy to "bet on yourself" for a chance at a better life. Then, you stay in the corporate world, where you will work for 50 years so that you can retire and live for 10 years before you die.

Money should be working for us, inside of investment vehicles. Retirement accounts, insurance policies, businesses, lending, etc. In the Bible Matthew 25th chapter, (the talent parable), Jesus told the two who traded and got more, that they were good and faithful, but he called the servant who buried the talent and gave it back to him, wicked and slothful. He even told his servant, "You could have at least put it in the bank and given me some interest. The servant allowed his fear to lead to his decision. He was fearful and didn't want to take any chances with his master's money, and for that, he was labeled wicked; and the little money he did have was taken and given to someone doing better than him. If you allow fear to run your life, you have a great chance of survival (because that's the purpose of fear, to let you know of danger), but you will not thrive. I am tired of simply surviving, and I am ready to thrive. Step forward despite the fear, better educate yourself to remove some of those small stumbling blocks, and begin your journey to financial freedom. YOU can be the catalyst for your bloodline. "If I don't come from money, money MUST come from me" You have everything to gain.

NOTES:____

DAY 344

Today is the day you should start whatever it is you want to do. If you're waiting on just the right time, or for the stars to align, you'll be waiting an extremely long time. Very rarely do things just so happen to line up in your favor. People MAKE their own "luck." The harder you work, the more you educate yourself, the luckier you seem to get. The more work you put in, the better skilled you become, the more you educate yourself, the more you begin to see the things that always eluded you, the more the gaps in the system are shown to you, and the more you know the rules, about what can and cannot be done. Take a step today towards your goals and watch how things begin to align. The more you walk towards your goals, the clearer your path will become.

Start today, start with what you have. If all you've ever been taught to do was save, then dig through your couch cushions, and that $0.17 that you find.... Put it in a savings account. The pennies you find, the ones people throw away, collect them and put them in your account. Start putting $5 per check in the account; if you can't afford that, do $1, but start somewhere, and start today. How badly do you really want it? Are you willing to cut out a meal or two a week, and save that? Will you get rid of a habit, like smoking, drinking, shopping, or any other number of vices???? And if you heard that and thought "Well, I've got to enjoy myself," you may not be ready, because enjoying yourself, is what most likely got you to where you are now. Start making the changes you need in your life today and stop waiting for a perfect tomorrow that may never come.

NOTES:____

DAY 345

Rich is NOT a dollar amount, rich is a state of being, it's a mental place of happiness. One definition of rich is having more than one needs. You may look at your current situation and see yourself struggling…. mentally, physically, emotionally, and financially, but it's all based on how you gauge your situation, and what you compare yourself to. If you stop spending as much, stop shopping, stop giving out your emotional dollars, and start saving your mental bucks, you'll find you have far more than you NEED. Can you send that new car back, can you downsize your living situation, can you get a roommate, how about, not dealing with those who upset, frustrate, and bring you down emotionally???? You're giving away all of your physical dollars to make others rich, while you struggle. You're spending your emotional coins making others happy, while you cry yourself to sleep because nobody is there for you.

Begin to learn how to cut back all of your spending. Lifting someone's spirits may be too expensive for you today, save those coins to build your emotional account. It may take a little time, but you can't give out that which you do not have. You don't need a million dollars to be rich, you simply need to open your eyes and change your mindset to see just how rich you are.

NOTES:____

DAY 346

Every person you come across isn't meant to be in your life for the entirety of your life. Some people are put there for a season, some for a life span, and some for a brief moment in time. It's up to us to figure out what timeframe they are here for. There are times when people are put in your life for one particular purpose, and that's it. We run into problems when we try to keep people past their expiration dates. It's like food, the further past the date it goes, the worse the food spoils; and if you leave it long enough, it can begin to rot other things close to it. If you find things falling apart around someone or something, it may be time to step back for a while and see if things change. If they do, maybe that was a major problem. Take the time to evaluate the people, and things in your life, and see if anything has "spoiled," or is no longer able to feed or serve you.

NOTES:

DAY 347

If you continue to do the things you know need to be done, you will continually make progress. Sometimes that progress isn't seen by everyone, all at one time. Some may see a little here, some may see a little there, and some may not see much progress at all. There may even be times when you don't see the progress yourself; but because of the goals you have, the vision you've seen, and the plan you've written down and followed, you know you're on the right path.

A close friend had been in the gym consistently for 2 years, had only lost a few pounds over the entirety of time, and didn't see his body changing, the way he thought it should have from working out consistently for that long. One day he was at work, lifting heavy boxes, and he was in sort of a funnel. He would pick a box up, and stack it, and somehow four more people ended up behind him, picking up boxes, and passing them to him to stack on the shelf. So, he would pick up his box, stack it, then grab one from each person and stack theirs. By the time they'd finished, everyone was winded, and tired except my friend; he wasn't tired, sweating, or even breathing heavily. Although he couldn't tell the difference, his body could when it came down to crunch time. He'd put the work in, and this one task showed him just how well it'd been working. We also must take notes of our small wins. After a brief conversation, I came to find out he hasn't pulled a muscle in 2 years, has no more small aches and pains, sleeps better, is off his CPAP machine, his skin and nails are clear, AND his blood pressure is down. Those two years were simply his foundation being built. The next two years he will be where he needs to be. Keep doing, keep pushing, your time is coming, and you're just building your foundation.

NOTES:____________________________________

DAY 348

Surround yourself with such solid people, that even if you are the leader or boss, and you are wrong, everyone has the conviction to stand firmly against you. Nobody in history built anything by themselves; there was always a team of people doing a myriad of jobs, and even though one may have not been an expert in your given field, there were enough conversations, meetings, and knowledge, to know when you weren't doing what you were supposed to be doing. When you keep valiant, strong, dependable, smart, capable people around you, not only can you lean on them, and rely on them to accomplish tasks, but they can also keep YOU in line. In a group, we are a system of checks, and balances against each other, to accomplish our common goal (whatever that may be).

When anyone in the group isn't pulling their weight, or going off script, there should be no problem with the other members "pulling on their coattails" and getting them back in line. You surround yourself with quality people for a purpose, a reason, and that is to make sure you can spot when I'm off and help to get me back on track. Those you keep around you are even more important than yourself because they are the ones who protect you, who look out for you, who cover you, and who do all the things that you can't do. Make sure those in your inner circles aren't just there for a good time but are there to help build, strengthen, and produce for the long haul. Be able to disagree, and still be able to come back together to finish the goal.

NOTES:____

DAY 349

The people you choose to listen to can be a valuable roadmap to your success, or they can be a weight around your neck dragging you down into oblivion. Whomever it is you're listening to make sure the roadmap they are trying to get you to follow is 1) Where you want to eventually end up, there's nothing worse than following something/someone, only to find out that you're nowhere near where you thought you'd be. 2) Make sure their road map has a good starting point from where you are. Even if we are headed to the same destination of New York, but I'm starting in Miami, and you're starting in California, my map and directions are still no good to you.

Follow those who can give you direction and leadership based on YOUR specific needs, and situations. Simply following someone else's direction blindly, just because they "made it" can lead to a disastrous ending. You may be thinking, that because you grew up around them, they came from where you came from; but their directions started in their parents' basement, rent-free, with no children, and no bills, and they were taught financial literacy. Their parents died and left them an insurance policy, and a paid-off house....none of which applied to you. So, if you are taking their advice, and trying to do what they did, you'll be trying to ice skate uphill.

Do your research and look into people's backgrounds before listening to them, ask questions, and see if what you want, and where they're trying to lead you coincide. A good mentor is a cheat code to life, and a bad one will pave the road to destruction for you. The good thing is that no matter how far you get off track, you can always readjust, and get back on course. You'll be a bit wiser for your next encounter; and maybe one day, YOU can be a mentor to someone.

NOTES:____

____

____

____

____

DAY 350

We all have to learn to accept people for who they are. Our problems come into effect when we want to turn these people who are hammers into wrenches. People are who they are; and instead of forcing people to be who we want them to be, let them be who they truly are, but learn to keep them in certain areas of your life. When you need a certain wrench, you don't go to the garage, grab a hammer, try to forge it, and mold it into a wrench, then throw it on the ground, curse it, and scold it for not being a wrench. You simply grab the wrench off the shelf.

Don't use people in your life out of sorts, we are only upsetting ourselves; go find the person/people who fit the job you're looking for. Using that hammer to do the job of the wrench will only deform the hammer, and almost assuredly break whatever it is you're trying to fix. Compartmentalize all those around you. Don't take the party friend, to business meetings and get mad when the deals fall through. Don't expect the friend who you know is selfish, to be the giving friend, and the one who is going to put your needs first. Accept people for who they are, and not who you want them to be. When you learn to do that, you can remove so much anger, hostility, and hurt from your life.

NOTES:

DAY 351

Progress is a fickle thing. We are made to believe that progress is a straight never-ending line forward, or upward. This is so untrue. Progress is forever trying, never giving up. In order to progress you may lose 5 lbs. today and gain 2 tomorrow, but as long as you're still working, you're OK. Progress is filled with setbacks (also known as learning experiences). Progress looks like getting lost on the journey, but you also keep that in mind, because it will come in handy for another journey; and you can remember that you've been here before, so you already know the way. Progress looks like going broke, but figuring out other ways to sustain yourself, and finding out who's truly there to support you. If I go to cross the street and step back on the curb to prevent being hit by a bus, that's progress. Sometimes steps back, rest periods, and recovery times will prevent future damage, which is far better than just trudging forward. Progress comes in so many ways, and forms, that it's almost impossible to track them all. Just don't.... give....up.

NOTES:

DAY 352

When fathers stand up and draw a line in the sand to protect their families, we are demonized, ridiculed, and pushed out of the picture, because we tell people "No." NO, you can't go there, NO you can't go with them, NO you can't do that, NO you can't have that. When we discipline our children, we are made to look like devils, because we are trying to straighten out a flaw we see in them, that can be very detrimental to their futures. People think because the mothers say "yes" and give the children what they want, that they love the children more, but I feel as though that means you love them less. You're not guiding, protecting, or properly nurturing, instead, you're leading them to their impending doom.

To take over a city, you can go to war, have massive bloodshed on both sides, and POSSIBLY, win, OR you can find a way to get rid of their men, their warriors, and all you have to do is walk through the front gate. They are slowly but surely getting the real men out of society. They are making anyone with a backbone the bad guys. If you stand up for what you believe, and it goes against societal norms, you'll be ostracized. Allow the fathers to guide, love, and nurture their children. Yes, it's tough, yes, it's hard, and yes, there will be many nights where you will want to jump in and stop everything; but WE are building a better, stronger, healthier generation for a better future. Very few people honor and protect their fathers, very few people look at the protectors and ask, "What do YOU need?" or "How can we make YOUR job easier?" But we continue to do the things that MUST be done. Being a real father, a real man, is a lonely life for many of us, but we will continue to fight, and protect until our hearts stop beating, and we draw our final breaths. If you have a father in your life, or even a prominent male figure who has taken that role, appreciate them, check on them, and allow them to lead and protect you and yours properly.

NOTES:____

DAY 353

YOU are the problem in your relationship. Most of us have never been actually taught what love is, or how to love. We pick up what we can, from past relationships, what we've seen or heard in movies, TV, music, and from other friends, and try to piece things together the best we can. Before we can point the finger at others for what they are or are not doing, we've got to learn to focus on ourselves. Self-improvement, self-enlightenment, self-progress, and self-love. Some of us don't know how to love ourselves but expect someone else to give us what we cannot even give ourselves. The more self-growth you focus on, the more you'll learn what it is that YOU need, and the more you learn what it is you need, the better you will be able to navigate through life and relationships.

The more you learn about life and self, the more you begin to notice different avenues, and choices that you'd never seen or noticed before. Things won't affect you as much as they used to, and there are so many things that you will be able to simply walk away from. One thing I heard that stuck with me during my self-building process was "Not my monkeys, not my show." It is a simple saying that means, "That has absolutely nothing to do with me, and the outcome doesn't affect me in any way possible, so I'm going to mind the business that pays me and leave them to their own business." This has saved me so much frustration, and so many headaches, I can't even begin to count. Your problems are just that.... YOUR problems. Learn to build yourself, and work on YOU, so that you can learn to maneuver differently, and make the adjustments you need to keep your peace. You will NEVER get the world to adjust to you, but you can make adjustments to the world.

Stop complaining about the rocks being thrown at you and learn to duck and dodge; and as you begin to do more self-work, you will learn to pick up the very rocks that are thrown at you, meant to destroy you, and build a fortress from them to protect yourself.

NOTES:____

____

DAY 354

Last week I had a slow leak in my tire, so I went to the tire shop to get it fixed. I could have done it myself, but.... just didn't feel like taking the tire off. When I pulled up, he asked if I had a nail, and I said, "I don't know, I guess." Then he had me turn my wheel and slowly roll back, and sure enough it was a nail. He grabs a pair of pliers, pulls the screw out, plugs the tire, and fills it with air. It took all of 3 minutes and $25. All I'd ever seen was taking the tire off to put a plug in it. It never crossed my mind to plug a tire while it was still on the car, because I'd never seen it. There are so many simple and basic things that could make our lives easier, better, richer, and fuller.... if we just opened ourselves to newer possibilities and opportunities. Put yourself around new people, see what they have to offer, go to different places, change your routines, and see what happens.

We don't know, or understand some of the simplest things, all because we've never been exposed to them. Expose your children and grandchildren to as many things as possible, not just the things you did as a child. Who knows where their young minds may take those opportunities, or what they may turn them into? Try some things you've said no to before and listen to someone who you normally don't listen to. (be wise about this one, don't listen to an idiot). You never know where the road of change may lead you, open yourself up.

NOTES:____

DAY 355

Hurt people hurt people. While this statement is true, it's very strange to me that only the negative statement rings true, and gets notoriety, because while hurt people are hurting people, loved people are loving people, fixed people are fixing people, and people who've been cared for are caring for others, and helped people are helping others. If you look for more positivity in the world, I promise you'll find it, you just can't believe all of the negativity that's being pushed on you. And if you can't seem to find any peace, joy, happiness, or laughter in the world, then make your own, and pass it along to someone else. Be the love you want to see in the world today. Love the hurt out of yourself.

NOTES:

DAY 356

Many people around the world pray to whatever God it is that they see fit. I wholeheartedly believe in prayer....to a point. Prayer is simply having a conversation with GOD, a back and forth about things, kind of like talking to your parents. You won't always get what you want, but the conversation opens up avenues and possibilities that may have never been there without the prayer. Even with this conversation with GOD, you're still not going to see the results you need if you don't do something. Even in the Bible, James 2:17 says, if you have faith, and don't do anything about your situation, it's pointless (paraphrasing of course). In Nehemiah 4:9, Nehemiah prayed to GOD, that his enemies would not harm him and his people. But he didn't stop there, he set a watch amongst the people, with shields and weapons to look for their enemies' attack, he made sure all the workers worked, with a weapon on them at all times, in case of attack.

Prayer isn't enough, SOMETHING has to be put into action. GOD can make a man out of dirt, but he needs the dirt, he can make a tree that reaches to the heavens, but he needs the seed. You have to give GOD something to work with. My knees hurt me my entire life, and if I ever ran, played basketball, or overtaxed them too badly, they'd hurt for an entire week. I prayed to GOD to take my pain away....and he never did until I came across a workout program directed at knee pain. I've been following the program for about a year and a half now, and when I awake, there's no pain; walking up and down stairs, there's no pain, and I've recently tested out running on the treadmill.... no....pain.

GOD will give you the tools necessary to solve most problems, and you have to work them to the best of your ability. It's hardly ever easy, but it's well worth the time and energy you put in. GOD won't give you the million dollars you ask for, but He will give you a job, and people to tell you how to properly save, manage, and invest your funds… The action behind your prayer is like steroids to a bodybuilder, watch how you'll begin to flourish.

NOTES:____

DAY 357

It's hard to move to the next city, almost impossible, if you keep packing your things, getting on the road, then turning around, and going back to the old home every time there's traffic, or you think you're going to run out of gas, or you see some inconveniences on the trip. I'm sure many people would read this and say to themselves "Well duh, of course, it is." But we all do this every day of our lives. We see where it is we want to go, and as soon as we get started, some small thing turns us around, and we are back at square one. We start going to the gym, and our body hurts, so we stop; it's too crowded, so we don't go; we aren't seeing the results we want to see, so we turn back around; it's harder than we thought; we aren't getting the support we thought we'd have; and so on, and so forth.

We have to stop turning around on our journey and push through the seemingly tough times. The better we plan, the better chance we have of reaching our goals. An emergency is only an emergency because we haven't properly planned for it. Your money's short, because you haven't saved enough, so start saving more. You haven't lost weight because your diet and exercise haven't been planned out. It takes such a long time to get to your destination, because you just started driving, and didn't plan out the route. Proper planning prevents piss-poor performances. If we plan our life journey better, we'd have far fewer reasons to turn back on our goals, and we'd be better prepared for the mishaps of life. Even if you're in an unplanned event now, and you're ready to turn back, don't give up, because you'll only have to start again. Grit your teeth and will yourself to your goals. Stop starting back at square 1.

NOTES:______________________________

DAY 358

I've been asked and have had several conversations about being remarried. My answer is always the same, "Yes, I would get married again. I don't have a problem with marriage, I was just married to the wrong one." But this time I wouldn't marry for love, that's on the back burner for me. As I begin to come into my own, I have more goals, dreams, aspirations, and standards for my future, and for those behind me. So now, my main criteria for marriage are collaboration, trust, unity, and honesty. Can you help me achieve the goals I have planned, can you add to those plans, or show me where I may be mistaken? Can we build a strong foundation together?

Love is insignificant in my book, because love comes and goes, and feelings will dwindle; but our goals, and dreams, will constantly be there, and they can be consistently worked on, no matter how you feel. Whether I love you or not, that light bill still needs to get paid, the mortgage is still due, the business paperwork still needs processing, and the investments still need to be funded. Can you still properly operate when you're upset, fallen out of love, not talking to me??? To me, THESE are the things that marriage requires, not butterflies, flowers, and sweet talking. Can you process when we are in the mud, muck, and mire? Can you persevere when your feelings have long been gone??? That's a marriage in my book; feelings aren't even in the same league when it comes to cooperation.

NOTES:____

DAY 359

I was watching a video of a woman explaining what it is that she looks for in a man. It doesn't matter what her specific list was, what matters is that she actually started with a list. So many people don't have a list of things they want out of ANY part of their lives. Their spouse, job, children, body.... nothing. Countless studies show that the more you write something down, the higher your percentages are of getting said thing. What also caught my attention, was the things she named, were all commendable things that I believe a man should have.... BUT, I began to wonder, if SHE had those same qualities that she was looking for. This is not sexist; it goes BOTH ways. Can you supply what you require? Some will say "Why do I need to invest if my partner invests?" How can you help me, support me, and help build our legacy if you don't know about investing? If I want to make moves, and you're fighting against me, because you think you're supposed to buy stocks when the price is high and sell everything when the markets crash, then how can we move forward? It's difficult to want a healthy spouse if you don't know anything about health, what meals to cook, what portions to eat, etc.

You can't just WANT things in life and expect things to happen for you, because you will get exactly what you ask for, then blow it, because you aren't what you were asking for, and you didn't know how to maintain it. If I put you in a clean house, and you're a nasty person, you will destroy that house. The same rings true when you ask for things that you can't handle. You'll ruin that man, woman, job, house, child.... just about anything you touch. At a minimum, you have to be the person you want from others.

NOTES:______________________________

DAY 360

At some point, you have to stop asking people why they are doing things, and just realize WHAT they are doing, and how they are operating in your life. It doesn't matter how someone was raised, what trauma they went through, or how bad they've had life. If they can't treat you how you see fit, it's time to reevaluate your relationship. If you have to tell someone who says they are broke to stop spending, or to work overtime when it's available, don't waste your time. We are adults, and people are making conscious decisions to either do or not do the things they do. It's who they are, it's what they do, and it is up to YOU to decide whether or not you will deal with what they are offering. If you're looking for a vehicle, it doesn't matter WHY there's something wrong with it, just the fact that there is, and you're not going to pay full price for it.

People are the same way, you can take your time trying to figure out why they are broken, what happened, how long it happened, how they've tried to cope, etc., or... you can visit the lot on the very same block. If you've asked, talked, had conversations, and arguments, and the person continues to do the things you're unpleased with, it's definitely time for some deep reflection on your part. People in life treat you how YOU allow them to, and they continue to treat you, how you've taught them to treat you.

NOTES:____

DAY 361

If you are not ready to have a joint bank account and unveil all your secrets and inner thoughts, are you really ready for marriage? When it gets down to brass tacks, you and the person you choose to marry are ONE, you are a union, the heads and tails of a coin. There isn't yours and mine, there's only OURS. If you make more money than your partner, it's all one big pot. It's not 90% mine and 10% yours. You all are a soup, a mixture of things brought together, and the longer you mix together under a little heat and pressure, the better you can turn out. But it takes both of you to be all in.

Hiding things, secrets, and having separate accounts, are all signs that maybe you're not ready for the wedding vows. Can it work...sure it can, but would it be its best? Find the one you can be open with, vulnerable with, share accounts and passwords with, the one with whom there are no secrets, and make sure these actions and feelings are reciprocated.

NOTES:____

DAY 362

You are who you are, and you have what it is that you have to give. Sure, we can all better ourselves, but this is where you are today, and if that isn't accepted by someone, that's OK, keep moving. Everything isn't made for everyone. Who you are today, may not fit the needs or wants of others, but don't let that stop you from being you. You will find the ones who are meant to be in your life. Everyone CANNOT afford a Bentley vehicle, and everyone WILL NOT purchase a Honda. The people who are meant for you will show up. They probably won't come as you think they should, but they are there. The ones who tell you about yourself, don't let you get away with foolishness, and keep you straight and focused are the ones who are sent to help you.

Be you, grow you, build you, and the people and things that are for you will present themselves. You don't have to change who you are to fit into someone else's puzzle, and you don't have to dim your light so others around you can shine brighter. Continue to walk in your essence and chase your dreams. Everyone will not like you, but that's fine because it's not their story. Even Jesus was a villain in someone's story.

NOTES:

DAY 363

We've all been hurt, we are all scarred, and we all have healing to do, but it's HOW we grow, heal, and learn to deal with our traumas that's important. We will consistently get hurt until the day we die…, that's not the question. It's about how we handle that hurt, how we cope with that hurt, and how we teach others to deal with their own hurt. We have a tendency to pass on our horrible coping mechanisms to our children, friends, and even other family members. Not only are we all not the same, but some things we've learned ourselves are just plain wrong. We've got to make conscious efforts to be better people, first of all to ourselves, and secondly, to those around us.

What your parents told you, probably isn't the best way to handle things, but we won't know unless we begin to search ourselves, and other coping mechanisms. Most of us were raised on survival, struggle, pain, divorce, and hardships, and we are trying to figure out how to operate and live on love. When our mindset is stuck in survival mode, it's difficult to operate in love. I'm asking you love questions, and you're giving me survival answers. I was renting a room to a person once, and he asked why I walked around the house with my gun on my hip. I looked at him and said, "You've never had your door kicked in have you?" There was a clear difference in the survival aspect from me that he couldn't understand. Because I've been there, my survival instinct says, protect yourself. He's never been there, so he feels if you lock your door, it's OK. Neither is wrong, just different. But in the wrong household, my suggesting a gun could be deadly to the inhabitants.

When you focus on YOUR personal growth and determination, you set yourself on a completely different trajectory, and everything around you can begin to blossom and grow. Don't focus on what's done to you, focus on how you reacted. When things aren't going your way, don't stand there and fuss, fight, and argue.... remove yourself from the situation and regroup.

NOTES:____

DAY 364

I saw a statement that read "To love means to give someone the power to destroy you and trust that they won't." As I thought about that, it made me think about "HOW" we love individuals. Usually, our love (at least the love I've come by) is built off of the way people make us feel, and/or the things that people do for us. If you think about those you love and WHY you love them, I'd bet 85% of your reasoning falls into one of those 2 categories. But to love in that capacity, you have to know each other deeply; you have to have so many late nights filled with talk… so many situations come up that you can talk through and work out…. and you must have so many experiences together. We must know each other intimately, on a level that's far greater than "what you do for me, or how you make me feel." Are you made of paper or a brick, maybe thin aluminum, or steel, and if steel, are you a thin sheet or a solid block??? What hurts one of these materials, doesn't necessarily hurt the other materials. So, to put that type of trust in someone, you need to ensure that you've given them all pertinent information, on as many aspects of your life as possible and gone over as many areas as you can think of; given them bits and pieces of you, little by little, to see how much they can handle. You have to know the material each of you is made of. If I'm a brick, and you're a sheet of paper, my natural existence will hurt you and tear you apart.

To be truly in love is more than about what you do for me, it's about intertwining and weaving ourselves together, on a spiritual, mental, and emotional level. Feeling our partner's pain, knowing and understanding their thoughts, and emotions. When something happens, your first thought is about your partner and what they would think or say. Love isn't a feeling; love is a state of perpetual action. I love you, not because of what you have done for me, but for the fact that I have opened myself to you; and how I have bared my soul, my vulnerabilities, my fears, and all of my worries, and you have NOT used them against me; you have NOT voided my trust, NOT, swept my legs from underneath me, or betrayed me like Judas, and shared my innermost feelings. Love isn't what you have done FOR me, but more about what you have NOT done TO me.

NOTES:____

____

DAY 365

There's a saying "If you hang around 4 broke people, you'll be the fifth, and if you hang around 4 successful people, you'll be the fifth." Now, absolutely nothing about the world changes, the same opportunities are there, the same chances, everything is the same; the only differences are the things YOU choose to focus on. Everything you need to make your life better is already in front of you, it's just in the choices you choose to make. When you go buy that favorite outfit, you see others already had it; but you didn't notice until you bought yours. You look up a store to purchase something, and it tells you it's on your route to work, so you stop there, and they say they've been there for years; but you never noticed it, because you weren't looking for it.

When you choose to look for success, you will find it. Some success takes changing your circle, some success takes opening your eyes, some success takes educating yourself, but all success depends on changing YOU. Your success is just waiting for you to come find it. It's around every corner and every decision you choose to make. Make better decisions and choose better people to be around. The more you hang around bad-decision people, the more you're going to focus on making horrible decisions. Rise above the clouds.

NOTES:____

DAY 366

Sometimes when I travel home, my family gets together, and we play board games throughout the night. I usually destroy them and take home gold. One evening in particular, they all decided to band together and make a pact. "We will not let you win; no matter what, you're going down tonight." Throughout the game, they kept their word and stuck together, making choices and decisions to make it tougher on me. Then someone got close, where it was possible that they could win. They saw the finish line and made a mad dash for it, and then everyone else began breaking ranks and seeing who could win first. But what they all quickly forgot was.... the goal wasn't to win, but to keep ME from winning. As they all gathered their pieces into their home spots, everyone stopped watching and defending against me, and I ended up winning yet again.

When we get into situations, we all start with the best of intentions, but little things distract us, and we take our eyes off the target just long enough, that when we look back, WE Have moved the target, and we don't notice it. We tell ourselves different things to make it ok, we see the finish line and make a mad dash for the win, but we forget that the goal was never to "win," but to set stuff up for the ones behind us. We took the money today, telling ourselves we would save the next deal for the future when we should be using this deal for that purpose. We'll say, "I know I shouldn't be eating this, but I'll make up for it tomorrow" or "I know they wanted me to do this, but I'll make it up to them later because I really want this thing now." We move the goalposts ourselves, and in the end, we are in a worse position, AND our ultimate goal was never achieved.

Write your goals down so you never forget them, keep people close to you, who can remind you of why you started a thing. Don't get distracted, stay focused, keep pushing. It's not about you winning, it's about completing the task at hand, in this case, it was keeping someone else from winning.

NOTES:____

BONUS DAY 1

Most people are out searching for gold (a good partner to build with) but don't know the first thing about mining (dating). Not many of us have actually been TAUGHT how to date, how to pick a partner, and what conversations need to be had. We ourselves, unless we've looked inward and done some type of actual self-reflection, don't really know what it is that we're looking for in a mate. We often go through life dating, and having sex, and find out what it is that we DON'T want, but it's hard to find out what it is that we DO want. I ask you this.... what are you looking for in a spouse? Think about that and write it down. Most people have rarely thought about it, much less written it down. And many people will give a few basic answers, not realizing how deep they need to actually be digging for that gold. What age range do you want; what height and weight specifics, and what kind of shape do they need to be in; do they need a job, and if so, how much should they make; what about raising children, do you both agree on the number of children, will there be more??? Who does the cooking and cleaning, and at what frequency; how do we split the bills; who carries the insurance; does the man need to fill your car up Sunday before the work week; how often do we have sex? Are we saving for the future, how much comes out of the checks for that, one account, 2, or 3? These are all BASIC questions that anyone looking for a long-term relationship should be asking. There are far more, but I'm sure I've used up all of your attention span with just these few questions.

Begin to do some self-reflection and think deeply about who you want in your lifelong term. And if you're already married, ask these questions. You may be surprised at the answers. Deep conversations, to UNDERSTAND are key. We're not here to argue, but to get a deeper understanding of each other, and for our futures together. Gold isn't just lying on the surface; it's buried in the earth. If you want the nuggets, you have to put them in the work.

NOTES:____

BONUS DAY 2

Everything that a tree needs is inside of itself, in the seeds that it produces; everything that a watermelon needs is inside of itself, in the form of seeds. Everything that YOU need is inside of you, in the form of seeds or gifts that God has given you. Our problem is that we have never been taught how to cultivate, nurture, and grow our own seeds and gifts. I am no expert, I am still working on myself, and learning how to grow my gifts, but what I can tell you is that it takes some self-reflection. You have to look inside yourself, and have serious conversations with yourself, about what you want out of life, what you're willing to give to get to that point, AND what you're willing to sacrifice. I am a firm believer that if you do what you know to do, things will be added along the journey. I don't know anything about farming, but I do know, that if I take a seed, and put it in the ground where it'll get sunlight, and put some water on it, something is coming out of that ground.

We as people work the same way. If I make some changes in my life, SOMETHING will be evident in the near future. If I read more books, or listen to tapes, and put things into action, more changes will happen. People will see the work being done on you, and the changes; and some will come to offer suggestions and help, which will lead to more help and other suggestions.

In my personal life, I began making financial changes such as making a budget, cutting back on spending, sticking to the budget (pretty close anyway lol), trying to figure out other streams of income… and now I'm in a good financial spot. My credit card balances are lower than they've ever been, I'm no longer stressed about bills and due dates, and all of my debt is now manageable. I can't wait until I have no credit card bills and zero debt, but that's for another day. It didn't happen overnight, but there were seeds of financial abundance in me that I just had to begin to cultivate and grow. Figure out what seeds you want to grow inside if you.

NOTES:____

____

____

BONUS DAY 3

We often get mad at people for saying one thing, and then doing what we deem as another thing. People tell us they love us, and act in a completely different way than what we expected, or they tell you how much drive, and passion they have, then you see them lying around most of the time. It's not that they don't have drive, or love you, or whatever you may see as contradicting to your beliefs, it may simply be.... you haven't talked to them and asked them what they see as drive, what love means to them, or what passion is in their book. You see love differently than I see love, you see drive, and passion differently than I do.

My sisters and I were all raised in the same house, by the same parents, and went to the same schools and the same churches, but yet, we are all as different as night and day. So how much different are 2 people with completely different backgrounds, and upbringings???? When someone tells you, how they feel, or they make statements about anything, ask them what they mean by that, and what is their outlook on a particular situation. People can love you, just not in the same manner YOU think it should be.

Unspoken expectations will destroy relationships. SPEAK the expectations you expect, nobody can read your mind, and nobody thinks exactly as you do. In your day-to-day activities, find ways and people to speak your expectations to, and allow them to speak their expectations to you. Begin a healthy dialogue with others, so that there are far fewer unhealthy dialogues.

NOTES:____

____

____

____

____

____

____

____

About the Author

Joseph Saxon Jr. is the youngest of four children, born February 5, 1980, and raised in the suburbs of Chicago. Growing up, he was a mischievous young lad... not quite a troublemaker but he did have his share of run-ins.

Over the years Joseph built a solid foundation of faith, hard work, and tenacity through weekly church services, sports, and volunteer services. Upon his high school graduation, he immediately enlisted in the U.S. NAVY, where he began his career path as an electrician.

In 2000, while stationed in Jacksonville, Florida, Joseph met and married his first wife, and they had three children. Sadly, after 10 years, the marriage ended in divorce. Since his divorce he has been traveling across the United States, continuing in his electrical trade.

To those closest to him, Joseph is known as a teacher, who tries to impart his knowledge of life, health, and finances to those he loves. He's also known as hard-working, dependable, transparent, knowledgeable, and fun-loving.

Joseph spends most of his free time reading, exercising, and learning, as well as helping his closest family and friends build their financial literacy. Upon discovering his new passion as a writer, Joseph Saxon, Jr. has published his first book: ***Challenge Yourself to Change: 365-daily Inspirational Messages to Bring Out the Best You.***

Printed in the USA
CPSIA information can be obtained
at www.ICGtesting.com
LVHW021249121124
796387LV00015B/746
9798991736206